DATE DUE

DEMCO 38-296

Broken Silence

» » »

BROKEN SILENCE

» » » » » » » » » » » »

Voices of Japanese Feminism

SANDRA BUCKLEY

UNIVERSITY OF CALIFORNIA PRESS

Berkeley » Los Angeles » London

University of California Press
Berkeley and Los Angeles, California

University of California Press, Ltd.
London, England

Library of Congress Cataloging-in-Publication Data

Broken silence : voices of Japanese feminism /
Sandra Buckley.
      p.   cm.
   Includes bibliographical references and index.
   ISBN 0–520-08513-2 (alk. paper).
   ISBN 0-520-08514-0 (pbk. : alk. paper)
   1. Feminists — Japan — Interviews.   2. Feminism — Japan.
3. Feminist theory — Japan.   I. Buckley, Sandra, 1954–
HQ1762.B76   1997
305.42'0952 — dc20   95-51306

Printed in the United States of America

9 8 7 6 5 4 3 2 1

The paper used in this publication meets the minimum
requirements of American National Standard for
Information Sciences — Permanence of Paper for Printed
Library Materials, ANSI Z39.48–1984.

*For my mother, Ellen Buckley, and
my sister, Lynne Jarvie — they
opened so many doors for me and
were always there to give me a
gentle push when I hesitated.
With love and thanks.*

Contents

»   »   »   »

Preface and Acknowledgments

» » » »

A male academic colleague once phoned me to ask why there was no feminism in Japan, "at least no serious feminist theorists." A long discussion ensued at the end of which, to my frustration, he concluded, "I'm not convinced. I've looked everywhere, and I just don't see feminism in any form I can recognize." Several months later I was in Japan and discussed my colleague's question with a group of Japanese feminists. One of them commented, "He must have been looking in all the wrong places." We went on to discuss the fact that Japanese feminist theory and practice have — not unlike their European and North American counterparts — generally developed outside academic institutions, which have for the most part remained indifferent, even hostile, to this intellectual and political movement. Because feminism has not "evolved" in such familiar Western contexts as women's studies centers, panels at academic conferences, and specialized academic feminist journals but has preferred to channel its multiplicity of voices through a mixture of nonmainstream and informal publications, a person looking for "familiar forms" may find it less immediately locatable.

I am sure that the reader will agree with me after reading the works of the ten women collected in this volume that they are indeed "serious feminist theorists" even while recognizing that the contexts (historical and contemporary), platforms, motivations, and priorities of their feminisms may not always be familiar. Yet only two of these women are full-time academics. Each of the others has made a conscious strategic choice to locate various aspects of her work outside the academic institution and closer to specific sites of cultural or political activity. For example, in addition to being a practicing lawyer and founder of a women's legal cooperative, Kanazumi Fumiko ran in the 1989 national elections as co-leader of the newly formed political party Club of the World. Nakanishi Toyoko has focused her activities on feminist publication and translation projects developed around her Kansai women's bookstore. Matsui Yayori is known as the most senior woman in the Japanese newspaper industry and as an avid writer, but despite a very hectic life she has maintained a high level of political activism around issues concerned with Japan's relations with the developing world and the international sex trade.

In our discussion my Japanese feminist colleagues and I went on to consider why there is such a continuing sense outside Japan that feminism is neither active nor viable in that country. Different women in the group described meeting foreign feminists at overseas conferences and being both amused and dismayed by the level of surprise that these women expressed when they realized the extent of feminist activities in Japan. Two major concerns of our discussion were the limited number of Japanese feminist materials available in translation and the dominant modes of representation of Japanese women in both feminist and nonfeminist Western texts. We focused our attention mainly on North America. A woman in the group described one such mode of representation as the "cameo" approach — a collection of personal stories or mini-biographies. With this approach, the voices of Japanese women are usually diffused in the author's attempt to contextualize and interpret. Passages in a first-person narrative or interview format are framed and mediated by an authorial presence. The reader's sense of the intimacy between interviewer and interviewee, or between author and subject, somehow obscures the act of interpretation and re-presentation.

Another mode of representation was found in more scholarly or academic works. In this approach individual Japanese women do not occupy a speaking, subject position. Rather, they are displaced by a category of "Japanese Woman," which becomes the object of study or analysis, and a particular theoretical or methodological framework often dominates. While these works have an obvious contribution to make to academic discourses, their pursuit of a specific research goal can threaten to dematerialize the individual women whose lives are the "material" of the text. Ironically, through a process of analytical scrutiny, individual identities are dissected to the extent that all that can finally be reconstituted is the wholistic "Japanese Woman," who bears little resemblance to any of the women out of whose fragmented experiences she is composed. These two dominant modes produce, on the one hand, the collectable curiosity and, on the other, the patch-work Everywoman.

Discussions such as this, where my Japanese feminist friends and colleagues lamented the fact that so little was known outside Japan of that country's feminism(s), led to the conception of this book. The question of how to choose which Japanese women to approach to participate in the volume was a major consideration from the outset. Ultimately, the decisions were based on a series of consultations with both Western feminist colleagues working on issues relating to Japanese feminism and Japanese feminists whom I had known through their writings. Vera Mackie (Melbourne University, Australia) and Rebecca Jennison (Seika University, Japan) offered crucial advice and assistance in identifying possible feminist contacts in Japan beyond my own circle of acquaintances. During visits to Japan in 1987 and 1988 I met with twenty-three women who it seemed might be interested in participating. Aoki Yayoi proved to be extraordinarily generous, despite her own busy schedule. Anyone who is familiar with Japan will know how difficult it is to function without a person who is prepared to provide introductions and act as a go-between. I was extremely fortunate that, in addition to suggesting women who might be willing to be interviewed, Aoki also offered her active support and encouragement throughout the project. With characteristic openness, she helped me to meet and talk with feminists from a wide range of backgrounds, who often worked in quite different, even opposing, directions from her own. Aoki's efforts on my behalf were an important factor in bringing this collection to fruition.

Of the twenty-three women with whom I first met and discussed the project, ten decided that, while supportive, they did not feel in a position to participate, because of ill health, publication deadlines of their own, concern over their material appearing outside Japan, family obligations, existing translation contracts, or in one unusual case, a reluctance to be associated with one of the other women in the volume. Of the remaining thirteen women, three initially agreed to participate and were interviewed but later decided to withdraw. Two of them withdrew for reasons of deteriorating health and lack of time due to a move into a political career. In the third case the participant, a poet, felt compelled to return to a previous strategy of declining public interviews. She decided that a frank discussion of her lesbian identity would be too painful for her family should it ever be translated back into Japanese, and that she could not describe her work and life adequately without mention of her sexuality.

The remaining ten women are collected here: Aoki Yayoi, Ide Sachiko, Kanazumi Fumiko, Kōra Rumiko, Matsui Yayori, Miya Yoshiko, Nakanishi Toyoko, Ochiai Keiko, Saitō Chiyo, and Ueno Chizuko. Each was prepared to make the commitment of time and energy that this project required if it was to be genuinely cooperative and collaborative. Over the period from 1988 to 1991 I interviewed all ten women, and in consultation we selected the materials that would accompany a translation of the interview. Each of the interviews took place under quite different circumstances. In two instances the interviewee preferred not to be recorded (Miya and Nakanishi), and I had to brush up on my very rusty speed writing. There were also the inevitable technological problems; one interview could not be recorded completely and was also supplemented by notes (Matsui).

These interviews required the most consultation with the interviewee at the later editing stage in order to ensure that there were no misunderstandings or errors. Both the interview with Ide Sachiko and the one with Ueno Chizuko took place in a mixture of English and Japanese. All the other interviews were held entirely in Japanese and translated into English from transcripts.

The location varied significantly for each interview. The meetings with Miya, Matsui, and Ochiai all took place in coffee shops. It is not at all uncommon in Japan for meetings to be held away from someone's home or office, and a favorite, quiet coffee shop is a popular alternative. The atmosphere surrounding these interviews was often somewhat less relaxed as we found other customers being drawn toward the scene of a foreign woman interviewing a Japanese woman. The people around us were curious about the content of the interview and strained to hear better. In two separate instances, a waitress and a customer at an adjacent table interjected their own opinions at some point in the interview and asked about its purpose. Aoki, Kōra, and Ide all met with me in their homes, while Nakanishi, Saitō, and Kanazumi chose to meet in the workplace. The interview with Ueno was perhaps the most unusual, for our own interview was recorded by a reporter doing a story on Ueno for a popular Japanese publication. His interview blurred into ours, with questions to me about Ueno's reputation outside Japan and my view as "a foreign feminist" of some of the domestic criticisms of Ueno's work.

The process of translation and consultation was slow but central to the nature of the project. Each of the women was encouraged to suggest changes in the translations of both the interviews and their original written materials. I attempted in the translations not to merge the diverse voices into a single one that would merely echo my own in style or theoretical perspective. A close comparison of the English with the originals would show some discrepancies that reflect my own decisions as translator to exercise license, on occasion, in an attempt to capture the mood or intention of the original in a way that a literal translation could not accommodate. Variations from the original Japanese are, however, more often the result of suggested changes from

the authors. Sometimes these changes were due to the author's preference for a different English word or expression, but there are also
many situations where an author chose to edit or alter the original for
English publication. Changes of this kind include decisions to drop
names of individuals, to modify or intensify a criticism of someone
else's work, and to delete Japanese wordplay or references that might
be lost to a non-Japanese reader. This highly interactive process took
a good deal of time, but it also resulted in a constant review of my own
relationship to the women and their works over the course of the
project. The experience of undertaking translations on this basis has
foregrounded for me the politics of interpretation/translation and the
impossibility of "disappearing" myself from the texts. On more than
one occasion I caught myself modifying or misreading a passage in
ways that could only be explained by my own discomfort with a
specific idea. The women chosen for the volume were not selected on
the basis of consistencies between their works or between their work
and my own. Rather, they were selected to emphasize the multiplicity
of Japanese feminism(s). Thus, in presenting the works of such a
diverse group it is inevitable that I have disagreements with certain
positions and that they have been, and continue to be, openly discussed. I have chosen, however, not to engage these differences here
but have described elsewhere my own position on many of the issues
raised by these ten feminists.

The inclusion of a chronology of recent events in the history of
Japanese feminism was a response to the need for a context within
which the reader could situate the specific issues and themes developed in the interviews and articles with a minimum of intrusion. An
expanded historical introduction seemed fraught with potential problems, given the overall goals of the project. After discussions with the
ten contributors and other colleagues, I decided that even though a
detailed timeline inevitably involved subjective selection and editing,
it would offer a reasonable level of contextualization with a minimum
of interpretation. The selection process and sources are discussed in
more detail in the brief introduction to the timeline. I hope that the

reader will find it a valuable and convenient resource both when reading this volume and in the pursuit of other research projects.

A glossary has also been included, which lists information on proper names for people and historical periods, events, and movements, as well as explanations of specific terms and Japanese expressions. It is my hope that the glossary, in combination with the timeline, will render the book accessible to readers who are unfamiliar with Japan. The list of feminist and related women's organizations was included to offer readers a means of pursuing further any interest they may develop in particular areas of Japanese feminism by guiding them toward channels of direct contact with relevant Japanese women's groups. The list was drawn from a range of feminist networking publications released between 1990 and 1993. Wherever possible, the contact information has been updated and confirmed. This list should be a useful resource for people who would like to collaborate with Japanese feminists in academic research or political activism.

In the end, I hope that I have created a collection of interviews and writings that allow the reader to grasp the diversity of feminist practice and theory in Japan and the complexity of the history of feminism over the last several decades. While each of the interviews and writing selections is quite distinct from the rest, this does not, I hope, result in disjointedness as each piece weaves its way in and out of a multi-textured narrative of Japanese feminism. The women speak to quite different issues, but certain threads emerge — the politics of language; the construction of the gendered body in medicine, the law, the family, and other dominant institutions; the relationship of Japanese feminists to "Western" feminisms; the political future of feminism in Japan; and the Japanese feminist critique of Japan's role in the third world — to name only some. Several of the women interviewed are engaged in public debates with one another over particular theoretical or political issues, and these differences surface here in their interviews and writings. The issue of reproductive technology is a good example. Kanazumi's demand for strict controls on new technologies;

Aoki's call for a carefully researched feminist platform on technology; Nakanishi's concern that women be given the opportunity to make informed medical decisions in an environment committed to the right to self-determination; and Matsui's focus on the different configurations of power, race, and gender in which Japanese women and Southeast Asian women negotiate their relationship to new technologies exemplify the fact that there is no singular Japanese Feminism but rather a rich cacophony of voices constantly redefining and renegotiating the boundaries of feminism in that country. I hope that the points of convergence and divergence in the women's various approaches work to create a "wholeness" in the volume without slipping into wholisms.

From the outset the goal was to create a space in English translation where Japanese feminists could speak in their own voices. This volume does not attempt to speak for all Japanese women or to mediate the voices of Japanese feminists. Nor does it attempt to construct a favored theoretical position as an organizing principle for one more re-presentation of "Japanese Woman." There are various marginalized groups of women whose voices are not directly represented here — lesbians, Korean Japanese, Burakumin, physically handicapped women, Okinawans, sex workers, and others. Issues of concern to these marginalized groups are discussed in the book, and some of the ten women in the collection are members of one or more of these communities, even if they have chosen not to claim these identifications here. But the volume could not realistically be all-inclusive. This statement is intended less as an apology than an invitation to others to continue the process of translation and circulation of Japanese feminist materials outside Japan.

This project began in Bev Smith's garden. Long summer days, tea, and talk nurtured ideas into action. They say that angels never die, they just take flight, but I miss Bev still.

The material for the book was collected and translated over the six years from 1987 to 1993. I wish to thank the Social Science Research

Council of Canada for its funding of the early stages of the project. The editors and staff at the University of California Press have been supportive and endlessly patient throughout. Thanks to Colleen Ovenden, Natasha Pairaudeau (I got it right!), Kaye Broadbent, and Cathy Burns for their patience at the keyboard and for organizing me. Kerry Bingham was there for me during the best and the worst times, when I was still unsure of where it was all going. I am proud to be the father of her child! Tomita Nobuko leapt into the fray in the final stages of editing, helping to tie up many a loose end in Japan. Sakai Minako worked with endless enthusiasm as my research assistant for the historical timeline and list of feminist organizations. Margaret Lock, whether she realizes it or not, continues to be a remarkable and treasured role model. Rebecca Jennison has been a source of constant encouragement and support in both the pursuit of this project and the thrills and spills of motherhood. Kim Sawchuk could always see a way through and kept me smiling. Audrey Kobayashi's warmth and gift for listening beyond the words helped me over many a hump, professionally and personally. And always Brian.

Last, and most important, I offer my heartfelt thanks to all of the Japanese women, friends and colleagues, who have offered their support at various stages in the gestation of this project. They are far too many to even begin to name here. All I can hope is that as our relationships continue to grow over the years to come, I can offer the same encouragement and openness to them that they have provided me in this endeavor. A shared commitment to the politics of collaboration is at the heart of this book. And above all I wish to thank the ten women who saw this volume through to the end for all their patience, effort, and ongoing commitment: Aoki Yayoi, Ide Sachiko, Kanazumi Fumiko, Kōra Rumiko, Matsui Yayori, Miya Yoshiko, Nakanishi Toyoko, Ochiai Keiko, Saitō Chiyo, and Ueno Chizuko.

This book is more theirs than it is mine.

AOKI YAYOI
Independent Scholar and Critic

» » » » » » » » » » » »

THE FREELANCE WRITER and *hyōronka* (social critic) Aoki Yayoi is one of the most widely known feminists in Japan. She has published extensively on topics ranging from the cultural construction of sexuality to abortion rights, new reproductive technologies, women in the workforce, teenage sexuality, and women and the arts. She is in high demand as a public speaker on women's issues and as a university guest lecturer. Although she has accepted short-term appointments in tertiary and community colleges, she intentionally maintains a noninstitutional and nonaffiliated status rather than face what she considers the inevitable compromises of a strategy of "working from within." Aoki is also known for her strong interest in the rights of indigenous peoples, particularly in the southwestern United States, and has published two books on the Hopi. From her experience as an art and music critic in the 1960s came a continuing commitment to the feminist analysis of artistic production. She has recently published the second of two major works on Beethoven.

In the 1980s Aoki was one of the first Japanese feminists to theorize the relationship between the imperial system and the contemporary conditions of women's lives. The piece translated in this volume,

"Feminism and Imperialism," constructs a gender-based analysis of the symbiotic relationship between the Japanese imperial institution and the patriarchal *ie* (household) system. Aoki traces the continuities between the status of the emperor and the imperial household and the status of the husband/father and the domestic household. She describes the organic linking of the two as a central strategy in the construction of the modern Japanese nation-state. Aoki interprets the model to be patriarchal and based on systematic exclusion and aggression that inevitably marginalize women. Written in anticipation of the Shōwa emperor's death, the piece attempts to shift attention away from the popular preoccupation with the question of the emperor's responsibility for the war. It raises instead the far more provocative issue of the imperial institution's very legitimacy in contemporary Japan, and the implications of its continued existence for the family, and for women in particular.

Aoki became involved in a major public debate with Ueno Chizuko starting in the mid-1980s. In what became popularly known as the "Aoki and Ueno Debate," Aoki was criticized for promoting the concept of the "feminine principle" within a theoretical framework characterized as eco-feminism. Ueno and her supporters argued that Aoki's call for a return to the "feminine principle" as a strategy for rejecting the predominantly masculine mode of the existing structures of power was an essentialist move that risked romanticizing an already problematic construct of the "feminine." There was also concern that Aoki had conflated the "feminine" and female identity. In combination with Aoki's strong critique of reproductive technologies, it was easy for her critics to represent her position as revisionist and technophobic. Ueno published her major critique of Aoki's work in a book entitled *Can Women Save the Earth?* In fact, a close reading of Aoki's work on the question of the "feminine principle" and eco-feminism shows that much of the criticism was not founded on her actual writing but on an oversimplification of specific terms taken out of context.

Aoki's analysis of reproductive technology cannot simply be dismissed as technophobic. Her research is thorough, and her conclusions regarding the potential risks to women of an unmonitored technological revolution in reproduction are consistent with those of similar studies by feminist scholars outside Japan, in particular in the third world, where women tend to greet new technologies with caution. One of her specific concerns has been the impact of new technologies — whether reproductive, biogenetic, or informational — on the lives of third world women. Much of her work in this area actually seeks to complicate the distinction between the first and the third world in the current global geopolitical environment. Technofeminists might disagree with her conclusions, but it seems preferable for them to keep the dialogue on technology open rather than simply to reject alternative positions out of hand.

One of the strengths of Aoki's work is her constant insistence on the historical and local specificities of feminist politics and theory, a practice that she identifies as originating in her experience of Japan's imperialist era. She does not claim that women can "save the earth." Rather, she calls on feminists to extend their critique of technological and ecological reform to incorporate a more thorough and sensitive analysis of the differences between women. Aoki argues that we must consider the significantly different contexts within which women develop a relationship to technology. A Japanese woman's encounter with a specific reproductive technology may be liberating or empowering while a South Indian woman's experience of the same procedure may be involuntary and dangerous. There is no doubt that the technology debate among Japanese feminists will continue over the years to come. Aoki's voice is sure to continue to complicate and challenge the assumptions surrounding women's relationship to the contemporary formation of knowledge. Her analysis of the emperor system is grounded in this same assertion that power is negotiated through knowledge of technologies and technologies of knowledge.

Interview

SB: One of the things I find difficult to deal with in Japan is the distinction between male and female speech and the power politics of honorifics. I prefer not to use women's language and yet not to do so produces a whole other set of problems.

AY: What's interesting to me is the recent resurgence of honorifics. If you went out into the countryside in, say, the prewar period or even the years just after the war, the old men and women working in the fields together made no distinction between male and female speech. Back in the home the daughter and mother would use respectful speech when talking to the grandparents, but the grandfather and grandmother usually spoke to each other as equals. When a senior member of the village — say, the village head — came to visit, then the grandmother might introduce some honorifics into her speech. The rest of the time she'd happily refer to herself as *ore*.

All this recent proliferation of women's language coincides with the rise of a class of people determined to establish their own credentials as an elite, sophisticated social class. Ironically there are a lot of incorrect usages in vogue — hyper-corrections. There's a basic difference between the use of honorifics in the male and female speech of today, and what you find in the classical literature.

SB: How would you describe the difference?

AY: In contemporary society, where a woman's role is essentially limited to reproduction and even that is given no value as labor, women seek means of enhancing their status in whatever way possible, striving to achieve some positive recognition of their existence. Female speech amounts to an effort through language to reinforce the difference between male and female, and that difference is then invested with the value of femininity. The greater one's skill in feminine speech, the greater the difference and the greater the femininity. Of course, the difference produced by such tactics is a difference that grows out of a preexisting discrimination and only serves to replicate and reinforce the inferior status of the female speaker. This tendency to glorify or aestheticize the feminine reached its peak in the samurai culture. In that society, the distinction between male and female was cultivated over hundreds of years. The expressions used today for "wife," *okusan* and *kanai*, literally designate women's place as within the house. I understand that these terms date from the period of the rise of samurai culture. However, this designation was only true, even in those times, for samurai women, certainly not for the women of merchant or rural households. These women moved freely in and out of the house. They say it was the prostitutes of the pleasure quarters who first started to imitate the language of the samurai class, and then the practice spread slowly from the pleasure quarters out into the town culture of Edo.

It's not unusual for a social group to imitate the language of a higher-ranking one. With time the "upper-class" or "polite" language of the samurai became a mark of social standing. This seems to have been particularly true for women.

SB: I met an old woman in Gifu Prefecture some years ago who had spent her whole life in the same rural household. As she had no brothers, her family had adopted her husband into its family register. Her own daughter and son had left Gifu to live in Tokyo. She explained to me that she felt sorry for her daughter, a married woman who had given up her office job to raise children. She said she preferred her life to the one she saw her daughter living. She explained how she and her husband had worked the ricefields together. She felt they shared a deep closeness and saw each other as equals. She also described how she had raised silkworms to earn extra money, which both she and her husband acknowledged as her own, to dispose of as she saw fit. She saw her daughter's life in Tokyo as a life of dependency and boredom. While I recognize the dangers inherent in romanticizing the past, I was struck by what she said.

AY: I agree that there are risks in romanticizing traditional lifestyles and the past. Whenever I'm tempted to romanticize the traditional rural life, I force myself to picture the old country women whose bodies are permanently bent at a 90° angle from years of working the ricefields. What the old woman was describing is a good example of what I've heard you call power politics, isn't it? The urban Japanese wife has very limited power. She's caught within a system in which her primary role is reproductive-nurturing, but she can only fulfill this role in a position of dependence on a male. That's the system that's emerged. Any power the modern Japanese housewife has is delegated to her and can be withdrawn. She manages the household but doesn't control it. Even in cases where the wife works, her income is usually supplemental and considered secondary to the husband's. There have been various surveys that have documented clearly the Japanese housewife's sense of the limited range of her decision-making power. Occasionally, conservatives will claim that the Japanese housewife has become too sure of herself, too pushy, but statements like this ignore the whole picture. You can't discuss the status of women just within the household. It has to be put in the context of the whole society. The power relations between men and women in the family are determined by external conditions. The action of the wife within the household will always be curtailed by society's intolerance of a woman who has been rejected from a household. What she perceives to be the limits of her power will be determined by the available options. And what are the Japanese wife's options? We have to be just as ready to critique the idealization or mythologization of the status of the contemporary Japanese housewife.

SB: *The power the woman yields in the private domain doesn't transfer into the public domain, while on the other hand the power of the man operates in both.*

AY: To be powerful only in the private domain is not to be powerful in any real political sense. Another interesting thing is the division of labor within the household. What a man does and doesn't do in the household is very clearly demarcated. There has been some breakdown of this at a superficial level lately, but fundamentally the divisions are intact. When I was active in the peace movement, I was struck by the fact that even when women moved into the public domain, into the realm of politics (as many women did in the 1960s and 1970s), the domestic division of labor of the private sphere carried over into the public. Women were expected to perform the same kinds of domestic duties for men as they would at home. The fundamental nature of the power relations of gender is not so easily broken.

SB: A woman member of the socialist party I spoke with recently complained that she had felt like the tea lady for years after joining the party. I wonder if things changed under the leadership of a woman, Doi Takako. I don't think this is a problem particularly unique to Japan.

AY: Oh, no. However, I do think there is a greater proclivity here for accepting the situation as normal, even desirable. In situations where I have seniority by virtue of age and/or experience, I still frequently find my male colleagues reluctant to accept that I am an able spokesperson or public representative. Of course, there are some exceptions. The test I think is always the homefront. All too many open-minded, radical young men go home to their wives and sit down and wait for their dinner, demand their cigarettes, or shout for another cup of tea.

SB: Japanese women are politically active in relation to such issues as environmental pollution, the antinuclear movement, and consumer affairs. They also play an active role in electing left-wing municipal and prefectural governments. At the national level they generally outnumber male voters, and yet at this nonlocal level they show a marked conservative tendency. It actually appears to be women who keep the conservatives in government.

AY: It's true that women will vote differently in local and national elections. Another interesting point is that women's responses to opinion polls and their voting in national elections are often contradictory. While both an opinion poll and an election vote are anonymous, there may be a perception that the poll will have no direct consequences. In the case of an election in Japan, there are so many considerations other than the stated political issues operating to influence the choice. An election vote is less an individual choice than a household issue. Questions of obligation, business and personal relations, and regional or community interests may affect a voter's choice. Many of the issues may be determined by the public status of the male household head, his employment, personal links, and so on. I have no statistics, but I think that you'll find many women are influenced in their choice of candidate at the national level by their husband's opinion. Japanese election results don't represent a national preference so much as the state of regional rivalry, the internal politics of the LDP, and the complexity of the network of human relations in Japan.

SB: When I spoke with Saitō Chiyo of Agora *magazine, she said that she feels Japanese feminism is at an important turning point. She sees it as crucial that Japanese feminists assess how best to react to the new conservatism and complacency among middle-class Japanese women.*

AY: I agree. I don't believe we can go on talking in terms of such simple divisions as conservative and radical. I think that the recent emphasis of politicians and parties on guaranteeing a high quality of life is indicative of the new face of politics in Japan. Most Japanese people have come to believe that a certain level of comfort and prosperity is their due. Ideology becomes a secondary issue. Talk to people of restraint, and they will vote "no." Talk of prosperity, and they will vote "yes." What needs to change now is the basic, individual value system, the dominant value system. Otherwise we will all — radical and nonradical alike — be drawn into the new conservatism. It's this preoccupation with comfort and prosperity that is the greatest political threat. I've been involved with various peace groups over the years, but when I've asked other members why they are antiwar, all too often they respond that they lived through the war and suffered the food shortages and other hardships. The objective becomes not so much peace as the maintenance of a given quality of lifestyle. This is no basis for a serious political resistance.

For example, what if our leaders inform us some day that the supply of oil to Japan is threatened. Without oil we can't continue our temperature-controlled existence with air conditioners in the summer and heaters in the winter. The only way to protect our oil supply is to send the Japanese Self-Defense Forces into the Strait of Malacca to protect the tankers. Another example is atomic energy. Without atomic energy, we can't sustain the power grid necessary to run all the air conditioners and refrigerators in Japan, or so the authorities tell us. How many of our young Japanese could ever imagine life without a refrigerator? Regardless of the possible risks, atomic power plants have gone into operation in Japan with only a murmur of public resistance.

SB: Do you see any possibility of change in the future?

AY: At the risk of sounding flippant, I grew up without a washing machine or a refrigerator, and so did many other people. That's not to say we should do away with technology but rather that we should do away with the current state of technological dependence. What needs to be revised is the prevailing perception that a high quality of life is one that requires no manual labor or exertion. Unless there is some return to a more self-reliant system of existence, we will just go further and further down the path of technological dependence, and that can only lead to political apathy.

The risk of war or nuclear disaster will only get higher. An LDP slogan before a recent election said it all: "Carefree, safe, secure." One newspaper report after the election quoted a woman voter as saying, "It's not that I particularly like the LDP, but I couldn't see anything specifically wrong with them either. My life is comfortable and convenient these days, so why change?" This is the political reality in Japan.

Perhaps the biggest single problem in our society today is a lack of imagination. We carry on our daily lives enjoying the comforts of electricity, ample food, and commodity and resource imports, but we don't pause to consider the economic structure that all this rests on. So much of our present way of life depends on exploiting the peoples of the third world. We enjoy our lifestyle at the expense of the environmental heritage of future generations. Individuals need to take stock of the fact that their quality of life is achieved only at great cost to others. The famines and droughts in Africa are man-made, not natural, disasters. The conversion of whole regions to cash crop mono-cultures has destroyed both the land and the traditional way of life. We can buy cheap coffee for our enjoyment, but at what price to others? Someone once said that we throw away paper with ease, but if we stopped and imagined the paper was a photo of a starving child we might hesitate before wasting another sheet.

It's this kind of imagination, the ability to make connections between our own lives and others' that is lacking. The current education system works to repress rather than to encourage such flights of imagination. Parents need to recognize that this is what happens to their children in school. I suppose it all comes down to consciousness raising. I believe that in our society it is women who presently are most in touch with the nitty-gritty details of everyday life. Even if they don't immediately recognize the discrimination they suffer as women, it is difficult for them not to recognize the more general level of discrimination against others that supports their own existence. It's no accident that the women's movement in Japan has been closely associated with questions of human rights and the environment, the antinuclear movement, Southeast Asian prostitution, and anti-Apartheid activities.

A growing awareness of the reality of sexual discrimination at the level of individual experience goes hand in hand with the recognition of one's implication in the existing systems of global exploitation and discrimination. I disagree with the basic motivation behind a recent campaign among Japanese women's groups to send blankets to Africa, for example. It goes no further than a sense of one's own good fortune in the face of someone else's misfortune. It doesn't begin to recognize our own direct responsibility and involvement. It is our own value system that is contributing to the destruction of the sociocultural and economic foundations of the African nations. Until Japanese women recognize their own complicity in this process and act to counter it, there can be no real women's liberation.

SB: There have been several books written in English lately on Japanese women, and each one has its own version of the origins of Japa-

nese feminism; but there seems to be a general tendency to trace an influence back to the Occupation and then, later on, to the American Women's Liberation Movement.

AY: It's not unusual for social or political movements to occur independently of one another yet at the same time. However, with each occurrence a movement can take on a new form, a new expression, while each of its manifestations need not exclude or contradict the rest. At the same time they need not be, and seldom are, mere imitations of one another. While the beginnings of feminism are generally recorded in America and England, there was also an early, first wave of feminism in Meiji Japan.

It began with the problem of child prostitution. In the late nineteenth century, twelve- and thirteen-year-old girls (especially farmers' daughters) were being sold into prostitution by their parents to meet family debts. It was the Christian women's groups that first mounted a protest against this practice as a basic infringement of human rights. In those days a father could dispose of his daughter in any way he pleased, and she had no protection. Early attempts to draw the attention of politicians to the problem failed. Women didn't constitute an electoral interest group. Without the vote they had no direct political influence. Thus, out of the initial movement against child prostitution eventually emerged a suffrage movement to obtain the vote for women.

This all happened quite independently of the English or American movements of the same period. Over the ensuing years I think Japanese feminists have learned a lot from Western feminists, but I don't think they have imitated them. Even the second wave of feminism in the late 1960s and 1970s, although it took on the name of "women's liberation" and was accused in the mass media of copying American women, in fact had its own quite distinct origins in Japan. Tanaka Mitsu, one of the early leaders of this second wave, said to me once that she can still remember her own sense of amazement when she discovered the existence of women's liberation in America. She had already found her own identical ground before this. For Tanaka, and other early members of the women's liberation movement in Japan, the beginnings of the movement, the earliest stirrings of a feminist consciousness, came from our experience of the anti–Vietnam War movement as it was manifested in Japan. At the most basic level there was a discovery that the rhetoric of freedom and liberation did not extend to the lives of the women within the movement. At another level, for me personally, there was a growing sense of doubt about what constituted civilization. Here was a civilized society, a democratic nation, waging warfare in another land, denying the rights of the people of that region, experimenting with various forms of chemical warfare. And all this in the name of democracy and civilization. I began to question whether women and men would govern in the same way, whether women politicians would make the same decisions. I began to sense the need to open up the way for a reassessment of our society, a new way of seeing the world, from the perspective of women.

All this was happening well before any contact with the American women's movement. It was at about the same time, the mid-1960s, that the first campaign was mounted for the reform of the Eugenics Protection Law. The women who fought against the reform bill were not radicals or necessarily even feminists. Their major concern was with the basic human rights issue involved in the proposed reforms. The combination of the anti-Vietnam and the anti-Eugenics movements sparked the possibility of Japan's second wave of feminism as the women who came together around these two issues began to recognize their shared experiences and goals. This all happened at the same time as, but without any direct contact with, the beginnings of American feminism.

SB: Were there attempts in the early years of the movement to cooperate with American feminists?

AY: Unfortunately, American feminism, or Women's Lib as it was called then, was introduced to Japan through the mass media. The women in the movement were presented as eccentrics. The media focused on such isolated events as bra-burning ceremonies and the

violent protest at the Miss America pageant. That was Japan's first
exposure to the American movement. Japanese feminists were not
anxious to be identified with all of this, given the media environment
of the day. They were wary of giving the media any excuse to represent them in the same light.

*SB: You talk in various of your works about the problem of the me-
dia representation of women in Japan.*

AY: In the past in Japan, in traditional Japan, the endless stereotypes of male and female determined what women should do and
think, how they should be. This is still true but not to the same extent. It is more obvious in some areas of the media than others. For
example, the image of women presented in commercials is a very
clear attempt to define the nature of womanhood: images of happy
women contemplating their perfect, white laundry, voice-overs of
"Just like mother's cooking" for rice commercials, etc., etc. If you
take any one advertisement in isolation, it doesn't seem like much,
but a constant input of these images works to reinforce, at a conscious or unconscious level, the sense that a woman's place is in the
home, working for the happiness of her family, deriving her satisfaction from providing them with hot meals, clean, crisp laundry, and a
sparkling house. The accumulated impact of the combined verbal
and visual images is difficult to ascertain, but there has been a lot
of research done recently in this area. The advertising companies
and their clients are clearly convinced that there is some measurable
result.

I don't think there is any real doubt that over time women do internalize elements delivered to them through the media. And this col-
lage of media images works to reinforce the aestheticization and
glorification of femininity. It is the process of internalizing this image
of "what it is to be women" that is most frightening. Something that
starts out as ideology is gradually transformed into an aesthetic and,
thus internalized, becomes "natural." People speak of the power of
the written word, but I think all the media have the same influence
today. Japanese consumers are especially naive in relation to the me-

dia. There is an absurd level of trust in anything seen or heard on television.

SB: I'm particularly interested in the problem of internalization because of my own work on popular culture.

AY: Ideology is not intrinsic to the individual. In that sense, it is external to the individual and can be resisted. However, when it comes disguised in the media as self-determination, choice, or taste, like a sugar-coated pill, it's difficult to identify and counter. It is this process of unconscious internalization that is politically dangerous. One's thoughts and beliefs seem to be one's own and yet . . .

SB: In direct response to the mass media, Japanese feminists have developed and sustained an alternative network of communication — the minikomi.

AY: I don't think one can overestimate the importance of the *mini-komi* system. However, I have some reservations. I think what concerns me is that, while there are so many independent publications in circulation, many of them address the same issues. What I don't sense is that the women behind each publication are addressing one another closely enough. There seems to be a high degree of fragmentation. Many of the publications are still working at the level of individual experiences and self-discovery. I think that Japanese feminism has gone beyond the state of self-declaration or self-affirmation. The feminist project is clear; what is missing is the strategy.

That is what I would like to see as the new focus of the *minikomi*. We live in a country where access to international news is minimal. What we need are alternative sources of news that will provide what we don't get in the major dailies. Even *Newsweek* gives a better range of news and more detail than the Japanese press. Our three major daily newspapers don't offer us the news we need. For example, the fact that only Japan, Russia, and France are still actively pursuing nuclear power as a future energy source is far more useful than another French recipe in the women's supplement. The *minikomi* network is well established and would be an excellent means of circulating alternative news sources in Japan. We need access to news that goes beyond individual or local issues to give us the information we need to put our imaginations to work, to develop new strategies that recognize the intricate links between women's liberation and questions of human rights and the environment.

SB: If so many minikomi *publications are still focusing on individual experiences or local issues, perhaps feminism is at a different stage of maturity or development among different groups of Japanese women.*

AY: Of course, there is always a risk in generalizing. "Japanese women" — that's a very diverse group. It's probably true that for many women it is still important to have access to a channel of self-expression and networking along the lines of the existing *minikomi*. The kind of alternative news network I'm describing need not displace what is already there but could coexist, using the *minikomi* network as one means of circulation.

SB: The ecological movement in the United States shifted to a more local level of political activity in the 1980s, but what you're describing seems to be a blend of ecology and feminism that would move away from the localized activities of the minikomi *toward a larger political strategy at the national or international level.*

AY: The primary focus of much of Japanese feminism has been the economic independence of women. This is a crucial factor in the liberation of women. However, if all it achieves is the right of passage of women into the existing male social structures and practices, I don't know that we have achieved very much. An example of the risks implicit in this course would be Margaret Thatcher. I don't believe we can achieve any real liberation for women until we have some vision of an alternative lifestyle, some other way of existing, not just between man and woman but between humans and the environment. I think that we are seeing the first signs of an alternative value system emerging in such movements as the ecological feminism of Denmark and the Green Party in West Germany.

SB: *Reading recent articles in* Agora *or* Chihei, *I get the impression that there are already the beginnings of such a movement in Japan.*

AY: Yes, and these date back into the early 1970s. I mentioned Tanaka Mitsu before. She and the young feminists who gathered around her at the Shinjuku Ribu Sentā had a deep sense of ecological issues and their significance for a feminist project from the outset. When other feminists were shouting slogans for the legalization of the pill, Tanaka Mitsu's group cautioned against a blind acceptance of the virtues of new technology. What they defended was every woman's right to self-determination in all matters relating to her sexuality and her body. They expressed concern that the pill was not a guarantee of liberation but was potentially an extension of the existing mechanisms of control inherent in so much other scientific and technological progress. They considered the pill one more way that technology would touch and alter the nature of female sexuality. This kind of ecological critique dates back then to the early and mid-1970s.

SB: *Were they actually opposed to the legalization of the pill?*

AY: No, not at all. Of course, the legalization of the pill is still a major issue even today, more than two decades later. They were arguing that the pill should not be seen as the answer to the problem for either sexual liberation or women's liberation. They also wanted a more coherent statement of the possible risks or side effects. Because they were in favor of self-determination, the issue was not the banning of the pill but access to adequate information so that each woman could make an informed decision for herself.

SB: *A common complaint among American grass-roots feminists is that academic feminists are out of touch with the concerns of most women, that they constitute a new elite. You stand in an interesting position somewhere between the two here in Japan.*

AY: Until some ten years ago there were no academic women to speak of. There were a few exceptions — for example, Nakane Chie, but her work couldn't really be called feminist. The academic woman and the academic feminist are a relatively new phenomenon in Japan. The gap between these women and grass-roots feminists will be a problem in time, I suspect, but is not evident yet.

My own position is somewhat unusual. My feminism grew out of my participation in the grass-roots movement from its early days, but now I'm moving closer to the academic world. I have no formal affiliation with any one university, but recently I've found myself increasingly drawn into the world of academic feminists. I suppose I have one foot in each camp these days. I've received a considerable amount of criticism from the academic camp on the basis of my promotion of ecological feminism and what I've termed the "feminine principle." There is some concern that my use of this expression, the "feminine principle," is no different from the traditional concept of "femininity." Another common criticism of my work is that it is antimodern or revisionist. Most academic research is tied to the belief that all technological advances are positive and progressive. It is not surprising that academic feminists have inherited the same prejudice. However, my own point of departure is different. I started out doubting the virtues of the doctrine of modernity and progress, and I remain doubtful. This seems to be the fundamental difference that separates us. I think the controversy is good for the movement, for Japanese feminism.

Feminism and Imperialism

Perhaps it is the passing of the sixtieth anniversary of the Shōwa emperor's reign that has led to the recent resurgence of the "emperor debate." Discussion of this topic—one that was previously considered taboo or rejected as ideologically unsound—is welcomed in the contemporary cultural environment. Some consider it overdue. It is

First appeared as Chapter 2 of *Feminism and Ecology* by Aoki Yayoi (Tokyo: Shin Hyōron, 1986). Translated with the permission of the author by Sandra Buckley.

extremely rare, however, to come across a convincing version of the "emperor debate."

Needless to say, I have not seen all the relevant materials, but among those I am familiar with there are some that abound in emotionalism and the pronouncement of assorted rash notions, and others that, by virtue of their idealistic positioning, promote potentially dangerous currents. As one who is concerned with the impact of the emperor system on daily life, both during and after the war, and its influence in the construction of a mass consciousness, I would like to offer the following observations.

THE MASSES AND THE EMPEROR SYSTEM

The existence of the emperor is as old as the history of Japan. Moreover, in ancient Japan the emperor was indeed considered to be the descendant of the gods. However, this belief came into being in an environment where the ancient Japanese also believed that the *Kojiki* was a record of the myths that had originated among, and remained the property of, the people. In the period following the systematization of political power under the Ritsuryō Reforms [A.D. 708–12], the environment changed totally. Needless to say, the meanings of the *Kojiki* itself also changed. Although the emperor has been a permanent presence, the rationale and significance of that presence are not located in some homogeneous continuum that traverses Japanese history. Given that history has focused until now only on what has been left to us in written documents, environments (or contexts) are often misread. For example, there is a theory that the deification of the emperor is directly linked to the emergence of a theoretical foundation for Shinto and is therefore a recent phenomenon. However, this view of the emperor is found only in occasional written records of the opinions of only a portion of the total number of Shinto scholars. It is completely unrelated to the undocumented sentiments of the people of the day. The *real* proof of this view lies in the fact that, prior to the Meiji Period, there were no shrines devoted to the worship of the emperor as a god, other than religious sites associated with imperial requiems and burials. If we accept that the people of ancient Japan chose as their object of universal worship that which had the oldest and grandest genealogy, then we have to acknowledge that this was always *o-tentō-sama* (the sun/sun deity) — the absolute creator of all things and the embodiment of all the heavenly movements. We find a testament to this in the observations of a foreign visitor such as Lafcadio Hearn. He described how in the Meiji Period Japanese treated the sunrise as a special event and referred to it as "The Coming of the Sun." Every morning they faced the sun and clapped their hands in a gesture of worship. There is no need to resort to such unusual sources for our information. Any Japanese born before the war will certainly recall hearing the elderly use the expression *o-tento-sama*.

Such popular practices as mountain worship (starting as it did with Mount Fuji) and pilgrimages to Ise Shrine spread across the entire country and can also be traced to sun worship. These locations were revered as sites where the sun deity was enshrined. When some people see the name Ise Shrine, they will argue that this was a stronghold of state Shinto, which had the function of worshiping the imperial ancestors. However, the classification of national shrines was the product of the imperialist historical view and thus a direct result of Japan's modernization. The people of pre-modern Japan knew nothing of all this, and it was of no real significance to them that the sun also happened to be Amaterasu, the ancestral figurehead of the imperial household. The following poem is said to have been written by the twelfth-century poet Saigyō and recited by him within the inner precincts of the Ise Shrine.

> I know not what he does
> but still I weep tears of awe.

In light of a poem such as this, we are left to wonder just what the emperor meant to the people. He was not looked upon as the ultimate god-figure, nor was he close enough to the people to be held dear to them. They went to the shrine to announce births or the coming of age, to pray for good crops or safe travel, because they believed that the emperor was the tutelary deity for all such matters. I have heard that there is an interpretation in folklore studies which claims that the emperor was considered a "wandering god," but I'm not familiar with the details of this argument.

During the period from the middle ages to the modern period, the emperor could be described as the most elite member of a nobility that traced its descent from the heavenly gods. Residing in the imperial palace in Kyoto, he was the high priest of etiquette from old. The "emperor system," which protected this role, also maintained a certain authority for the emperor, but he was not the source of either a power or a morality sufficient to control and restrain the consciousness of the people.

There is no doubt that the appearance of the Meiji emperor in full regalia and his generals carrying Western-style sabers represented a substantial break with tradition and came as a surprise to the people. The reign of the same emperor as an absolute monarch, having seized all right to rule, was also without historical precedent. Such unprecedented practices dated only from the enactment of the Meiji Constitution and the establishment of the constitutional monarchy after the dissolution of the bakufu, and the abolition of the position of shogun. From its initiation to its end, following Japan's defeat in the Second World War, this system lasted at most a mere half century. Nonetheless, after the Meiji emperor, the process of deification of the emperor was incessantly reinforced, to the point where it seemed likely to undermine the modernization of Japan. There was even a school principal who committed *seppuku* after a photograph of the emperor — one of the "Imperial Portraits" sent out to primary and middle schools across the country — was destroyed in a fire. Of course, this occurred during the Shōwa Period. This style of deification was, without question, unrelated to the individual identities of the successive historical emperors. Why then was it necessary to construct such a fabrication? I want to consider this question further from the perspective of the *ie* system and its diffusion.

THE "*IE* SYSTEM" AND THE SUPPRESSION
OF HUMAN RIGHTS

It is well known that the Meiji Restoration was led by lower-level samurai, but whether they were effective in dismantling the class system is less clear. It could be argued, in fact, that they universalized the Confucian style of morality they carried with them into the Meiji Period and that one consequence of their attempts to "raise standards" was a further intensification of their contempt for the people.

We can find a partial expression of this problem in a discussion by Professor Hozumi Yakka of the drafting of the Meiji Civil Code during a lecture on the subject of constitutional law. Hozumi was a professor at Tokyo Imperial University in the early Meiji Period. He believed that "the customs of farmers should not even be considered as customs. The farmers should seek to model themselves after the warrior and noble classes." This attitude was incorporated into the Meiji Civil Code almost verbatim. It was most directly expressed in the protection of the male bloodline within the structure of the institution of marriage — the "*ie* system."

In the intensely communal rural villages of Japan, contrary to what is generally believed today, the vertical relationship of power between blood parents and their children was not particularly close. In addition to the blood parents, children had numerous adoptive parents, starting with the godparents. As adults, almost none married a spouse chosen by their parents. It is said that it was the norm for couples to form within cohorts, and in such cases the support of the other young people of one's own generation was more significant than parental approval. Inheritance practices were also not strict. Cases of inheritance by the eldest daughter or even the youngest child were known across Japan. In other words, the portion of Japanese society that lived under the stoic morality of Confucianism and defended the patriarchal structure of parent-child relations and inheritance patterns — both essential elements of the *ie* system — was the warrior class, a mere 6 percent of the population. It is difficult to see how this can be described as

Japanese "tradition." We would do better to limit our understanding of who championed the Confucian "system" to the warrior class in the period that followed the feudalism of the Tokugawa* Period. Because some 90 percent of the population had to be converted, it is not surprising that they saw the need for new ideological and practical structures suited to the rapid and effective dissemination of these principles.

From the viewpoint of the people, the Meiji Civil Code enforced the will of a high-handed cultural minority. Under the new code the freedom to choose one's own spouse was scorned as a "wild match." The approval of the household head became necessary before marriage or employment. In no other period had the people experienced such an intensification of the master-servant relationship between the household head and family members, or such a disregard for the will of individual family members. Even the wife of the head of a household was in the same legal category as minors and the mentally incompetent (the latter group was also banned from procreating). This status of wives amounted to a total denial of their human rights. In an environment that required the birth of a male heir for the continuation of a household, young girls were discriminated against from the moment of their birth.

Despite the contemporary backdrop of the constitutional monarchy, the conservative parties of the early Meiji Period remained dissatisfied with the new civil code. Hozumi Yakka, whom I mentioned earlier, expressed this discontent in his "Birth of a Civil Code, Death of Filial Piety." The title itself makes his position clear. It is likely that the conservatives viewed the introduction of a legal system incorporating such concepts as rights and duties as a dangerous fuse that might ignite the people's consciousness of human rights. When the bakufu's stable and resilient structures of control collapsed, there was no guarantee that the traditional, indigenous energy of the merchants and farmers would not coalesce around an increased awareness of human rights generated by the climate of insurrection. A major concern of the policymakers of the time must have been to encourage the modernization of the society while containing change within the existing structures of control. What they did was designate a power to both the emperor and the household head beyond the scope of the law — the authority to require unilateral submission in accord with Confucian ethics. They disseminated this new family morality thoroughly under the appellate of "the beautiful and pure customs" of ancient Japan. They used a technique that had been successful at the time of the Meiji Restoration, "the brocade flag" — the borrowing of authority from the emperor. The Imperial Rescript on Education handed down in Meiji 23 (1890) was only the beginning of a process of implanting a national ethic into the hearts of the Japanese through the vehicle of compulsory education.

The modern reader may at first glance see nothing more to the rescript than a genuine statement of praise for the imperial family. On closer examination, however, it can be recognized as the first introduction into the national public domain of the concept of "nation-as-family" — Japan's peculiar kind of national polity, which is anchored in a family system that encodes the Confucian ethic of filial piety and the imperialist historical view together.

IMPERIALIST SENTIMENTS AND THE PRIVILEGE OF AGGRESSION

Within the Japanese system of "nation-as-family," the imperial household holds the position of the main house, and the people become the branch families. An adoptive relationship is formed between nation and family, and within this framework "loyalty" and "filial piety" are inextricably bound to each other at a structural level. Consequently, it became even more difficult to distinguish between the controller and the controlled in the modern period than during the feudal period. In the modern period, in matters relating to government (the emperor and the nation), the concepts of loyalty and "voluntary" self-sacrifice were internalized by the people as the ultimate virtues. This process provided a uniquely favorable environment for the internal systems of a late-developing country, keen to achieve the goals of national unity and industrialization. The union of nation and self-sacrifice around

the common goal of "Japan as number one" has formed the foundation of a Japanese work ethic that proposes low wages and overwork
as the raisons d'être of the individual worker. At the same time, this
approach has fostered the continued existence of selfless patriotism as
a key component of the Japanese national character. It was a primary
force behind the social predisposition toward giving priority to the
"public good" while placing social welfare on the shelf, a predisposition still apparent in Japan today.

Fundamentally, what the household head and the emperor had in
common was the fact that neither of them had the rights of a dictator
in the modern sense of the word. The authority they could claim was
only whatever came to them as the representatives of their ancestors.
It was not an autonomous authority, which they could claim in their
own right. And their responsibilities and duties were held not in relation to the individual members of their particular family group but in
relation to the ancestors they shared with that group. Within a group
organized on this basis, even if an individual member is sacrificed for
the sake of "family name," "company," or "country," the leader does
not need to suffer from any sense of conscience or responsibility. Not
only are vertical relations of political influence and power structure
clearly in place but it is also difficult for any oppositional relationship
to develop between victim and aggressor.

The social action taken by the Japanese people in August 1945 is
best understood in the context of this psychological makeup. Hungry,
burned out of their homes, and bereaved of loved ones — all for a war
fought in the name of the emperor — there was almost no one who
blamed the emperor himself. Some suffered the defeat as the direct
result of the incompetence of the people and took their own lives to
atone for what they considered a disloyalty that had endangered the
continuity of the imperial line. The majority of the people, rather than
identify themselves as victims and pursue those responsible for the
war, chose to try to close the door on the whole situation, referring to
it simply as "a crime of the people." While those who fought in the
war considered it a "senseless" war, they did not consider the young

war-dead "senseless victims." The people fashioned the dead into tragic "war heroes," enshrined them, erased their victim status, and exempted themselves from all responsibility.

The same general structures are found between men and women. If anything, the structural mechanisms are even more complex in the case of gender. For example, in the pre-modern warrior class, a woman's virginity was considered more important than life itself. The wives and daughters of the samurai class were educated to choose death rather than risk rape. If we consider that men of the same period who kept mistresses and frequented the brothels of the pleasure quarters were regarded as men of the world, we can discern a gross inequity. In the modern period there are practices related to the status of the female that are even more difficult to comprehend. It has to be seen as a modern irony that the burgeoning trade in young female bodies from the Meiji Period onward was a consequence of the poverty caused by the downfall of the old samurai families and the impoverishment of the farmers. There were many young women who lost their freedom through a system of prepaid labor that sold them into the spinning mills—the location of so many "sad histories of working women"—but still worse off were the girls sold into brothels. Why was the traffic in female bodies possible in an environment where the prevalent sexual morality continued to claim that it valued virginity over life? A filial ethic has come into play here—"for the sake of the family"; "to save the household from ruin." Though the daughters could probably predict the ultimate fate of their bodies once they were sold, if they refused to go, they would be branded as unfilial; and, as the Imperial Rescript on Education stated, filial piety and loyalty were inseparable components of the national ethic. For young girls, whose position was already weak, there was no hope of defeating this ethic. They threw themselves into the world of prostitution, taking their only solace in the fact that they would be the future heroines of tales of filial piety. In exercising their "parental rights," the parents themselves ended up in exactly the same position of victim as their daughters. They were no more able to question their role of aggressor than the daughters could question their role as victim. There are even records of praise for this unification of parent and child in the act of self-sacrifice:

> What is needed today is beauty of the human heart. It was evident in the many brothels in the days of the Yoshiwara. In this time of emergency we must sustain our national ethic, built as it is upon the memory of the beauty of such human devotion.

These words were spoken by Funeda Chu, a Diet member, in an address to the Special Congress of the National Federation of Brothels in the year Shōwa 10 (1935), when Japan was mobilizing for war.

From a modern perspective, it is nothing short of grotesque that a Diet member should have praised the prosperity of brothels as an aspect of the national ethic and then gone on to aestheticize the sale of young girls' bodies as representing "beauty of the human heart" as Funeda did. But this structure, where the compassion of the powerful is prerequisite to the self-sacrifice of the powerless, is a special characteristic of a Japanese style of discrimination nurtured within the emotional climate of imperialism. This structure is still in place today. Incidentally, the same Diet member, Funeda, continued to be active in the political arena after the end of the war and, if my memory serves me correctly, served as speaker of the Lower House.

THE ANATOMY OF DEPENDENCE AND THE FAMILY-EMPEROR SYSTEM

Doi Takeo argues in his *Anatomy of Dependence* (1971) that the ideology of imperialism is an ideology of dependence. According to Doi the first hint of this association came to him through the remarks of a law student who had been coming to him as a patient. The student announced that he wanted to confide the cause of his nervous breakdown to someone but that no one was willing to be his confidant. He recognized, according to Doi, that his desire for *amae* was not being met. And as for his recovery, he hoped for the advent of "a person to replace his mother," a person whom he also referred to as "someone who will act as my aide." Doi explains that it was the patient's peculiar choice of the word "aid" — he chose a term used in the Meiji Constitution in the specific context of "aid to the sovereign activities of the emperor" — that led to his discovery of the psychological significance of the emperor's status. The emperor's position is such that there is nothing he decides or resolves for himself, and yet at the same time that he is totally dependent on the aid of those around him, he also occupies the highest position in the land. Doi goes on to claim that "only someone who is the pure embodiment of the dependency of the infant can qualify to stand at the pinnacle of Japanese society." And, he continues, "there is no essential difference between" the Meiji Constitution's declaration that "the emperor is divine and not to be disobeyed" and its stipulation that "the emperor is the symbol of the Japanese nation."

Though I may not agree with all that Doi has to say, he has certainly pinpointed a certain aspect of the Japanese mentality as it concerns the relationship between authority and servitude. The point made by Maruyama Masao in *Japanese Thought* (1961), that "the imperial system is responsibility-free," is relevant not only within the history of political thought but also from the point of view of social psychology.

The psychological structure identified by Doi, wherein the person at the top does not take responsibility for decisions made but depends on the advice of "aides," is not limited to the example of the emperor and his immediate "aides." This structure can also be found operating between the head of a household and the family members or between corporate executives and their subordinates. One could go even further and argue that this deep structure is at the very heart of the "Japanese spirit," the soft structure of Japanese society that has sustained such traditional units as the *ie*, the "company as family," and the very concept of the "nation." It is possible that the underlying foundations of the alternative "maternal" structures, which have gained such currency of late, can also be traced back to this deep structure. Since the Meiji Period, Japan has constructed what is clearly a patriarchal legal system, and yet, as stated earlier, over this same period the relationship between the controlled and the controller has become increasingly unclear.

We must not forget that beginning in the Meiji Period, when Japan set itself on the path to modern constitutional statehood, this society has been rigidly administered under the patriarchal principles of the West. Japan's rise to the top in the classroom of modernization has been measured solely by the extent and speed of the process of Westernization. Because the proliferation of patriarchal principles meant an ongoing systematization of the processes of selection and exclusion, advances in Japan's modernization saw the status of the individual increasingly determined by such factors as education, family lineage, and financial status. The result of all this was a reshuffling of the existing class system.

Rapid social change such as this can give rise to extensive problems of identity crisis — more for males than for females. In the Japanese case, the sentiments surrounding the emperor system offered, at two separate levels, life rafts for the victims of the crisis. First, the status of "subject of the emperor" guaranteed a racial identity. Second, the creation of the concept of "maternal desire" provided a foundation for the potential coexistence of the contradictory functions of male dependency on the female and male exploitation of the female. Seen from a female point of view, the "family-emperor" system required not only that a woman devote herself to an overbearing husband but also that she take responsibility for offering aid in accord with his dependent male role. Moreover, she was expected to take responsibility for the countless concerns of the family/household. Despite all this, women were categorized, together with children, as intellectually incompetent and unaccountable under the law. In this way, women were effectively excluded from public life. These contradictory "traditions" still cast their shadow over contemporary Japan.

THE IMPACT OF FEMINISM

The continually intensifying process of estrangement of the human heart is the natural outcome of a totally efficient industrial society.

Psychologists were predicting this phenomenon as early as the 1930s. By the 1950s, however, we find, in such examples as Herbert Marcuse's advocacy of a shift from a logos- to an eros-based civilization, that this process of estrangement has been redefined as an effective cure for the ailing condition of industrial society. Either way, today sexual oppression and its offshoot, sexual prejudice, are leading us down a blind alley. The problem is how to escape. In the Japanese case, there is a particularly high risk that an ideology of the mother will surface. For example, in discussing the phenomenon of estrangement, Doi Takeo suggests that Goethe predicted this condition early in the nineteenth century. He goes on to quote from the ending of *Faust*, "He will be eternally drawn to the feminine." Only a few lines further on, Doi refers to the shift in human pursuits from logos to eros saying, "As suggested at the end of *Faust*, there is a *longing for a maternal being* or, to put it differently, we are drawn toward *amae* [my emphasis]." In other words, the companion sought by Doi's patient (the law student) was not merely someone of the opposite sex — a female — but the Mother. Doi himself, the analyst treating the patient, has unconsciously transformed the "feminine" into the image of the "maternal," and this in turn is transformed into the concept of *amae* as the layers keep shifting. Would it be going too far to say that here, in the equation feminine = mother = *amae*, we can glimpse the deep psychological layers of desire of the modern Japanese.

If, as Doi claims, the systematization and rationalization of infantile dependency (the seeking of an "aide") is a product of the ideology of the emperor system, then it must be said that the related concept of "maternal desire" is rooted in dangerous ground. At the risk of oversimplifying, if an individual, for one reason or another, has embraced a sense of "lack" that arises from some childhood experience and has also developed a sense of unsatisfied desire because of this lack, we can reasonably acknowledge that such an individual might emotionally, if unconsciously, equate the comfort and security of the relationships of "aid" implicit in the ideology of the emperor system with the desired maternal substitute. Whether male or female, the individual who harbors these unsatisfied desires will create a vicious circle within which it is difficult to sustain an equal relationship with a member of the opposite sex. Herein lie the links between the ideology of the emperor system, the ideology of the mother, and their common agent, the ideology of *amae*.

In the case of Goethe, the final lines of *Faust* refer to the "feminine" and *only* that—not "woman" and certainly not the "Mother." It is possible, in fact, to interpret Goethe's proposed ultimate salvation of humankind, the "feminine," as a recovery of the "female principle" in each of us. A complete reassessment of values is needed in order to restore relativity to the foundations of existence. Only in this way can we hope to retreat from nihilism and restore equilibrium to the lives of people who have been transformed into either "monsters of ideas" or the reverse of the same coin, "monsters of pleasure"—both expressions of the unilateral dominance of the male principle. At the very least, however much of a compromise it might be, this would result in a continuation of the existing patriarchal ideology but one that has been freed of the present insidious structures of the world of "*amae*-ing" ("aid-ing") mothers. But if we give no thought to our own individual development and unquestioningly accept the dominant stereotypes of maleness and femaleness, each seeking either the Mother or Father as a partner, we are only a short step away from a return to the ideological nationalism of the emperor system. For this reason feminism, with its dual aims of equality in human relations and the dismantling of patriarchal society, has the potential to have an impact on the current tide of "maternal desire" in Japan.

Finally, I would emphasize that, whatever their underlying objectives, those who argue that the emperor system is a convergence of the religious sentiments and the way of thought of the Japanese people risk encouraging a revitalization of the imperial myth. Furthermore, when the people of contemporary Japan, having far outpaced any process of Western modernization to occupy a seat as the people of a major economic power, use the name of "multi-culturalism" in an attempt to force their style of imperialist culture on other countries, they must realize that what they are really describing is cultural imperialism. Just as true internationalism is not a homogeneously Western

world, neither should it be a global flaunting of the cultural peculiarities of the Japanese. Surely what we should be striving for is the
construction of a new paradigm of solidarity within which we learn
from the humility of the cultures of Central and South America, Africa, and Asia — the cultures of the third world — in order to better
decode our own culture. It is only by valuing our mutual differences
that we can take the first steps toward decoding the ideology of imperialism at the levels of both the family and society as a whole.

Selected Works

Ai no densetsu — Geijutsuka to joseitachi (The Legend of Love: Artists and
    Women). Sanichi Shobō, 1968; new ed., Kōsaido Shuppan, 1989.
Bosei to wa nani ka: Atarashii chi to kagaku no chihei kara (What is Mother-
    hood? From the Horizon of the New Sciences and Knowledge). Kaneko
    Shobō, 1986.
Feminizumu no uchū (The Universe of Feminism). Shinhyōron, 1983.
Feminizumu to ekorojī (Feminism and Ecology). Shinhyōron, 1986.
Harukanaru koibito ni — Bētōben: Ai no kiseki (For My Sweetheart — Bee-
    thoven: A Trace of Love). Chikuma Shobō, 1991.
Josei: Sono sei no shinwa (Women: A Myth of Gender). Orijin Shuppan Sentā,
    1982.
Keizai sekkusu to jendā (Economic Sex and Gender). Co-authored. Shin-
    hyōron, 1983.
Sensō to onnatachi: Onna no ronri kara no hansen nyūmon (War and Women:
    An Antiwar Primer Based in Women's Logic). Orijin Shuppan Sentā, 1982.
Shinguru karuchaā: Posuto famirī no yukue (Single Culture: The Post-Family
    Age). Yuhikaku, 1987.
Yasashii kankei (Gentle Relationships). Kōsaido Shuppan, 1992.

All the publishers are located in Tokyo unless otherwise indicated.

IDE SACHIKO
Professor at the Japan Women's University; Linguist

» » » » » » » » » » » »

A PROFESSOR OF LINGUISTICS at Japan Women's University, Ide Sachiko is one of the two women in this book who is a full-time academic. She has published extensively in both English and Japanese, especially on the issue of women's language in Japan. Ide's interest in the comparative analysis of women's speech and honorifics in Japanese and English has led her to spend considerable research time in the United States at such institutions as Harvard, the University of North Carolina, the University of Wisconsin, and the University of Hawaii.

From her experience abroad both as a graduate student and as a professor, Ide has developed a strong awareness of the significant differences in the status of academic women in the United States and Japan. She is intensely aware of the gender politics of the university and speaks openly of her own attempts to develop successful strategies for survival within that institution in Japan. For Ide, language plays a crucial role as individual women construct these strategies, an even more crucial one in Japan than in North America because of the high level of gender coding that permeates every level of the Japanese language. Ide has explored the implications of the densely inflected nature of women's speech in Japan through both the detailed analysis of the linguistic construction and functioning of specific gendered forms and the location of these forms in the sociolinguistic context of case studies. She is particularly interested in questions related to women's manipulation of language in such diverse forums as the family, shops, classrooms, formal and informal social events, conferences, meetings, and interviews.

Ide is also concerned with the advantages and disadvantages of applying Western feminist models and criteria of analysis to Japanese contexts. There is an obvious engagement with Western linguistic and feminist scholarship throughout her own book *Women's Language, Men's Language*. The examples she presents in the section of that book translated in this volume support and develop the work of such Western theorists as Dale Spender and Robin Lakoff while also demonstrating why she considers gender coding to be even more intense in Japan than in the West.

Ide is aware that she is constantly struggling to describe the nature of Japanese women's language from within, and her analysis is always shaped by this inescapable "insider" status. In this context, her discussion of the experience of writing in English rather than in Japanese is striking. As a woman writing for a Japanese academic audience, Ide is constantly questioning the choices she must make regarding the gendered level of her writing. Is the adoption of a standard academic voice an erasure of her voice as a woman or a rejection of the disempowered value of feminine forms? Can feminine forms be reclaimed or redefined positively, or are they indelibly marked as inferior? When Japanese women speak and write in new contexts, how can they negotiate their way through the linguistic minefield of women's language in order to develop the strategies of self-expression and self-representation that suit their lives? During our interview Ide and I shifted from her office to her home, where an older woman was engaged in some domestic work. Ide immediately pointed out the multiple contexts of power in which she finds herself speaking daily as she moves through a variety of roles that include mother, wife, employer, employee, teacher, senior colleague, and junior colleague.

In both the interview and the book chapter translated here, the question of women and power arises. Ide argues for the need to complicate the notion of power, regarding it as something that is not given or static but negotiated differently in the multiple contexts of women's lives. For Ide, language is at the heart of the gender politics of this process. The concept of power seems to be less fluid than this in her book as she attempts to describe the complex workings of gendered syntactic and lexical repertoires in the Japanese language. Ide acknowledges that in *Women's Language, Men's Language* she found it necessary to reduce the unpredictability of individual linguistic performance to generalized rules and categories. It is clear in the interview, however, that this simplification of power within the project of describing specific sociolinguistic codes of appropriateness does not reflect Ide's usual understanding of the day-to-day complexity of the circulation of power between speaking, gendered subjects.

Some critics of Ide's work have pointed out that her descriptions of the conditions of women's lives are often rooted in dominant stereotypes, but Ide responds that her descriptions of women's practice and experience fit the stereotypes because they remain representative of the conditions of daily life of most Japanese women. The real myth, she argues, is the notion that the stereotypes are no longer true. An important distinction needs to be drawn here between what women do and how women represent themselves. Most married women in Japan today work outside the home, often in part-time, low-paid, unskilled jobs — jobs traditionally marked as working-class. However, in their nonwork environments the majority of these same women would identify and represent themselves as middle-class and upwardly mobile. For Japanese women in the 1990s "class" is a slippery notion. In the often-contradictory or multiple contexts in which they find themselves, language — in particular the presence or absence of feminine and honorific forms — is an important masking or passing mechanism in the process of self-representation.

The trend toward increased patterns of hyper-correction (the excessive and/or incorrect use of honorific forms) in young women's polite speech levels seems to indicate an intensification rather than the often-predicted rejection of popular markers of "feminine" and "appropriate" behaviors. Ide argues that Japanese women speakers need speech strategies that are more complex than those proposed in the work of Western feminists to obviate the "intrinsic" negative or disempowered quality of female speech. The chapter on gendered speech forms translated here was chosen because its detailed description of the functional differences between male and female speech patterns in even the most basic daily utterances illustrates the complexity and pervasiveness of gender differentiation to all Japanese communication.

Ide is one of a growing number of Japanese feminists who have identified the centrality of issues of language, in particular women's speech, to the challenge facing Japanese women as they seek to redefine their roles and status. It is striking how often questions of language arise in the interviews and writings of the other nine women. Ide's work offers a careful introduction to this issue of gender and language, which informs and contextualizes much of the rest of the volume. From the obvious sensitivity to the power and manipulation of language of a poet such as Kōra Rumiko to the detailed critiques by Nakanishi Toyoko and Miya Yoshiko of the role of language in the medicalization and management of women's bodies, the relationship between women and words is identified as central to a redefinition of the female condition in Japan.

Interview

SB: How long have you been teaching at Japan Women's University?

IS: It must be fourteen years.

SB: There are still very few women who hold a tenured position in a Japanese university. Are you conscious of any problems you face as a women in academia in Japan?

IS: I think my own case is somewhat the exception, for this university happens to be my alma mater as well as a women's university. In this environment I think I am faced with very few obstacles that I could attribute to being a woman or to any form of sexual discrimination. I realize, however, that women face many difficulties in more male-dominated and traditional institutions.

SB: I imagine that your own experience is important for the students studying under you.

IS: Yes, in the sense that I feel an obligation to do all I can to encourage my students to take their studies seriously and to pursue any possibility to travel and study overseas. Young Japanese women travel overseas a great deal these days, but usually on quick package tours. It's almost the equivalent of a "coming of age" ceremony, like the debutante ball. This isn't the kind of travel I am referring to. I encourage them to try to stay in a country long enough to gain some real sense of the way of life of a culture other than their own. I believe that study abroad is an extremely valuable experience.

I also find that my own experiences as a junior faculty member have a significant effect on how I treat younger colleagues when they join the staff. I recognize how important it is to encourage them in every way possible to develop their research and teaching interests.

SB: A frequent criticism of academic feminists in North America is that they are not in contact with the grass-roots feminism of the women's movement. Does the same criticism arise in Japan? I asked Aoki Yayoi the same question, and she felt that there is not yet such a pronounced gap in Japan.

IS: I think it is becoming more of an issue as the number of academic women increases. I can only really respond from my own point of view and experience. I think that all women, academic or non-academic, are overworked. Women who are full-time mothers and homemakers receive no real credit for the work they perform. Women who work outside the home as well are essentially carrying two full-time jobs. One is paid and the other not. There is so little time or energy left over that I know I make conscious decisions as to what I can and cannot take on above and beyond what I am already doing at home and at the university. I do feel a commitment to the women's movement and for that reason I am a financial member of various organizations, but I admit that my involvement is limited to financial support.

At this time I feel it is more important for me to be an active member of the Linguistics Association of Japan and to establish my reputation as a linguist who is also a woman committed to feminist research. My main objective at this stage is to establish my position in the male-dominated academy. This doesn't mean becoming the same as my male colleagues, but gaining recognition of a woman's right to participate equally in this environment. The intellectual domain is still very closed to women in Japan. I think this is an important area in which to work for change. The presence of a woman at the executive meetings of the Linguistics Association of Japan and the more active participation of women in its conferences have had a definite impact upon the internal workings of that organization. It is not that the women have to adapt to fit into this world but rather that the academic world is having to adjust to the reality of an increasing number of women entering its ranks.

SB: As someone who has lived for several years in the United States, do you perceive any differences between the ideological focuses of feminism in Japan and the States?

IS: I suppose one thing that comes to mind immediately is the emphasis placed upon *boseiai* (maternal love) in feminist discourse in Japan. I'm sure you are aware of this concept.

SB: Yes, in fact it was the focus of a considerable controversy at the 1984 Australian Asian Studies Conference in Melbourne. In response to a question from the floor, Ueno Chizuko stated that Japanese women have a far greater awareness of the value of motherhood than "Western" women, a position I have heard her reiterate in various situations since then. Her statement created quite a furor at the time, and several Australian feminists commented on the essentialism of the claim. Ueno countered that the concept of bosei *was not a simple equivalent of the English "motherhood" and had to be understood in the context of its development and application in the specific environment of Japan.*

IS: I can see how such a claim might generate accusations of essentialism, but at the same time I think there is something fundamental to Japanese feminism and questions of female identity that cannot be fathomed without reference to *boseiai.* When I speak about the concept in English, even though I know that "maternal love" is a perfectly reasonable translation, I still resort to the Japanese expression. There is something quite specific about its significance within Japanese society and gender relations.

The function of *boseiai* is not limited to the relationship between mother and child. The bonding of couples is often founded on *boseiai.* It is a fundamental social relationship, which is central to the female identity in Japanese society. Women don't consider *boseiai* as oppressive or something to be overcome. After all, it is preferable that the maternal or nurturing function should be one of the basic structures of social relations rather than more aggressive — what might be characterized as masculine or patriarchal — forms of power. I think that, on the whole, American feminism has been critical of placing too much emphasis on the link between female identity and the maternal or nurturing role. This has possibly led to a devaluing of the maternal role. This would have to be one of the basic differences between Japanese and American feminists.

For me, the practice of *boseiai* is not limited to the domestic or private world. I see myself extending that role into my professional world as well. In the past men ran universities, departments, and committees according to a style that depended on more traditional notions of power and position. I feel, as a woman who is committed to the values of *boseiai,* that it is appropriate for me to use my own preferred style when taking on the same responsibilities within these institutions. When I have a committee or project, I do see myself in a maternal role, and this means that I approach the members of the group in a quite different way than a male colleague would. I think this is good. I am in no way apologetic for taking on a mothering role. I suspect that a statement like this might be frowned upon by some of my American feminist friends, but this is one important way of introducing change into academic institutions and practices.

SB: As a non-Japanese woman speaking Japanese, I think the aspect of the language I am most conscious of is honorifics and the use of women's speech. I am constantly making choices about which situations do and don't warrant polite forms. The choice is always compounded by my own sense that these decisions are at some level political ones intimately related to questions of power and gender. I also have to keep reminding myself that, as a foreign woman in Japan, I am in a privileged position of difference that can create a higher level of tolerance toward the choices I make.

IS: Yes, I think it's probably true that you may be allowed to be more playful, even defiant, in the choices you make. Gender marking of speech in Japan, where there is a clearly defined concept of women's speech, makes the area of language a far more complex one for feminist analysis. It also adds a whole other level of complexity to women's daily lives. You know Robin Lakoff's work, I'm sure. When I first read Lakoff I was struck by how extreme the Japanese case was compared to what Lakoff was describing. There is one line I still remember very clearly, where Lakoff says that for a woman to succeed in the professional world she must be bilingual — that is to say, she must be fluent in both men's and women's language. This summed up my feelings of some twenty years.

On a personal level I know that when I write for an academic journal or prepare a public lecture, I strive to achieve a style of language that is substantially different from the language that I speak or write in other contexts. I don't believe that this same gap exists for my male colleagues. Written and spoken language are not the same, I know, but this is definitely something else again that is occurring at the level of gender. It amounts to a form of bilingualism on the part of women who want to move out into the public domain.

SB: There are many different attitudes toward women's language among feminists. Some people argue for the abolition of all forms of discriminatory language usage and consider women's speech to be inherently discriminatory — Dale Spender, for example — and some argue that women's language is a resource to be protected and nurtured. Hélène Cixous calls women's language the last ground that is not colonized by men.

IS: What comes to mind immediately is the business lunch I just left. I was meeting with the president of the university and several guests. The president is a scholar of Japanese classical poetry and has a Ph.D. in literature. She's a well-respected scholar and someone I admire deeply. Whether at a formal lunch or trying to deal with the aggressive style of certain of my male colleagues in a faculty meeting, she always maintains a perfect level of women's speech. By this, I don't mean flowery language but a very graceful and sophisticated style. She never resorts to excessive levels of politeness but establishes a distance between herself and the others through the very careful selection of her speech levels. It is this distance, which she is always in control of, that enables her to manage the atmosphere of any situation no matter how tense or difficult. Her use of women's language is brilliant. You could never argue that she is in any way lowering her own position in relation to those she is speaking with. She makes the tradition work for her. Owing to her high professional and intellectual status, she has access to a whole range of honorific forms that are unavailable to any one else present, especially the men. This distinguishes her from everyone else, and she is able to manipulate it into a strong mechanism of influence. Her language is beautiful to listen to, and the effect it has is remarkable. I recently asked her if in the future she would keep not only written copies of her speeches but also tapes.

SB: You made a distinction before between women's language in the private and the public domain. Clearly your president has been very successful in developing an individual strategy, but what is the situation in a more general context? You describe the negative characterization of women's language in great detail in your book Women's Language, Men's Language; *do you see the prejudice against women's language lessening in recent years?*

IS: I think that considerable progress has been made. Until the early 1980s only men read the news on NHK, the national television station. Then, gradually, women came onto the scene but usually only to read domestic news or the weather. By the late 1980s, the concept of a woman news-anchor was no longer a novelty.

SB: *Is this a reflection of some change in attitude toward women's language, or are these women bilinguals in the sense you were just talking about?*

IS: The distinction you're making is a good one. The language of the news hasn't changed. I think what this represents is progress in the public acceptance of the female voice in the public domain. Just the sound of a woman reading the news would have been an enigma to many only a few years ago. The change is coming slowly, but that is not a bad thing. We suffer less major setbacks this way. The progress is most obvious when you look at the young. I have an adult daughter. When I listen to her speaking on the telephone to her male friends, I notice a tremendous difference between the way she talks with them and the way I spoke with my male friends at the same age. It's sometimes not obvious whether she is speaking to a male or a female friend. That is perhaps the strongest evidence of change. If I listen to a woman of my own age talking on the telephone, I can almost always say with certainty if it is a man or woman at the other end.

SB: *Do you think that this changes when a young woman marries and enters into the social relationships that surround the family in Japan?*

IS: I think that it doesn't change. I hope not, anyway, but the social pressure on young women to adjust their lives to the new role of wife, daughter-in-law, and mother are strong. It's an interesting point. Only time will tell. We will just have to observe future generations.

SB: *One thing that becomes clear very quickly when examining performative situations for honorifics in Japanese is the fact that gender is only one determining factor. Among women, class and authority also dictate the levels of politeness to be observed. There are situations in which these other factors override gender. I heard an exam-*

ple this morning while walking in my neighborhood, when a woman of about sixty, dressed very well in traditional kimono, opened the door to her home and addressed a delivery man in anything but polite or respectful language.

IS: These other factors are also important, but listening to you just now reminded me of your earlier question about the differences between Japanese and Western feminisms. I noticed while I was in the United States that power and authority are central concepts there in much feminist analysis. This is another major difference. I don't believe that Japanese feminists place so much emphasis on questions of power. What I'm saying now ties back into my earlier point about *boseiai*. To value, and work within, the structure of *boseiai* would quickly be interpreted as accepting a low power position by many Western feminists. The same might be said of my president's choice of working within women's language. I think that Japanese women are more ready to look at alternative structures of social relations that are not based on power — at least not a simple, singular notion of power. There is a willingness to recognize power as something that is in process or negotiation, something that shifts levels and balance from context to context rather than remaining static. In a sense, this Western feminist privileging of power with a capital "P," as both a tool of analysis and a political objective, can only lead to duplication, more of the same. It doesn't offer any new direction.

There is an old saying in Japan to the effect that the future of the country is decided on the laps of geisha. There is still some evidence for this today. It conjures up the image of the politician lying cradled in the arms of a geisha. This is *boseiai*, too. Within this system men are always little boys. They are dependent on their mothers until they marry, and then the wife takes up the *boseiai* role in relation to the husband, and later toward her children. This role is the fundamental thread of all social interaction in Japan, and Woman is at the center of it, in a position not of weakness or power but of influence.

SB: In your own work you are obviously trying to introduce certain Western theoretical approaches into the study of Japanese women's language. What risks or problems do you perceive in the application of Western theory to Japanese contexts?

IS: It's surprising that you should ask me that question as it is the exact issue I have been considering these last few days. I have been reading several pieces in English that deal with the questions that surround taking a theory outside its own cultural context and wondering what its significance is for my own work. I would like to work on this question further from the perspective of a Japanese researcher. I want to explore how the Japanese case can modify Western theory. This reverse encounter intrigues me. In general I think that it would be foolish to ignore Western theory and all that it can bring to the study of language and women's speech in Japan, but at the same time I think that this theory has to be applied with a degree of sensitivity to the cultural variants operating in the Japanese context. The adaptation, not adoption, of Western theory is what is required. How do you deal with these theoretical questions as a Western woman doing research on Japan?

SB: It's a constant issue in my own work also. As a non-Japanese woman coming into Japan to do research on Japanese women, I can never forget my status as outsider. I agree that some of the most interesting results are the adjustments that the Japanese case can require of the Western theory when the two come into contact. If the theory helps develop new readings of gender construction in Japan, then the politics and practice of gender in Japan can also help to develop the theory in new directions. Flexibility is the key, I think. The most frustrating situation for me is to be faced with the statement that I won't be able to understand something because I am a non-Japanese woman. Once this is said, there is nowhere to go.

IS: This is an unfortunate line that Japanese resort to too often. It is foolish in that it only blocks communication and learning. I think, as you say, that flexibility and openness are the key on both sides. Just the fact that we are having this exchange bodes well to me.

SB: You mentioned before we began the interview that you had recently completed a three-year research project on women's language funded by the Ministry of Education. What was the nature of that project?

IS: We developed a theory of the causes of performative variation in women's application of honorific patterns. The study was based on the analysis of a large quantitative data set. Three main variables emerged. The first was gender-related. Women are generally more deferential to men than to other women. We explained this not in terms of power but as a reflection of psychological distance.

The second factor we identified was true for both men and women. In a social context the sender will choose a speech level that reflects a higher degree of deference to the addressee than they would show to that same person in a work context. If you introduce gender into the second situation, you find a higher overall occurrence of polite speech levels among women than among men because women are less often involved in the work environment and more often involved in social contexts. We can tentatively predict that a decrease in the frequency of polite speech forms among women will accompany an increased flow of women into the workplace.

The third factor is closely related to the first and second. We described it as linguistic inflation. We found that the more a woman uses polite speech forms, the less these forms register for politeness. She will develop increasingly higher and more inflected levels of politeness to accommodate the necessary performative range of her daily speech interactions.

Another interesting point we found was that working women have a far wider vocabulary and range of politeness levels than nonworking women, whose activities are largely limited to private and social contexts. I think that findings such as these begin to show how complex the issue of women's language is in the Japanese case, where it is never absent from any speech interaction. In studies of this kind we can begin to look at what Western theory can bring to our analysis and what our findings can do to test and expand the theory.

SB: Possibly because in Japan women's language is so visible — I suppose audible is a better word — feminists here have mounted several campaigns around questions of language. These campaigns have been been based on a recognition of the political nature of language. The most well known case was the fight to change the characters used to write the word for prostitution.

IS: It was Lakoff who said that we are used by language just as much as we use language. In this context I am not sure how women can achieve political change through language reform. Such a project assumes that we can manipulate language from a position outside language. I suspect that such reforms can only affect the surface of language and not its structure, which is the level where it is intrinsically linked to the political. In 1979, when I wrote my book *Women's Language, Men's Language,* I think there was a purpose to listing in detail the types of sexist language common in Japan. It was a strategy suited to that period. I have to admit, however, that when I recently canvassed students in order to look at the contemporary use of discriminatory language, I was surprised to find how much change there has been. There has also been an obvious improvement in the major daily newspapers. Such reductions in the most overtly discriminatory language don't, however, necessarily correspond to any change to the deep structural differentiations between men's and women's speech that I document in detail in that work.

The point is that the fall in the frequency of sexist language has not led to any shift in the importance of women's speech in certain contexts. This brings us back to your point about young females today. Will they continue to use fewer of the polite forms associated with women's speech, or will they change their speech patterns after marriage? Another question is whether the statement I made before about my daughter's telephone conversations takes into account the issue of performative context? I suspect not. A young Japanese university student wouldn't speak with the same level of honorific inflection when addressing a professor, a fellow female student over the telephone, or her grandparent. Yes, I think what I said before may have been too much of a generalization, perhaps even a little optimistic.

SB: Until now we have been talking mainly about academic feminism rather than grass-roots feminism. I know you said that you have had only limited contact with the women's movement, but could you make any comments on the state of the movement in Japan?

IS: I feel I have to be sensitive when commenting on the movement as I am in a sense an outsider, despite being a woman and a feminist. It's my impression that in general the women's movement in Japan is not committed to radical change. There is a fear of going too far, of being too feminist. Many Japanese women are deeply frustrated by the limited lives they lead as wives and mothers, the traditional *okusan* role, but they are not about to leave the family structure or challenge the values at its foundation. It is one thing to fight for the principle of equal employment opportunity but quite another thing to pursue your own individual right to a career. At the same time that the *okusan* who participates in a local women's group is attracted by the language of liberation, she is also devoted to preserving the conservative structures that her life is built around. To begin to undo them would be a very frightening and dangerous process. It is not surprising that such local groups tend to steer away from radical action. The same reluctance helps to explain the tendency for Japanese women to be politically active at the local level, to vote sometimes for the Communist Party or Japan Socialist Party in municipal or prefectural elections, but to vote conservatively at the national level.

I have tremendous admiration for American women who have had the courage to act on their feminism, to divorce their husbands, to raise their children alone, and to make new lives for themselves outside traditional structures. These women have carried a very heavy burden. Far fewer Japanese women have been prepared to take that radical step and move from words into action. Those Japanese women who have done so have had to pay a high price for their decision. Are the rest cowards or clever? I don't know. It is so much easier to follow than to lead.

I should put this more in context so as not to be misunderstood. Japanese women make these kinds of decisions knowing that their average life expectancy is approximately eighty years. They know that there is little or no state support for the elderly, and they can expect to live at least the last decade of life as widows dependent on their children. The decision to take or not to take a radical action that will alienate you from traditional structures of support is made within this long-term framework. The American system is far more flexible and offers more support mechanisms to women who go out on their own.

Another difference between Western feminism and Japanese feminism is the status afforded the *okusan* role. Domestic labor seems to have been devalued by feminism in North America. A woman who chooses to stay home to raise her children feels almost apologetic. This is sad. There has been no equivalent of this in Japan. The *okusan* role is almost revered in this society. It is the working woman who still has to deal with a social stigma, especially if she has school-aged children.

SB: To go back to your own research, how has your work on women's language been received in Japan?

IS: Women's language is so obviously a part of life in Japan that there is no difficulty in getting the concept itself accepted. Problems begin to arise when — say, with my first book — I try to analyze the role language plays in structuring social relations or when I attempt, as in the latest study, to develop a theory to explain the frequency patterns of women's speech. Some critics might go so far as to ask whether women's language even warrants such attention. I just ignore this type of comment. One of the more interesting reactions I have noticed to my work has been the frequency with which my own writing style is mentioned. The most common remark is that I say things in a more straightforward way than a male academic would feel free to do. I'm sure you're familiar with the very vague and noncommittal style that Japanese academics use in their publications. Different critics have commented that the way the "softness" of the women's diction comes through in my writing allows me to say things directly without appearing too forceful. I am not conscious of this when writing, but once it was pointed out to me I could see what they were refering to. I suppose that over the years I have unconsciously developed my own strategy for saying what I want. I think every woman has to find a voice of her own.

Excerpts from *Women's Language, Men's Language*
FIRST PERSON PRONOUNS

When we observe male and female usage of first person pronouns in everyday speech contexts, we find that in identical situations a male speaker uses *watashi* and *boku* while a female speaker uses *watakushi* and *watashi*. Because women are required to be more polite, the parameters for using the formal *watakushi* are greater in women's speech. Even in situations where the social status of the collocuters is the same, the woman is expected to adopt the more humble stance and resort to the formal form. In so doing she signals her respect for the other participants in the conversation.

In Japan appropriate language has a similar function to appropriate attire. At a wedding reception or funeral, out of respect for those concerned, one wears attire that is as formal as possible. The formality of dress acts as an expression of the extent of one's respect for the event. The more formal the attire, the more formal the posture adopted by that individual. Language has a similar relationship to decorum.

It is worth noting that the informal feminine pronouns are all variants of the formal *watakushi*. *Atakushi* replaces the *wa* of *watakushi* with an *a*. *Watashi* simply deletes the *ku* of *watakushi*, and *atashi* replaces the *wa* of *watashi* with an *a*. In other words, while the informal form of the masculine first person pronoun is derived differently than the formal form, the informal forms of the feminine first person pronoun are all contractions of the formal form.

The application of first person pronouns reveals a pattern of male

Translated with the permission of the author by Sandra Buckley.

speakers using various less formal or relaxed forms, such as *boku* and *ore*, in contrast to female speakers who use more formal forms. This pattern can be understood in two ways. First, because the status of women is lower than that of men, women's language is required to reflect this inferior position through the use of formal speech items. Second, one could argue that formal speech reflects the level of refinement and dignity of the speaker. There is a common expression in Japanese, "After all, she's a woman . . ." which is frequently used in criticism of behavior outside the accepted etiquette for a woman. The implication is that as a woman she should know better. The expression "After all, he's a man . . ." also exists, but its usage has nothing to do with criticizing breaches of a male code of etiquette. Rather, it is used in situations where a man is criticized for cowardice or weakness. If a woman chooses a personal pronoun that does not fit the formality of an occasion, her impoliteness is likely to be criticized with the expression "After all, she's a woman." She is expected to know better. The correct choice of personal pronouns and a sensitivity to context are extremely important to women. Therefore, in certain contexts they are likely to focus more on the manner of their speech than on its content.

Individuals placed in situations of the same level of formality will select first person pronouns based on their relative status. For example, in an all male panel discussion two of the participants use *watakushi* while the third uses *boku*. From this we discern that the panelist using *boku* is superior in status to the other two, not only because he chooses to represent himself with the informal designator *boku* but also because he does so in the comparatively formal context of a panel discussion. He is of a sufficiently high status that he is "allowed" to use the informal *boku* in this formal context. In order to show the correct level of respect, the other two panelists cannot use *boku*, for this would be a breach of politeness and inappropriate in the context. Thus, the selection of the first person pronoun, or one's method of self-representation, shows the extent to which the relative relationships of collocuters are psychologically determined. The result is that men's speech is capable of being more flexible, humorous, and relaxed than that of women, for whom gender always adds multiple layers of relational complexity.

TERMS OF SECOND PARTY ADDRESS

In the Japanese language, pronouns are not the only means of designating a second party. For example, in the case of doctors, teachers, Diet members, and other respected individuals, the term *sensei* is used instead of a second person pronoun. A title such as *shachō* (president of a corporation) is also frequently used instead of a proper name or personal pronoun. It is possible to designate a person of higher status by title only, but the same is not true in the case of someone of lower status. A suffix indicating a relationship of respect (*sama*, *san*) or intimacy (*chan*) is also commonly used to designate someone in the second person. The suffix is used in combination with either the family or given name of the person depending on context — for example, Satō-*san* (family name + *san*), Yōko-*san* (given name + *san*), Yōko-*chan* (given name + *chan*).

One can only use a second person pronoun in situations where the referent is of the same status as oneself or lower. It is considered impolite to use a second person pronoun when addressing someone of higher status. *Anata* is the form of second person pronoun most frequently used by a male speaker in addressing somone with whom he is not well acquainted or when speaking in a formal context. (The use of *anata* by a man to address a woman with whom he is romantically involved is a special case. In this situation *anata* has the value of a term of endearment not unlike the English "darling" or "dear.") Depending on the social class of the speaker, *anata* may be contracted to *anta*, which is used more by working-class male speakers. *Anta* is also frequently used in regional dialects. The most commonly used alternative form of the second person pronoun is *kimi*. The speaker who uses *kimi* must be male and of a status equal to or higher than the person whom he is addressing. *Omae* is extremely informal and generally limited to exchanges between males in a close personal relationship. The form *kisama* implies the speaker's sense of superiority over the person spoken to and is usually limited to arguments and ridicule.

At all levels of formality, women are generally restricted to the use of *anata*. There is no situation in which a woman should use *kimi*. The only other acceptable second person pronoun available to women is *anta*, and this form has an inescapable nuance of condescension when used by a woman. Women consistently use the formal form of the second person pronoun more than men. By contrast, when a male speaker is being ostentatious or when he is expressing anger at a second party, he can use the informal *ore* to refer to himself, and when he is expressing condescension he has access to the derogatory second-person pronoun *kisama* (which is ironically derogatory because it is an excessively polite traditional form).

It is quite common for couples to use the second person pronouns *omae*, *kimi*, and *anata*. The husband uses *omae* or *kimi* to address his wife, and the wife uses *anata* to address her husband. The fact that *anata* is more formal than *omae* or *kimi* reflects again the polite posture women adopt in relation to men. This remains true even within the context of a marriage. Because the inferior status of women to men is axiomatic in Japan, it is the norm for women to adopt polite speech. Moreover, when a husband calls his wife, he can use her personal name without a suffix. In Japan this is generally only allowed when a superior addresses an inferior and when individuals share an extremely close relationship. The case of a husband's using the form toward his wife is an example of the former rather than the latter, as evidenced by the fact that a wife would never call her husband by his personal name alone. She would always use a suffix.

How do individuals learn to apply the various forms of personal pronouns? Do female and male children learn distinct applications from the very outset? Or do they use all the forms randomly at first and then acquire the appropriate distinctions during the process of socialization? At first, most children use the form of "given name + *chan*" to designate another child in the second person (e.g., Ken-*chan*, Yōko-*chan*). Very young children use this form to designate both the first person and the second person. There are, however, some very young boys who use the self-referent *boku* from the outset. This is possibly attributable to the mother, who is in close direct contact with the male child, consistently using the form *boku* when she addresses him in the second person pronoun — for example, "Ken-*chan*, boku mo iku?" (Are you going, too, Ken-*chan*?). Although *boku* is the first person pronoun, it functions here as the equivalent of the second person pronoun (*anata*). Perhaps it is the close psychological relationship of the mother to her male child that invites this pattern of usage. It is in fact also very common for people other than a male child's mother to use *boku* to replace the second person pronoun when addressing him, even though they know his proper name.

In this androcentric society the form *boku* seems to have accumulated the value of the favored status of the male (in this case the male child). *Boku* has in fact become so widely used as the second person masculine pronoun that it is not uncommon to hear the compound *boku-chan* used as a proper noun. There is no equivalent to *boku* in the case of female children. The first pronoun used by girls is *watashi*, but it is usually not learned until later than the age at which a boy begins to use *boku*. By the age of three, the majority of boys use the pronoun *boku* as the first person pronoun. By contrast, girls of the same age generally still use the combination of "name + *chan*."

By the time a girl enters kindergarten (at four years of age), she will have learned that she should use *watashi* (or *atashi*) for the first person pronoun and *anata* for the second person. It remains the norm, however, even at this age, for a girl to continue to use "name + *chan*" for both the first and second person pronouns. She generally only uses *watashi*, *atashi*, or *anata* in a formal context. For children, entry into kindergarten means being placed into a more formal context. Girls know that when speaking in public or to a teacher, they are expected to use *watashi* as the self-referent.

Boys use several different forms for the first and second person pronouns in the kindergarten environment. As a self-referent they may use *ore* as well as *boku*, and they also learn to use *omae* for the second person pronoun. *Ore* and *omae* are used to address a close friend or when a boy assumes a superior position. Once again, there are no pronouns of equivalent function in the lexical repertoire of female children. The only variable learned by girls of kindergarten age is the extremely formal *watakushi*. Even from this early age girls recognize that they should use this form in any particularly formal situation. Soon after this age boys learn the form *kimi* as a substitute for the earlier form of "name + *chan*" for the second person pronoun in contexts where they are designating an equal or inferior/junior. From a very early age the repertoire of pronouns and the criteria of selection are significantly different for boys and girls. When a boy says *ore*, he is displaying his masculinity. A four-year-old girl uses *watashi* to indicate that although she is still young, she is a "young lady." Her performance conveys the message, "I know what kind of language to use in a formal situation like this."

From a very young age Japanese boys can already use pronouns to express their own masculinity and power. From about the age of four, when they have developed an awareness of sexual difference, both boys and girls link this awareness to their use of pronouns. In the process of applying gendered forms, they reinforce their individual consciousness of sexual difference.

ZO, ZE AND WA, NO

Final particles reflect the mood and feelings of the speaker. Through the use of final particles, a speaker can add tone or emotion to what is said. Final particles are generally used in informal speech. People tend to avoid final particles when in conversation with someone of a higher status because the use of such informal language would be impolite. Among the numerous final particles in the Japanese language, some are clearly marked for female use and some for male use, but most can be used by both sexes in different contexts. Here, however, I will focus on the final particles that can be used by only one of the sexes. In other words, I am concerned with final particles that exhibit a clear gender marking.

Zo and *ze* are used only by male speakers. Both have the function of drawing the attention of the other party by adding emphasis. Both sound strong (or powerful), and both can be interpreted as showing condescension toward the other party. *Ze* is an even more emphatic form than *zo*. There is also a third form — *yo* — which has the same function but does not carry the connotation of superiority and is, in this sense, somewhat more neutral. Thus, a man could use any of the following: *Omoshiroi zo* (M, -f), *Omoshiroi ze* (M, -f), *Omoshiroi yo* (M, -f) ⟨⟨It's interesting⟩⟩.

When a female wants to attract someone's attention, she uses either *wa* or *yo*. *Wa* softens sentences and is used only by female speakers. By placing *wa* before *yo* at the end of a sentence, a woman can both soften it and add emphasis: *Omoshiroi wa yo* (F, -f). A male speaker has a choice of *zo*, *ze*, and *yo*. The type of final particles available to male speakers indicates their comparative freedom to express themselves strongly and with less concern for politeness. *No* is a final particle used only by females: *Omoshiroi no* (F, -f). It both softens a sentence and adds a quality of cuteness or quaintness. Young boys also use *no* but stop as they grow older: *Omoshiroi no* (F, -f). With the final particle *no*, a sentence is rendered softer, cute, or even childlike. *No* frequently occurs in combination with the emphatic *yo*: *Omoshiroi no yo* (F, -f). In summary, male speakers may use *zo*, *ze*, or *yo*, and female speakers may use *wa yo*, *no*, or *no yo*. *Wa* and *no* are both marked as feminine forms. An American feminist has written that the formation of a question by the intonation of a sentence final particle or suffix is a characteristic of women's speech in various languages. She writes that this function "contributes to the general impression that women's speech is more polite than male speech. It demonstrates politeness at one level while avoiding any sense of pushing a point of view or ideas, and it also allows the other party to feel they have the freedom to agree or not." In Japanese speech *wa* and *no* have this effect in that they soften the impact of a statement by rendering it more polite, less definitive, and unobtrusive.

Here "M" designates a masculine speaker, and "-f" designates informality. "F" designates a female speaker, and "+f" designates formality.

DESU AND DA

Desu is the formal form of the copula, and *da* is the informal form. Male and female speakers use the former, but the latter is generally limited to male speech: *Kore wa hon desu* (M, F, +f), *Kore wa hon da* (M, -f) ⟨⟨This is a book⟩⟩. In an informal context a female speaker can use the copula *da* plus the softener *wa* or replace the copula entirely with one or more final particles: *Kore wa hon da yo*; *Kore wa hon yo*; *Kore wa hon na no* (all = F, -f). With these forms women can avoid using an unmodified *da* in conversation and satisfy the social requirement that women should not use decisive language. The softness in women's speech is thus not limited to tonality but also extends to forms of expression. It can be extrapolated from this that women are not allowed access to informal or decisive patterns of speech. If a woman specifically wishes to take up such forms, she can deliberately choose to use *da*, but this choice will lead to what is seen as unfeminine or inappropriate communication. Because women's speech is required to be soft, it is not possible for women to participate equally in a serious conversation and abide strictly by the sociolinguistic rules. This situation rests on the strong expectation that the social role of women is to be gentle, to promote a bright and pleasant atmosphere for others, and to never put themselves forward in any way.

TABENASAI AND TABETE

Differences can also be found in the male and female use of directives or imperatives. In addition to the imperative verb endings *nasai* (M, F) and *rō* (M), the form *yō* can also be used to indicate the imperative. Whereas *nasai* designates a standard imperative, *rō* is used for a strong and frank order and can only be used by a male speaker addressing someone of lower status than himself: *Tabenasai* (M, F, +f, -f), *Taberō* (M, -f), *Taberō yo* (M, -f) ⟨⟨Eat!⟩⟩. Here again, women cannot use the informal forms. Nor is there any equivalent in women's speech for *rō*. Whether the situation is formal or informal, a woman can only use the imperative form when addressing someone of lower status than herself. What then can women use in an informal context instead of *rō* and *rō yo*? She can use a contraction of the form *-te* + *kudasai* (dropping the *kudasai* and only using) *-te* ⟨⟨please⟩⟩ as a verbal suffix. In this case the contraction creates an incomplete sentence and is thus rendered indecisive or unconvincing: *Tabete kudasai — tabete* (M, F, -f) ⟨⟨please eat⟩⟩. The form *tabete* is a soft or weak request, which amounts to no more than a watered down order and suggests that the speaker is in a low power position. Once again the norm for women's speech emerges as soft and lacking in self-confidence or assertiveness.

THE TOLERANCE LEVELS OF THE PREFIXES *O* AND *GO*

The more formal the situation, the more polite the language. The higher the status of the addressee, the higher the level of honorifics. Honorific or polite forms can also be used to show respect toward a person who is not known to the speaker. Honorific forms are generally more widely used by female than male speakers. An inferior adopts a polite position in relation to his or her superior, and this position is reflected in language. From a slightly different perspective, a woman's correct use of polite language and honorifics reflects her "good breeding" and refinement and is considered a virtue. The use of beautiful language and sensitive responses to relative statuses and contexts are considered virtues in a Japanese woman. However, it can also be argued that this attention to politeness and the form of language leads to a deficit in content. Whether one chooses to look at it negatively from the perspective of sexual discrimination or positively from the perspective of feminine charm, honorifics or polite speech is an important mirror for understanding both how women are seen by society and women's self-image.

O and *go* are decorative prefixes that can be added to nouns, adjectives, adverbs, and some other forms. Both males and females use them, but the frequency is far higher in women's speech: *Sensei no hon*

(M, +f, -h), *Sensei no go-hon* (M, F, +f, +h or M, F, -f,-h), ⟨⟨the teacher's book⟩⟩.

The use of the prefix *go* for the teacher's book indicates the speaker's respect for the owner of the book (a teacher, whose position is higher than that of the speaker). For an adult woman the use of the polite *go* is mandatory in this context; however, if a man were to use *go* here, it would appear excessive, even feminine, unless the teacher was in a clearly superior position or extremely formal circumstances prevailed. A male speaker only uses *o* and *go* in situations where it is necessary for him to be especially deferential toward his collocuter. In other words, the tolerance level for male and female use of these two honorific prefixes is different. It should be noted that *o* and *go* have the same function and level of politeness, but different words take one or the other and they are generally not interchangeable. Which words take which prefix cannot be reduced to a single rule. Let's compare two sentences: *O-shokuji o issho ni shimashō* (M, F, +f, +h), *Shokuji o issho ni shiyō* (M, F, -f, -h) ⟨⟨Let's eat together⟩⟩. Here we are comparing the two verbs *shimashō* (polite and formal) and *shiyō* (informal). The former would be used not only when a woman speaks to a man but also when she speaks to other women. However, a man in exactly the same context can be expected to use *shiyō* when speaking to another man who is not of significantly higher status. Interestingly, a male speaker will probably use the more polite *shimashō* when inviting a woman to eat with him, as a way of verbally gesturing symbolic, if not real, status to the woman. When requesting something politely, one usually uses a higher level of formal language structure than the norm, thus lowering one's own status and elevating that of the person from whom something is sought.

While honorific language is not limited to women's speech in Japanese, the degree and frequency of honorific and polite forms do reflect the nature of sexual difference in Japan. A Japanese woman is always

---

The categories +h and -h designate the presence and lack of politeness, respectively.

expected to demonstrate a higher level of politeness and to use honorifics more frequently than a male speaker. Even those of us whose mother tongue is Japanese find the correct application of honorifics difficult. Because honorifics are intimately linked to context, their usage is learned through daily life. For people who engage frequently in formal situations requiring honorifics, their usage seems relatively easy. Honorific frequency is highest among women of the upper-middle class. Women aspiring to upward mobility within this group use honorifics with greater frequency than the norm—even to the extent of hyper-correction or excessiveness. They are attempting to demonstrate their "good breeding" and refinement. The incorrect or excessive application of honorifics is generally limited to women's speech, with the notable exception of male salesmen. The use of honorifics has two distinct dimensions, a demonstration of respect toward the other party and a demonstration of one's own social pedigree.

THE UNSUITABILITY OF CHINESE SCRIPT FOR WOMEN'S USE

It is said that a characteristic of women's speech is a lack of words of Chinese origin (*kango*). I am referring to words written in Chinese graphs (*kanji*) as opposed to the Japanese syllabary and which originally came to Japan from China. Sei Shonagon, the famous woman writer of the Heian Period stated, with some irony, that the sound of Chinese words was unbecoming to a woman. That point of view is still in evidence today. Various contemporary scholars have undertaken research into the modern use of *kango* by men and women and have found that the frequency in female speech is indeed much lower than in male speech. Men in their thirties use *kango* most infrequently, while its use increases exponentially for men in their forties and fifties. Men and women in their twenties rate almost equally.

The occurrence of *kango* increases with the level of formality of the context. The more important the topic of conversation, the higher the frequency of *kango*. Its compound words often represent complex and difficult concepts and can thus be perceived as heavy or stiff.

Women seldom use this type of *kango*, leaning more toward a "softer" sounding vocabulary. It is through the use of *kango* in Japanese that one is able to express one's thoughts precisely and succinctly. Even though a woman may speak at some length, what she says will often have far less content than what a man says in a similar number of words. Their lack of familiarity with the use (as distinct from a lack of knowledge) of *kango* vocabulary may explain why women find it difficult to participate actively as equals in conversations dealing with conceptually complex subject matter. This is often evident among a mixed group of university students and should be interpreted as an indication of access and familiarity with certain modes of linguistic performance rather than as a reflection of comparative intellectual abilities. Women are also often described as less academically inclined because of this same lower frequency of *kango* in the more feminine style in which they write. A woman who wishes to be considered feminine and also write good scholarly works must employ two different styles in order to do both. In other words, it is far more difficult for women to participate seriously in the whole range of social forums than it is for men.

CONCISE LANGUAGE AND MODIFIERS

Women are said to speak more emotionally and more softly than men. In English a woman might use the softer interjection "Oh dear!" where a man would say "Damn!" Japanese women show a similar preference for softer forms of interjection or exclamation. Such forms as *ara, mā,* and *waā* are generally limited to woman's speech and express the speaker's surprise or pleasure with both good taste and feeling. The equivalent forms used by male speakers — *yō* and *hē* — have a coarser, less refined, more energetic sound to them. Males, with their higher status, have access to a repertoire of less refined expressions.

Women use modifiers frequently. An analysis of essays written by male and female students between the fourth year of primary school and the third year of high school showed that the female use of modifiers was far higher than that of males. The female students had a tendency to add emphasis through the use of qualitative adverbs. Adjectives such as *suteki* ((wonderful)) and *osoroshii* ((awful, frightening)) and adverbs such as *totemo* ((very)) and *sugoku* ((extremely)) were typical of the language of the female students. Moreover, in sentences of the same length, the females used far more modifiers and fewer nouns and verbs. Though the sentences of the male students were of the same length, they generally incorporated more content.

The same study showed that while males used positive conjunctions — conjunctions that create positive and/or causative relations, such as *soshite* ((and)) and *dakara* ((therefore, so)) — females showed a preference for negative or discontinuous conjunctions such as *demo* ((but, however)). Less willing to show confidence in what they are saying, the female students express themselves hesitantly and modify or qualify their opinions with less decisive forms such as *demo*. It is widely thought that men do not like women who are sure of themselves and express themselves confidently. The ideal woman is one who adjusts her own opinions to those of others, who gracefully accepts all ideas that are put to her, and who doesn't exhibit the confidence to hold a strong personal view of life. Women's choice of conjunction, adverb, adjective, interjection, and other patterns of language use consistently reflects this social ideal of the feminine.

THE LEXICAL REPERTOIRE

Everyone has a repertoire of specialized vocabulary that is linked to their areas of particular interest. For a Japanese woman those areas of interest might include cooking, needlecraft, makeup, fashion, and childcare. For example, an older woman with an interest in kimono would know the color word *hōsōshoku* (a subtle shade of green like that of a leek). By the same token, a young girl would be familiar with the Japanized version of certain English and French color words such as *bēju* ((beige)) and *neibī burū* ((navy blue)). Older women have an extensive vocabulary related to the aesthetics of kimono and fabrics, while men of the same generation predictably have only a limited knowledge in this area.

Women usually give far more importance to standardized expressions of greeting or politeness and tend to use these forms diligently. Such language items are numerous in Japanese, and they are important in maintaining human relations. For example, when invited as a guest to someone's home, one must say *O-jama shimasu* ⟨⟨I am intruding⟩⟩ on entering and *O-jama shimashita* ⟨⟨I have intruded⟩⟩ on leaving. When giving a present, one must say, "It's really nothing but . . ." even if it is a valuable gift. It is correct for the receiver of the gift, on meeting or speaking with the gift giver later, to say, "Thank you for your gift of the other day." If a man uses these standardized expressions of politeness incorrectly, it is generally overlooked, but a woman who misuses or neglects these forms risks social ostracism. Mothers teach their daughters correct usage by example in daily life. A daughter's mastery of these forms and an appropriate lexical repertoire are indicators of her properness and "good breeding." Through indirect processes such as these, women's strong concern for social forms manifests itself as an important dimension of language in Japan.

ASOBASE KOTOBA

Asobase kotoba (exaggerated politeness) is a specialized form of honorific or polite speech used only by women wishing to emphasize or draw attention to their femininity. Because women of high social rank use this language, one might anticipate a decline in its frequency as class distinctions diminish in Japan. The *asobase* form is created by adding the word *asobase* to the end of a polite verbal inflection in the second or third person. Because this is an honorific form of address, it cannot be used in the first person. Consider the following examples: *Sensei ga kuru* (M, F, -f), *Sensei ga oide ni naru* (M, F, +f), *Sensei ga oide asobasu* (F, +f) ⟨⟨The teacher is coming⟩⟩. While the second and third sentences are of the same level of politeness, the latter has a particular nuance of refinement and softness, which can most probably be attributed to the sociolinguistic origins of the word *asobase*. How did this word become a form of honorific speech? One possible explanation is its close historical association with the leisured life of the cultural elite. The form was commonly used by women of the upper classes and high-ranking courtesans. By adding the verb *aso-basu* to action verbs in the second and third person, the user may feel that she is elevating the referee's status — even if only marginally — in the specific context of the immediate conversation by implying an association with a social elite, past or present. Once again the woman who uses the form also gains as she demonstrates her own refinement. Women who use the *asobase* form these days tend to live in grand houses, spend their husbands' salaries freely, and enjoy the more pleasurable aspects of a leisured life.

SOCIETY AS REFLECTED IN LANGUAGE

In one regard Japanese women's speech represents their lower status, their weakness and trivialized standing in a male-dominated society, which treats them as outsiders. At the same time, it is also understood to reflect their good breeding and refinement. Many Japanese today look on women's language differently, interpreting its characteristics positively. However, from the perspective of employment rights and the control of capital, the process of limiting women's power in exchange for a refined and comfortable lifestyle merely amounts to the belittling of women's value as human beings. There are those who recommend that, rather than use the male condition (the norm) as a starting point for reforms, we opt instead to use the female condition as the basis for setting criteria for major changes in the world we live in. From this perspective it has been argued that women, who have no concern with the workings of worldly affairs and are free to focus entirely on matters of art, music, nature and love, are in fact well placed to achieve the highest possible levels of cultural understanding. Women who never have to think about how their kimono are manufactured are indeed free to enjoy their status as women unburdened. The continued and extensive use of women's language only serves to reinforce this isolated way of thinking. As is well known, Japanese women generally regard their current status in very positive terms. One major reason for this is the fact that they have control over their husbands' salaries. In most Japanese salaried homes the husband hands over his paycheck untouched. The high value attached to the function of running the household means that, while women are officially isolated from worldly affairs, in reality they have considerable power and responsibility. At least within the exclusive domain of the household, women have total control over men.

These women don't attempt to concern themselves with the same things as men or to pursue the same social roles. They are content to enjoy life as "amateurs," free of any desire to pursue a career and its related responsibilities. The women's language they speak maintains this social function and, at the same time, imparts a quite different kind of dignity to their status than that sought out by men. This phenomenon can be explained in terms of the structure of Japanese society. Japanese form identities not as individuals but through their status or role within the group to which they belong. For example, a young married woman identifies herself more as a mother and wife than as a separate individual. In the domestic domain a man identifies himself as husband and father, but in the workplace he identifies himself as a person with a particular specialization (e.g., as a taxi driver or a teacher). Japanese characteristically give greater importance to their identity within the group than their independent or individual identity. And they are most at ease when situated in their assigned role within the group.

Most Japanese women perform their gendered role as women happily and even appear to take pride in choosing that role. Needless to say, the individual will and personality of each woman determines whether or not she decides to join the ranks of these "happy women." The language women use — feminine vocabulary, soft conjunctions, interjections, honorifics, feminine pronouns, the lack of *kango*, the exaggerated politeness of *asobase*, and so on — can all be understood just as well from this very different positive perspective. On the whole, we can say that the characteristics of Japanese women's language reflect the general characteristics of the feminine in Japan: formality, politeness, softness, and an attention to the emotional side of life.

Even though women demonstrate a definite propensity for conversation, there is not always a great deal of content in what they say. In public situations and "serious" discussions women are consistently overshadowed by men. Women are required to adhere to a strict degree of politeness. It is by beginning to uncover such characteristics as these in women's speech that we can get closer to the reality of women's lives. I have explored several different dimensions of Japanese women's speech from two different perspectives. People who think women are discriminated against and relegated to an inferior position will interpret these characteristics negatively and judge that women are trapped in a disadvantaged position. They will not be satisfied with what they consider to be women's powerlessness, limited opportunities, and narrowly defined feminine role. On the other hand, some people consider that women live a life apart from the worldly concerns that so preoccupy men and therefore enjoy a privileged lifestyle. These people will judge that the characteristics of women's language function to protect the feminine condition. Finally, these two different perspectives might be seen as interdependent, as essentially two sides of the same coin of gendered language.

Selected Works

"Discernment: A Neglected Aspect of Linguistic Politeness." *Multilingua* vol. 8, nos. 2–3 (1989).

"Formal Forms and Discernment: Neglected Aspects of Linguistic Politeness." In *Linguistic Politeness II*. Special issue of *Multilingua* vol. 8, no. 2/3 (1989): 223–48.

"Gender and Function of Language Use: Quantitative and Qualitative Evidence from Japanese." Pragmatics and Language Learning Monograph Series. 3. 1992. "How and Why Do Women Speak More Politely in Japanese?" *Nihon Joshi Daigaku eibungaku kenkyū*, no. 24 (1989).

"Introduction." In *Linguistic Politeness I*. Special issue of *Multilingua* vol. 7, no. 4 (1988): 371–74.

"Japanese Sociolinguistics: Politeness and Women's Language." *Lingua* vol. 57, nos. 2–4 (1982): 357–85.

"Preface." In *Linguistic Politeness II*. Special issue of *Multilingua* vol. 8, no. 2/3 (1989): 97–99.

"Preface: The Search for Integrated Universals of Linguistic Politeness." In

Linguistic Politeness III: Linguistic Politeness and Universality. Special issue of *Multilingua* vol. 12, no. 1 (1993): 7–10.

"Sex Difference and Politeness in Japanese." Co-authored. *International Journal of Sociology of Language* 58 (1985): 25–36.

"A Sociolinguistic Analysis of Person Referents by Japanese and American Children." *Language Sciences* vol. 1, no. 1 (1979): 273–93.

"Two Functional Aspects of Politeness in Women's Language." *Proceedings of the XIIIth International Congress of Linguistics*, 805–8. [City]: International Congress of Linguistics, 1984.

"Universals of Linguistic Politeness: Quantitative Evidence from Japanese and American English." Co-authored. *Journal of Pragmatics* 10 (1986): 347–71.

Josei no keigo no gengo keishiki kinō (Forms and Functions of Honorific Speech). Co-authored. Monbushō Kagaku Kenkyūhi Josei Hōkokusho, 1985.

Nichiei hikaku kōza — Daigokan: Bunka to shakai (Lectures on the Comparison of British and Japanese Culture — Vol. 5: Culture and Society). Co-authored. Taishūkan Shoten, 1982.

Nihongo no danjo sa (Gender Difference in Japanese Language). Co-authored. I.C.U. Language Sciences, 1981.

Nihonjin to Amerikajin no keigo kōdō (Honorific Expressions of Japanese and Americans). Co-authored. Nan undo, 1986.

Onna no kotoba. Otoko no kotoba (Women's Language, Men's Language). Nihon Keizai Tsushinsha, 1979.

Shufu no isshūkan no danwa shiryō-kaisetsu. Honbunhen oyobi sakuin hen (One Week of Dialogue in the Life of a Housewife). Co-edited. Monbushō tokutei kenkyū: Gengo no hyōjunka ni kansuru sōgōteki kenkyū. Sōkatsuhan kankobutsu, 1984.

KANAZUMI FUMIKO
Lawyer, Women's Legal Cooperative

» » » » » » » » » » » »

KANAZUMI FUMIKO IS A LAWYER in the Tokyo region who
founded the Women's Cooperative Legal Service in 1975. The aim of
the cooperative is to offer an alternative environment for women
seeking legal advice in areas where the law and the legal profession
have traditionally tended to disadvantage them. The cooperative
deals with a large number of divorce cases and has devoted considerable effort to overcoming the stigma attached to women who initiate
divorce proceedings. It has also worked to achieve the enforcement of
alimony orders and to bring to the attention of both the public and the
authorities the economic hardships facing single mothers in Japan
today. Like the feminist writer Miya Yoshiko, Kanazumi expresses
concern that the rhetoric of the "Japanese miracle" obscures the hardship of the lives of women who choose to step out of the dominant
family structure.

Kanazumi frequently asserts that all issues relating to the status and
freedom of women are fundamentally basic human rights issues. She
is firmly committed to both human rights and democracy, grounding
her activities as a feminist lawyer on these two principles. For Kanazumi, her politics and practice as a feminist are deeply rooted in her

personal history. She traces her own activism to the strength of her memories of a woman who taught her in school in the years immediately following the war. Kanazumi relates how, without ever mentioning the word "democracy," this teacher taught her students by example the importance of valuing oneself as an individual and learning to love and respect one another. Much of Kanazumi's efforts to create a positive and supportive environment for women in crisis has been based in the belief that women need to build networks within which they can develop an enabling level of self-respect and confidence. To this end she co-founded a divorce support group for women in addition to her work at the cooperative.

Kanazumi has also been extremely active both as a lawyer and an activist around issues of violence against women. Once again she is quick to relate this area of her feminist practice to personal history. Kanazumi is convinced that telling women's individual histories is a powerful strategy for breaking the silence surrounding women's issues, and thus she speaks openly of her own childhood experience of domestic violence. "Despite my mother's screams that she didn't want to bear another child, my stepfather threw himself on her and took her by force. Confronted by this scene as a small child, I experienced with my entire body the horror of the knowledge of the true nature of man's violence toward woman. . . . In the midst of such experiences and encounters, I came to realize that, for myself, a primary objective in life must be to facilitate women's desire and capacity to truly value their own worth and to build equal relationships with others, free from harm. . . . My mother, who had endured a life of suffering for the sake of her children, died a frail and thin old woman in the same year that I founded the Women's Legal Cooperative."

Kanazumi's interest in the relationship between sex and violence extends beyond relations within the family to include such issues as the rights of prostitutes and the antiprostitution debate, abortion law reform, and censorship campaigns related to pornographic and other media representations of violence. She is particularly concerned with the relationship between laws relating to these areas and issues of freedom of expression, individual rights, censorship, and the legal framing of the relationship between the public and private domains. Here, Kanazumi's interests intersect with Matsui's focus on illegal immigrant workers and prostitutes, Ochiai's exposure of the judicial system's treatment of rape victims, Miya's critique of the "anorexic family," and Aoki's recognition of the public nature of women's private role — areas in which public institutions such as the judicial and medical systems are actively involved in formulating policies for the management of women's bodies and sexuality.

Two years after the completion of the initial interview for this book, Kanazumi was persuaded to take up a position as co-leader of a new political party called the "Club of the World" and to run for office at the national level. She assumed the leadership in partnership with a man. Some people interpreted the party's poor performance in the elections as a rejection by women of what appeared to be a decision not to run a woman alone as the leader of the party. A far more likely explanation is that the structure of political fund raising and electoral campaigning in Japan makes it virtually impossible for smaller parties to remain viable. The fact that the "new coalition" government of Japan after the 1993 elections was no more than a reconfiguration of the previous map of political interest groups and party factions reinforced the sense of the impossibility of significant structural change in the absence of major electoral reform.

Kanazumi withdrew from party politics after this brief foray but has remained a central figure in campaigns for legal reform affecting the rights and status of women. She is a member of the research and action group "Women's Rights and Sexuality," which is involved in such diverse areas as health and welfare reform, abortion rights, and the human rights implications for women of new technologies. Most recently, she has focused her attention on the legal questions surrounding innovations in reproductive technologies and the feminist campaign to reform the antiprostitution laws. Utilizing her knowledge and experience of the law, Kanazumi develops careful linkages between single issues and wider reform campaigns. For example, her work on the antiprostitution law has been developed in close association with the formulation of proposals for sweeping reforms in the area of women's health and welfare.

Kanazumi's work in the area of new technologies is firmly grounded in her commitment to the law as a vehicle for the guarantee of human rights. Her rejection of certain reproductive procedures is an extension of the defense of the notion of self-determination that underpins her analysis of both women's right to choose an abortion and the rights of children. The concept of human dignity is central to her arguments for the guarantee and protection of human rights. Kanazumi's unproblematized use of the holistic concepts of human and humanity needs to be located in the Japanese historical context, where it has been difficult to legitimate or claim legal rights specific to women. Kanazumi's shift to the universal category of human/humanity as the ground for claiming women's rights is a strategic move intended to capitalize on the desire of the Japanese state apparatus to be recognized as a good global citizen. The same strategy was used in the 1980s campaign for the ratification of the Equal Employment Opportunities Act, when women used international media attention to embarrass the Japanese government into signing, and later acting on, a United Nations Treaty on Women's Rights during the United Nations Decade of the Woman. Kanazumi frequently appeals to international law and instruments of the United Nations to legitimate and document her legal arguments. In this way she sidesteps the lack of legal framing and precedent in Japanese law for the protection of women's rights and brings the weight of international scrutiny to bear on Japan's performance.

It is important when considering issues of legal reform in the Japanese case to remember that the postwar 1946 Constitution was drafted primarily by Occupation forces led by the United States. There are elements of the Constitution that the Japanese right continues to consider too "radical" or "permissive," particularly in areas directly related to the status of women (e.g., abortion access and welfare). As a result conservatives have repeatedly campaigned for reforms in certain elements of the Constitution. Kanazumi argues that some of the basic principles for women's rights encoded in the Constitution have more legitimacy in an international legal forum than they do in Japan, where they are only tentatively rooted in the contemporary sociocultural infrastructure. At the same time that Kanazumi emphasizes the need to monitor and respond to ongoing right-wing strategies for gradual legal reform, she also encourages women to look more closely at their own potential to negotiate for change within the legal institution. She is firmly committed to making the law work for women.

Interview

SB: I believe you established the Women's Cooperative Legal Service in the early 1970s.

KF: Yes. I became a lawyer in 1970, but the opportunities open to a woman lawyer at that time were limited. It wasn't clear even to me what my options were. Looking back I'd say that one of the more difficult things, one of the things I felt most strongly, was the lack of any model. My status as a lawyer and a woman was not even clear to me. I found myself dealing daily with questions of my rights, the limits placed on my free exercise of those rights in a predominantly male profession, what you might call a patriarchal system. The solution seemed to lie not in any struggle to fit in with my male colleagues but rather in a search for other women lawyers. It didn't take long to gather together a group of some thirty women. In our discussions we became more aware of the extent to which we shared the same problems both in and out of the workplace.

More important, as we talked we also became increasingly aware that the questions of rights and equality we had first identified at the individual level extended beyond our own particular experience and the shared experience of the group to the lives of all Japanese women, working and nonworking. We formed this legal service in 1975 with the goal of extending legal access to any woman facing a situation where her rights are denied or restricted. This was a personal as well as a political project for me. I was raised in Kagoshima, on the island of Kyūshū. It wouldn't be unfair to say that both economically and culturally Kagoshima lagged behind the rest of the country. My family was a traditional patriarchal household, and I grew up in the shadow of my father's violence toward my mother. From a young age I sensed the need to discover new ways, better ways, for a man and woman to live together. And until such new ways came into being, I wanted, as a lawyer, to do what I could to extend the practice of feminism and the law to the lives of women like my mother.

SB: *You seemed just now to make a point of emphasizing the status of both working and nonworking women.*

KF: Issues of women's rights, women's sexuality, these are all as true for the nonworking woman as for the working woman. The division is a standard one but is often made at the expense of the nonworking woman. The description itself is telling. Much of what has been said and done in the name of feminism in recent years has ignored the houseworker (full-time housewife). Feminism should extend into the private, domestic sphere of all women's lives. This was another central motivation behind the establishment of this office.

SB: *What types of legal cases do you deal with?*

KF: Occupational disputes related to wages, working conditions, and so on are usually handled by legal offices specializing in labor law, or in some instances unions represent an individual female employee in either direct negotiations with the company or in a legal action. Those disputes take place in the public domain. It's not surprising that by focusing our attention on the private domain, the life of the houseworker, we find that most of our cases are divorce-related.

SB: *The 1946 Constitution makes it very clear that there will be equal rights for men and women in both the choice of a marriage partner and access to divorce. After more than twenty years, what problems still confront a woman seeking a divorce in Japan?*

KF: At the most basic level, many male lawyers simply can't empathize with a woman who takes the initiative in seeking a divorce. Especially when the basis for her unhappiness relates to the nature of her day-to-day existence as a Japanese wife and mother. They listen to her description of her lifestyle and her dissatisfaction and can't see the point. What they hear sounds quite reasonable, even normal. They're incapable of recognizing the basic human rights issues at stake for the Japanese woman seeking a divorce.

SB: There's a publication called Japan Echo *distributed by Japanese embassy and consular offices overseas. It's a glossy journal-like publication with essays on various current Japanese topics. A recent edition carried articles on the family and included pieces that touched on the issue of divorce. There was a strong undercurrent of blame aimed at women who sought to divorce their husbands, even a suggestion that the modern Japanese woman is selfish and expects too much.*

KF: As you pointed out, the right of any woman to divorce is guaranteed in the Constitution. The problem is not the law; it's the public attitude. The United Nations Decade of the Woman had some impact. There has been a definite increase in the general awareness of the complex and diverse forms of discrimination that women face, and there has been some improvement in public attitudes toward divorce and other family or private/domestic issues that touch the lives of women. But on the whole, even among feminists, there has yet to be adequate recognition of the forms of discrimination, the infringements of a woman's basic human rights, that take place beyond the public eye. For example, the law calls for freedom and equality in the choice of marriage partners, and yet less than 30 percent of couples marrying in Japan today are "love couples" — nonarranged marriages. It's the gap between the law and reality, and between the law and public attitudes — in other words, public practice — that's the problem.

SB: A Japanese feminist once said to me that the system of arranged marriage was something a non-Japanese feminist should be careful of criticizing too strongly. She argued that it was a very straightforward

*contractual arrangement for the creation of a family unit and did
away with the eventual disenchantment or disillusionment of a
Western-style romantic match.*

KF: That may or may not be true traditionally, but marriages in contemporary Japan — arranged or nonarranged — take place in the
midst of the most amazing commercial fuss. The advertisements on
trains and in magazines testify to this. The message is that a young
woman's life all leads up to this one momentous event, that this ceremony is the key to her self-fulfillment. And her family pays a high
price, with multiple changes of kimono and gowns, flowers, gifts for
the guests, the reception, and the honeymoon. Weddings are big business. But again, it's the gap between the reality and, in this case, the
dream that's the problem. Marriage all too often doesn't offer self-
fulfillment; the dreams are left unmet. The extent of the commercial-
ization, the advertising hyperbole, the idealization of marriage in the
media, all this just adds to the depth of dissatisfaction and disillusionment of the young, newly wed woman.

*SB: There are two points I've heard made again and again in relation
to the status of Japanese married women. First, that the Japanese wife
has the power in the domestic sphere. The example given is always
the husband's handing over his pay packet to the wife. And second,
that there is not a problem of domestic violence in Japan. Does your
experience in handling divorce cases confirm these two assertions?*

KF: I'd say simply that both are myths. To start with, the practice of
the wife controlling the finances is a reflection not of her power but
of a change in the banking facilities in Japan. Computerization of the
banking system made it simpler for employers to deposit salaries directly into employee accounts. It's the wife who then makes the necessary withdrawals during bank hours. In some households this may
act as one expression of equality or trust, but it can just as well develop into a source of disagreement. It's often one of the issues raised
by our clients. When it comes down to it, the husband always has the
power to stop the deposits or override the wife's financial decisions.

The wife's economic power remains dependent on the husband's good will.

Another important aspect of this myth is the underlying assumption that economic prosperity, or at least a basic level of comfort, is the norm in Japan. There are plenty of stories in the newspapers about the plight of some salaryman who has lived beyond his means and lost everything, even in some cases committing suicide. This phenomenon was so prevalent at one stage that it earned the name *sarakin jigoku* (loan hell). It would go like this. A salaryman would not want to draw on the family finances for extra expenses but would feel a strong obligation to participate in all the entertainment functions related to his job — dinners, bar crawling, clubs, golf, weekend excursions, and so forth — and resort to borrowing from a loan shark who would accept his future salary as collateral but only at exorbitant interest rates. Borrowing to build a house or acquire something concrete is one thing, but to borrow over and over against your own salary and have nothing to show for it is sure to lead to disaster.

The whole structure of *asobi* (play or entertainment) in Japan, and the pressures it places both on men and their families, is another problem in itself. And then there's the pressure every young man is under to marry and create a household of his own. Again, advertising and the media play no small role in the process. The decision to marry is often made because of one's age and job profile. Needless to say, this does not foster a strong investment in the marriage on the part of the husband. Obligation is not the same as commitment. The wife faced with the frequent physical absence of her husband and his lack of emotional investment in the household often finds herself walking through our door in search of advice after years of putting up with a constantly deteriorating situation.

SB: And what of domestic violence?

KF: It all comes down to what you define as violence. In households where the primary wage earner is the husband, there can be a type of emotional or psychological manipulation that I consider a form of violence. The economically dependent wife is highly vulnerable — especially if she has no sense of her own rights. In my experience, emotional violence is a more frequent ground for divorce than physical violence. Too many husbands barely have a sense of their wives as human, much less any sense of their needs or rights. An important issue here is the failure of the husband, or Japanese society for that matter, to recognize the value of the wife's labor. A woman's place is not in the home: it just happens to be the primary workplace of many women. I'm not saying that there is *no* physical violence, by the way: that would be a mistake. I think the taboo against discussing domestic violence is still very strong, but as we've discovered in the Tokyo Rape Crisis Center over the past few years, once a taboo is broken, once a word like rape is brought out into the public domain, we discover that something we thought didn't exist was there all along but simply couldn't be spoken of.

SB: Rape and incest are two taboo topics that Japanese feminists have done much to bring into the public domain over the last decade. Is the law in a position to deal with the growing recognition of the existence of rape and incest cases, or have feminists jumped ahead of the existing laws?

KF: The rape legislation is clearly in place, but the existence of the law is not enough in itself. Again, public attitudes are a crucial factor. I'm sure this problem is not unique to Japan; but the rape victim is in a very vulnerable situation, and the stigma attached to the victim is a major reason for many cases not coming to trial. In situations involving divorce and domestic violence, technically the law could be extended to husband-wife rape, but the judicial system has not yet recognized the concept. The husband has the right to conjugal access. The law has yet to be successfully tested in this regard. But the time is close. In one recent case a husband was prosecuted when he and a friend raped his estranged wife.

And then there's the issue of incest.

SB: Recent public references to incest have broken a very deep taboo. The general implication seems to be that father-daughter incest is not a problem in Japan. Rather, the incidence of mother-son incest is high, and some argue that it even increased in the 1980s as a result of what Ueno Chizuko has coined the mazākon *(mother complex) problem among teenage boys.*

KF: Incest cases can, and have been, prosecuted under the rape legislation, but there is no law that deals specifically with incest. The situation is a complex one, especially in the case of mother-son incest. Because there is often little overt physical force or violence involved in these situations, it is difficult for the current definition of rape to include these cases. That mother-son incest is far from rare in postwar Japan is true. Whether it constitutes emotional violence and where the blame lies is far from clear. The answers are not as obvious as they may appear to some foreign feminists looking in from the outside. What I disagree with is the suggestion that father-daughter rape doesn't exist. I would argue that father-daughter incest has always existed but remains a strictly taboo topic. Mother-son incest is, however, closely related to the status of women and the changing nature of the family in postwar Japan. We all know the popular stories of the young boy initiated into sex by a female member of the household, but what we're seeing now is something else and it does have a lot to do with *mazākon.*

SB: How significant is the question of sexual satisfaction for the women who come to you for consultation? This has been one of the explanations offered for the occurrence of mother-son incest. The stereotype created is a sexually frustrated mother and wife who offers her sexual services to her son to help him through his own frustration while studying for the entrance examinations to a good university. At the same time she supposedly satisfies her own sexual needs. It's interesting to me that in discussions of mother-son incest, the concern seems always to be focused on the mental state of the son caught up in this relationship.

KF: There's been a lot of discussion about the *sei* [sexuality] of women lately, but I think that most feminists use the word in the sense of gender or sexual difference rather than in its other sense of sexuality — the awareness by an individual woman of her own sexuality, her own body. There has been some limited improvement, but on the whole I don't think there has been a significant increase in public or individual awareness of woman's sexuality.

SB: *There may be a difference here between the world of the wife and the world of* mizu-shōbai. *Although it's still the man's sexuality and his desires and fantasies that are "serviced" by the* mizu-shōbai *women.*

KF: Exactly. It's the man's desire that shapes sexual practice and a woman's sense of her own sexual expectations. Sexual awareness is not high enough yet for sexual compatibility to be a major issue in divorce cases in Japan. I can't help thinking that there is a link here between the need for a recognition of women's sexuality and the various forms of emotional and physical violence we see manifested in the Japanese family today. There is the mutual exploitation of mother and son, emotional and sometimes sexual, and at the other extreme there is the violence of children against their family. We've all been shocked by cases such as the one where a young boy attacked and killed members of his family with a baseball bat. And the one where a teenage boy stabbed to death his grandmother and both parents. This is the terror of modern Japan — the depth of anger or despair that must underlie such an act. Where does it come from? It would be different if these were isolated cases, but they're not.

There is something fundamentally wrong in the sense of human relations that is developing among children in contemporary Japanese families. This is the issue that runs through all the things we've been talking about here. What is missing in the modern Japanese family is any real sense of intimacy, any sense of emotion free of obligation or manipulation. The public and the media, in particular, are all too quick to point the finger at inadequate mothers or overly severe schoolteachers.

SB: *At a recent conference the National Teachers' Federation devoted a lot of time to the last case you mentioned. I believe it passed a resolution to work for better respect for the human rights of children within the educational system. The teachers seemed prepared to take the blame publicly.*

KF: Yes, but that's too easy. The blame is always placed somewhere other than on the family institution itself. It is not enough to shift responsibility onto the mother or the teacher. What is required is a total reassessment of the state of the family. Central to this is a frank reappraisal of the nature of sexuality and its role in child development and a reappraisal of the formation of family relations between husband and wife, and parents and children. It's not insignificant that in that particular case the boy killed his grandmother first. Just before the murders she is said to have found the boy reading a pornographic comic book and taken it away from him after shaming him over it. This seems to have been the crucial breaking point. Feminists and lawyers may be gaining a greater awareness of the relationship between gender issues and the law, but gender and sexuality are not the same even though they are intimately linked. The problematization of *boseiai* (maternal love) in recent feminist writings has created a polarization into pro- and anti-*boseiai* groups. However, the positive and negative aspects of motherhood in Japan today are not mutually exclusive; they're two sides of the same coin. What links them together is the issue of women's sexuality.

SB: You mentioned pornographic comic books a moment ago. This is an area of my own research. The antipornography law is very clear in Japan and is strictly applied to imported magazines and films (and occasionally Japanese films), but the proliferation of pornographic images in Japan is something foreigners always comment on. The most obvious and visible form is found in pornographic comics. These comics — particularly those titles aimed specifically at the teenage market — have become the focus of considerable protest from women's groups. How do you explain this particular gap between the law and reality?

KF: The law is seldom tested in the courts. The industry is largely self-regulating. That is to say, the publishers know how far they can go without risking prosecution. Of course, they are always testing and gradually extending the tolerable boundaries. The law is unquestionably self-contradictory. It tolerates comic books with the most violent, pornographic images and bans imported movies for explicit sex scenes. Again, the issue is largely one of public attitude, and this would seem to be shifting slowly. The incentive here is coming from the women's movement.

SB: Here, too, the question concerns the politics of sexuality.

KF: Yes. You mentioned before the interview that you had heard some attempts to justify or explain pornographic comics by linking them to traditional woodblock prints. You can argue for the traditional precedents of pornographic comics only if you forget about women's rights. From the point of view of women's rights, the presence or absence of any historical precedent is irrelevant. The current market in pornographic comics is a breach of women's rights and a denial of any sexuality other than the male reader's. This sense of outrage over pornography is new in Japan but definitely emerging into an antipornography movement.

Unlike America, we already have clearly defined laws in place; we need a shift in public attitudes sufficient to bring the laws into practice. There is a general concern in Japan, however, over any strengthening or extension of censorship laws. On the whole, I think the key is to alter the public tolerance of pornography. There have already been some results. Major daily sports papers have succumbed to pressure and moved their nude pinups from the front to the back section. It's a beginning. What counts is social attitudes toward basic human rights.

SB: Another, similar case is the abortion law.

KF: Yes. There again you have a law in place, however imperfect, and conservative moves to reform the law and withdraw access to abortion. At the moment women have recourse to the Economic Reasons Clause, but the right is arguing that no woman in Japan today should be able to claim sufficient economic hardship to justify an abortion.

SB: This claim in itself does not recognize the financial status of many Japanese women.

KF: It doesn't recognize the economic reality or the basic human rights issue at stake in any attempt to withdraw a woman's right to self-determination. Feminists counter that we need reforms that remove all crimes of abortion from the legal code and provide free access to abortion for all women without resort to any justification, economic or otherwise. The women's movement has done a lot to alter the public awareness of this issue. So far, it has been able to muster enough resistance to block all attempts to reform the abortion law or limit access.

SB: And the divorce law?

KF: There is still room for more change in public attitudes toward divorce, but this issue is ultimately related to the role of the family and individual rights, in particular those of women. Divorce laws are in place, but perhaps the single greatest deterrent for a woman considering divorce is the emphasis placed on marriage not as a relationship between a man and a woman but as the structure within which children are born and raised. I consider this a bigger problem for most women than economic concerns. More women work than do not these days, and a woman's reentry into the workforce after marriage or child raising has become far more common. That's not to say that there are no economic problems for a divorced woman. A woman's earning capacity is considerably less than a man's, but I still argue that this is secondary to the issue of her children.

Japanese society still locates all the responsibility for child rearing within the family unit. There is no public recognition of the range of influences shaping the development of a child — school, television, comics, playmates, and so on. Any aberrant behavior is blamed on the family, and more specifically on the mother. To divorce her husband and break up the family unit is a difficult decision for a woman who can anticipate that her action will be blamed for the slightest antisocial or disruptive behavior in her children. Her own self-expression and freedom are subordinated to her social role as a mother.

It's some fifty years since Japan became a democracy, yet we are still far from achieving a society in which all individuals, regardless of gender, have the freedom of self-expression and individual development. Japan has caught up with other nations in the area of economic and industrial development, but there has been little progress in the area of basic human rights. Seen from the outside by a Western feminist, it must be difficult to understand why Japanese women seem so unconcerned, seem to feel so little dissatisfaction. I think that awareness is slow in coming but will emerge as a crucial factor in the transformation of the status of the individual and the family, a transformation of the basic fabric of Japanese society. At heart I remain an optimist.

Problematizing Reproductive Technologies

1. WOMEN'S RIGHT TO SELF-DETERMINATION IN ABORTION AND REPRODUCTIVE HEALTH

A close look at the escalation of malpractice in the area of reproductive technologies leaves one with an acute sense of risk that both the state of medicine and society itself are moving in the opposite direction from what we women have hoped for. This is particularly clear when we consider the situation from the perspective of a woman's right to self-determination, a right we have won by our struggles over the last eight years or more: the recognition of a woman's right to choose to give birth or not. The central issue of reproductive health (i.e., the creation of legal and health systems that can guarantee the health of both women's sexuality and their reproductive functions) provides another important perspective on the current state of things. Using the category of basic human rights arising from the sovereign rights of the people, modern society has formulated a legal code that acknowledges the equality of men and women. However, in actual fact, in the interest of achieving efficient modes of production, most men and women have been reduced to the status of mere resources of

This is an unpublished public lecture.

industrial society and are organized at that level through the power of various systems of management and control.

The criminalization of abortion has deprived women of their right to self-determination in the choice to give birth or not. They have been forcibly confined to a procreative sexuality, thus limiting their lives to the resource function of continuous reproduction. There is no reason why the life and sexuality of men only should be emancipated under the law, while women's independence is compromised by the same system. Within this gender-based system of the division of labor, in which the inequities in the relationship between men and women are continually exacerbated, it was inevitable that the sexuality and lives of men should become increasingly violent. Within this system, working like a maniac is the one "worthwhile" lifestyle all men are pushed into.

The movement to establish a woman's right to choose dates from the 1970s. It was a product of the battle for human rights embedded in the new philosophy of women's liberation and epitomized in the call, "My body is my own." This call went out from women across the world. As the 1973 U.S. Supreme Court decision in *Roe v. Wade* made clear, if a woman's right to self-determination is recognized under the guarantee of privacy (in my opinion Article 13 of the Japanese Constitution also guarantees privacy as a basic human right in its reference to the sanctity of the individual), then the criminalization of abortion is unconstitutional and should be abolished.[1] What are the implications of decriminalizing abortion? Abortion-control advocates state that the motivation underlying the criminalization of abortion is the protection of the life of the fetus, and on that basis they oppose any termination of pregnancy. However, I believe that the real core of their opposition is their fear of a challenge to the status quo: where women are confined to domestic work; their role is confined to pregnancy, birth, and childcare; and the state has appropriated the right to determine matters of reproduction in the interest of fully controlling population policy. At the foundation of the notion of a woman's right to choose, encapsulated in the words "My body is my own," is the concept that if one is not the agent of one's own body, then one cannot be the agent of one's own life or the sovereign of one's own identity. I believe that this concept lies at the very heart of the philosophy of individual dignity, the dignity of human life. Of course, it is true not only for women but also for men.

As I continue, in the various groups in which I am involved, to debate and rethink the issues of women's self-determination and abortion rights, I am developing an overwhelming sense that, whether from the perspective of women's emancipation or human rights, this process of discovery of self-consciousness is likely to produce a Copernican revolution. That is to say, in a society where women are denied the right of self-determination, and the choice to give birth or not, the term "human" is essentially a designation for men only. Even if the law speaks of "human rights," it focuses on the rights of men. With the notion of "agency over one's own body" that is at the foundation of women's demand for the right to choose, we are moving, for the first time, toward a new horizon, a way of thinking grounded in individual rights rather than the rights of men.

The *Roe v. Wade* decision, which was based on the argument that human rights are recognized only after birth, freed women from having to pit the protection of the fetus against the protection of their right to choose. As long as the law posits the equality of men and women as a basic human right and at the same time criminalizes abortion, there can be no real recognition of the human rights of women. I see the U.S. Supreme Court decision as an affirmation of human rights through the principle of absolute equality between men and women. I predict that if people could internalize this interpretation of human rights as a profoundly just one, then the nature of society and our perception of the equality of men and women would be fundamentally transformed. It is essential that we construct and develop just such a notion of human rights.[2]

The philosophy of human rights is a precious cultural resource in the construction of humanity. Therefore, the creation of a universal theory of human rights is essential to the realization of an equal society, and I think that this should be just as evident to men as it is to women. Only at the point that human rights are understood as being one with the equal rights of men and women[3] will it be possible for men and women to enter a common arena, to engage in a global debate leading to a theory of existence that incorporates such fundamental issues as the dignity of life, human rights, and human dignity. Why should this be evident to all? Whether we are considering the lives of children, the value and sanctity of life, the protection of the world environment, the extreme disparity of wealth and poverty between nations, or the North-South problem, these are not questions of interest only to women or questions that women can deal with alone. The concept that "my body is my own" affirms an assertion of our self-identity — "I am what I am." I both feel and think that this approach incorporates, in an essential way, a philosophy of the dignity of *all* life.

A society that recognized a woman's right to choose and was grounded in the notion of "my body is my own" would have to reject the structure of a "control society" in which humans are reduced to things (resources) and manipulated as raw materials. I imagine that in such a society, men and women would function together as active agents, working cooperatively to build a system that guaranteed human dignity. Future societies will, I believe, seek change in this direction. It is for just this reason that the movement demanding a woman's right to choose in the issue of abortion has generated strong opposition from the center of power that adheres to the traditional, male-dominated, control society.

If we can expose the real meaning concealed below the surface of the call from abortion-control advocates to "protect the life of the fetus" and develop new arguments for gender equity to overthrow their position, winning away their capacity to gain massive public support in the process, then perhaps we can find peaceful means to move beyond confrontation. I would like to interpret the concept of reproductive health,[4] which is at the center of the current worldwide movement for women's health, as a campaign for legal and medical systems within which women can reclaim their status as agents of their own lives and bodies, a status denied them in a modern society that has stripped them of autonomy in matters of sexuality and reproduction.

2. REPRODUCTIVE TECHNOLOGIES TO PROMOTE BIRTHS AND THE PROBLEM OF SURROGACY

a. Reproductive Technology as Medical Practice

Reproductive technologies promote birth and thus function in an opposite mode from contraception, abortion, and other technologies of birth control (or prevention). The practice of surrogate motherhood typifies the various problems surrounding the new reproductive technologies. Reproductive technologies cannot be used without some form of intrusion into an individual's body. They should therefore take place within the parameters of approved medical practice and, as with all other invasive medical practices, fall under the jurisdiction of laws relating to the infliction of grievous bodily injury. It is clearly necessary and appropriate to take up the issue of these technologies within the framework of "Reproductive Technology as Medical Practice."

b. Questioning "Infertility Treatments"

Surrogate pregnancy takes place as a medicalized application of reproductive technology and is used as an "infertility treatment." However, the concept of "infertility treatment" defines infertility as an illness. There is a need to interrogate the notion that infertility is a form of illness that must be treated. This assumption is based on the value judgment that a healthy woman is one who gets pregnant and gives birth. The same value system underlies the notion that a male body that cannot "get a woman pregnant" is not a healthy body. A woman cannot be the agent of her own body within a system of legal and medical practices that does not allow her to experience that body naturally. If she cannot be the agent of her own body, then she also cannot be the agent of her own life. This is true for men, too. The concept that infertility is something that must be treated, and the popularization of this concept, infringe on the basic human right of self-determination in all matters related to one's own body, a right shared by men and women alike.

Infertility is not an illness but rather a feeling of sadness that arises from the inability to satisfy a specific desire — "We want to have a child." In this sense, infertility is an obstacle to fulfilling the desire to create a child (of the blood of one or both of the parents), but it is not an illness as such. When considered as a process to "meet the unsatisfied desire of an individual," the medical practice of reproductive technology has a lot in common with cosmetic surgery. Individuals who cannot create the necessary egg or sperm in their own body don't necessarily perceive of themselves as requiring "treatment." In this context reproductive technology merely functions as one more method of acquiring a child. In cases where the husband is infertile, it is common, instead of "treating" him, for the wife to undergo artificial insemination with the aid of donor sperm. In cases where the wife is infertile or cannot carry a pregnancy to term, instead of "treating" her, a surrogate mother is impregnated with the husband's sperm or implanted with the wife's egg fertilized by the husband's sperm through in-vitro fertilization. It would be a mistake to describe the husband and wife participating in these procedures as "patients undergoing infertility treatment," at least in any familiar use of the word "patient." In standard usage the term "patient" in a medical context designates an individual seeking treatment for an illness or disease afflicting his or her own body. Accordingly, in the past surrogate pregnancy did not fall under the legal umbrella of procedures designated as appropriate medical practice. Surely then we should question any contemporary move to recognize surrogacy as a form of medical treatment.

c. Reproductive Technology and the "Right to Give Birth"

The argument is frequently made that if we are going to demand the right of women to choose to give birth or not, then we must also be willing to recognize an infertile woman's attempt to realize her desire to give birth through available reproductive technologies as an expression of her "right to give birth." There is no question that Article 13 of the Constitution guarantees the basic right of each individual to the "pursuit of happiness." Article 25 also guarantees that the right to self-determination will not be regulated by the state (the individual right to freedom) and obliges the state to offer what support it can in an individual's pursuit of self-determination (right as a member of society). However, this should not extend to a guarantee (right) of access to reproductive technologies for purposes outside the treatment of any disease or illness afflicting the individual's body. Can we really say that resorting to surrogacy because of a desire to have a child should be recognized as part of the basic human right of the "pursuit of happiness"? The desire to have a child is not a "human (natural) desire." It is a compulsion produced by excessive social coercion — "If you marry, you have to have a child"; "A woman only achieves true womanhood if she gives birth"; "A man who cannot get a woman pregnant is not a real man."[5] I doubt that the desire to have a child is anything more than the emotional product of social pressure. The appropriate "treatment" for such a socially produced condition is not reproductive technology but support for an environment in which individuals who cannot bear children can live their lives fully and be at ease with their own bodies, free of any taint of "illness."

d. The Question of Surrogacy

Suppose surrogacy is considered in the context of the argument that both reproductive technologies and organ transplants are medical procedures undertaken in the interest of human dignity and the value of human life. Then it can be claimed that there is no problem if the individual who offers her body has given full consent. The same can be said in the case of organ transplants. Some people are of the opinion that it is wrong for anyone to object to or criticize what others do in good conscience. Whether we are concerned with organ transplants or reproductive technology, the issue is that one person is using the life and body of another as a means of satisfying a personal desire — be that the desire for a healthy body or the desire for a child of his or her own.

We need to approach the problems common to organ transplants and reproductive technologies from two perspectives. The first is the assumptions underlying the concept of a medical procedure undertaken in the interest of "human dignity," a term often used in relation to these procedures. The second is the issue of guaranteeing the right to self-determination to both donor and patient. When I think of medical procedures performed in the name of "human dignity," I have an overwhelming desire to reject any treatment that requires one person's body for the sake of another's "human dignity." My rejection is based in my belief that the concept of "human dignity," as that term is currently used in the widespread debates over surrogacy and organ transplants, implies and includes the reduction of a person's life and body to the status of a resource.

Medicine has, until now, identified the life of an individual with a single material body from the moment of birth to death. And human illness has been understood as something to be treated with all available medical instruments and medicines of a nonhuman origin. A medical practice that uses other people's bodies as a resource to maintain, prolong, or produce a healthy life seems to contradict the premise of human medicine. I would go so far as to say that this constitutes medical malpractice and that therefore we should be fundamentally opposed to the further pursuit of such procedures. Moreover, if a significant market or trade in organs and bodies (wombs) should develop, then the same human rights questions of "disrespect for human dignity" that were raised in relation to slavery and prostitution will have to be taken up again. It is inevitable that the proliferation of these procedures will encourage the impoverished and uninformed to donate (sell) their organs and rent out their bodies (wombs). Surely an argument can be made that "treatments" such as organ transplants and reproductive technologies could be eliminated if we demonstrated a modicum of self-restraint. I will return again later to the problem of the informed consent of both donors and recipients.

e. Reproductive Technologies and the "Rights of the Child"

One dimension of surrogate pregnancy is quite distinct from the issues surrounding organ transplants: surrogacy is a procedure for making a child. We need to problematize the rights of the child born through a surrogate pregnancy. In the United States, apparently, a child "produced" in this way has already brought a legal suit for damages against parents and physicians on the grounds that he would have preferred not to be born under these artificial conditions. This is a fundamentally different type of litigation from a charge of medical malpractice. It is a litigation that brings into question the very processes of childbirth (the ethics of life). A society that functions only to satisfy the adult desire for pleasure is a troubled society. Furthermore, in a world where the global environment and the future of the earth are at risk, people who utilize artificial means of reproduction should be held answerable for their action in the face of the hardship and pain endured by others, who struggle merely to hold onto their health or their life. In other words, because birth is the product of a natural or essential human process, we can concede that each person who is born has a connection to all the other people in the world who came into life in the same way. If a child who was born not out of a natural act of sex between a man and a woman but as a product of an artificial process of reproduction declares that he/she doesn't agree with the fact of his/her own birth, then the parents and physicians who created that child must surely have to accept responsibility.

Identity (self-autonomy, nature, subjectivity) forms the nucleus of human dignity. Reproductive technology disrupts society's shared sense of the meanings of legal parentage, blood father (source of sperm), blood mother (source of egg), birth (womb) mother, and parent-child relations. The right to know one's birth origin is an important guarantee of one's right of identity. I believe that this right is guaranteed under the reference in Article 13 to the dignity of the individual. The recognition of this right is implicit in the ratification of the International Bill of Human Rights and the Treaty for Children's Rights. It will be difficult to avoid the need to take steps to enact laws to guarantee the same right to know one's birth origin in the case of children born by artificial insemination or in-vitro fertilization involving one or more persons who may or may not be their legal parents.

Because these technologies are artificial methods of reproduction, they demand a careful consideration of the rights of the children born through them. We need to problematize the notion of "childbirth" within the framework of "human dignity." The right to be born into love has remained at the nucleus of our understanding of children's rights. Only if a person knows love from birth can he or she construct a self capable of respect for both others and self. If people are to develop a natural and personal knowledge of love, we have to draw attention to the importance of the act of sexual intercourse.[6] Given that both inseminations using donor sperm and surrogate pregnancies are artificial procedures, which create life between individuals who are not in a relationship with one another and do not involve sexual intercourse between a man and a woman, it seems appropriate to reconsider these approaches from the perspective of a child's right to be born into love. As with most social service activities (e.g., foster care), if the man and woman are parents who can gain pleasure from the act of raising a child, then there is no requirement that the child be their own by blood. There are countless children in this world who have been abandoned by their parents and fight to survive starvation from one day to the next. We ought to be able to reach out to these children with love. The continued escalation of reproductive technologies risks diminishing the right of human dignity in birth.

Eugenics-based birth control is a clear breach of human dignity and cannot be tolerated. For this reason Japan's Eugenics Protection Law[7]* should be abolished. As reproductive technology frequently involves the use of drug-induced ovulation, multiple births are not unusual. There is also a high risk of handicaps. A Surrogacy Information Center was established in Japan in 1991. According to information provided by its director, at the point of signing the surrogacy contract, the surrogate mother promises to have an abortion if the child she is carrying is discovered to be handicapped. If we support a woman's right to choose, then are we not obliged to recognize her right to choose in this situation as well? This ought to be a signal that we are dealing with something that is a mockery of human rights and the sanctity of human life, something that is the antithesis of human dignity: we know from the very beginning that if we continue to move in our present direction, we will arrive at a situation where certain kinds of birth will be considered not a natural event but an artificial procedure, in which it will be assumed, even required, that an "imperfect" fetus should be aborted. How can we approve of medical procedures that we know will lead to the desecration of human life, procedures that will treat life as one more commodity to control and manage? It should be clear from all of this that it is an abuse of the concept of "choice" to apply it in the case of abortions performed under these conditions.

3. THE LEGAL PERSPECTIVE

In Japan there is at present no law that directly restricts the practice of surrogate pregnancy as a medical procedure. However, within Japanese law the woman who physically gives birth to a baby is its legal mother.[8] If that woman declares that she does not wish to hand over the child, there is no legal basis for forcing her to do so. A contract in which she has promised to hand over the child is invalidated as a breach of "public order and fair practice" as soon as the birth mother announces her intention to keep the child. But the contractor (parents) can bring indirect pressure to bear around issues of payment.

According to announcements from the Japanese Association of Obstetricians and Gynecologists, reproductive technologies, including artificial insemination by donor sperm, are restricted to legally married couples (and also de facto relationships, in some hospitals), and surrogacy is not allowed. Married couples are also allowed to utilize in-vitro fertilization. However, as there is already access to artificial insemination using donor sperm, we cannot deny that there is also a potential for donor sperm to be used in in-vitro fertilization procedures so that both the sperm and the egg may be foreign to the parents and the actual fertilization may take place outside the body of the wife. In this context, it is not difficult to imagine an escalation in the direction of surrogate pregnancies in Japan. Recent government and academic approaches to the issue of organ transplants have displayed a tendency not simply to follow but even to overtake overseas practices. Given the continued increase in the number of Japanese women seeking surrogates outside the country (e.g., in America and Korea), there is a risk that the Japanese medical profession will move quickly to introduce surrogacy in Japan rather than have patients seek the procedure overseas.

In Japan, in order to establish that the child of a surrogate pregnancy is legally theirs, the couple who contracted the surrogacy would have to officially adopt the child under the Standard Adoption Law[9] or the new Special Adoption Law passed in 1990.[10] When a couple contract a surrogate pregnancy in America, there are some states in which the child is legally recognized as theirs at birth, and this recognition would presumably stand up under Japanese law. When a child born of a surrogate pregnancy is adopted under the Special Adoption Law, the identity of the original parent(s) is not available in the family register. For births by donor sperm and in-vitro fertilization, the identity of the donor (biological father) is not sought, and the child is automatically granted a birth certificate in the name of the parents who contracted the procedure.

However, if the right of a child to know his or her birth origin is recognized and pursued, then it follows that the identity of the biological father (sperm donor) or mother (woman contracted in a surrogate pregnancy) should be accessible. Moreover, in order to protect that right, it would be necessary to maintain records of this information, and this would in turn require the enactment of some form of legislation to ensure the documentation of such "extrafamilial" parent-child relationships. If the right of the child is acknowledged, then it will be difficult to repudiate the need for such steps. They would result in considerable confusion around issues of parentage, and the legal recognition of these parent-child relations would imply the recognition of associated rights of inheritance and child support. There would also be an increased likelihood of damage suits based on a child's rejection of the circumstances of his or her birth and stated preference not to have been born. In Japan, in the case of a child of an unwanted pregnancy caused by the rape of the mother, if the court recognizes paternity, then the obligation of child support and the child's inheritance rights are also legally enforceable. From the child's perspective, should not the same rights be enforceable in the case of reproductive procedures?

Next, I want to consider the issue of surrogacy from the perspective of informed consent — the guarantee of the right to self-determination of the patient. Informed consent is a concept that came into being in the wake of medical malpractice suits to guarantee the patient's right to self-determination. It has not been enacted into law in Japan, but the concept is generally recognized in this country, too. The nature of the explanations that are required in order to reach an agreement that constitutes "informed consent" raises different problems for reproductive technologies than in the case of general medical practice. In the latter case, treatments are performed "on" the body of the actual patient. However, in the case of reproductive technologies and in particular surrogate pregnancy, the man and woman (the married couple) who are undergoing "infertility treatment" and who will reap the benefits are not necessarily the ones undergoing medical procedures. The "patients" can include the sperm and the egg donors (either or both of whom may not be part of the infertile couple), and the woman who is "donating" her womb.

In general medical practice patients receive direct treatment for their own illness or condition; therefore, the explanations given need only include information relevant to their illness and the appropriate methods of treatment. However, a surrogate pregnancy does not necessarily involve the treatment of an illness of the actual "patient(s)" undergoing procedures but is rather an artificial technique for the production of a child. It will not suffice to offer the multiple patients involved the same kinds of explanations that would normally be offered in other medical situations. It is also essential to explain such problems as the rights the child may lay claim to after birth, the potential confusion surrounding the notion of parentage, and possible access to child support and inheritance. It is necessary to speak of the potential hardships that may challenge the mind and body of the child and the possibility of multiple births and handicaps that may result from artificially induced ovulation. In the case of such "mishaps," whether it is the doctor or the "parents" who are responsible for the choice of "damage control," the result remains a mockery of the sanctity of human life. And then we should consider those individuals who suffer great emotional hardship and confusion when they fall prey to symptoms of psychological disorders rooted in their obsession with the desire to procure a child. All the possible risks attached to the choice of reproductive technologies need to be adequately explained to all parties. In the absence of adequate information, resorting to reproductive technology carries the risk of being held responsible for medical malpractice. If we carefully consider the issue of reproductive technology from the legal and medical perspectives, it becomes clear that first and foremost it is a question of the medical profession demonstrating reasonable self-regulation.

4. IN CONCLUSION . . .

I wrote in the book *A Dangerous Reproductive Revolution* that infertility treatments should only be approved within the parameters of an established heterosexual partnership.[11] I also wrote that I believed that in-vitro fertilization and artificial insemination, if restricted to the egg and sperm of the man and woman seeking the infertility treatment, would not go against the grain of human dignity and could be accepted as both a reasonable medical practice and an alternative method of achieving a pregnancy. My position remains the same. Under these circumstances an appropriate level of information regarding the potential hardships and risks is necessary and any final decision should be made only on the basis of such information — informed consent.

By presenting here the characteristics of reproductive technology as exemplified in the specific practice of surrogate pregnancy, I have tried to show just how far we have traveled away from the type of society and medical practice that we all hoped for. Unfortunately, at present we are still living under a legal system that assumes the right of the state to control women's reproductive functions and a code of values that restricts women's sexuality to pregnancy and birth. As long as the number of people who share our concerns does not grow and the public does not increase its demands for change in the system, it is unlikely we can slow down the escalation in reproductive technologies. One possible method for achieving a consensus at this stage would be to create an open public enquiry.[12] No one would disagree that such issues as surrogacy and other reproductive technologies, the nature of medical practice, appropriate methods of birth, and the rights of children, are — like the related controversy surrounding the question of brain death — matters that go to the heart of our society's ethics. Debate around such fundamental issues should not be limited to the medical profession. We should demand that the direction for the future be determined on the basis of some form of national accord.

These issues are of deep significance for the human rights of women. It is therefore essential that women demand at least 50 percent of the seats on any public committee of enquiry. Moreover, I believe that this is sufficiently important that everything possible should be done to ensure that any final decision is ratified only on the basis of a national referendum.[13] We have surely reached the point where we must make sincere efforts to establish a system that guarantees the right of children born through reproductive procedures to know their complete birth origin. As we move in the direction of these unarguably essential steps, we will also gradually gain a wider public understanding for the perspectives that we bring, as women and feminists, to our analysis of women's health. And with time we may finally be able to guarantee the sexual and reproductive health of all women.

NOTES

1. The crime of abortion is stipulated in Sections 212–16 of the Legal Code. A key aspect of the law is the notion of abortion as a crime of the individual, as encoded in Section 212. The section states that "the use of gynecological or other forms of medication/treatment to induce abortion will incur a minimum one-year prison sentence." The criminalization of abortion in Japan dates from the beginning of modernization in the Meiji Period. Under the auspices of the imperial government policy of "National Wealth and Military Strength," an anti-abortion code was first enacted in Meiji 13 [1890]. At that

time abortion was prosecuted under the same law as the crime of bodily injury, but in Meiji 40 [1907] the law was revised to establish abortion as a crime in its own right. This law has been enforced from Meiji 41 to the present.

Until the early Meiji Period there had been no strong opposition to abortion. In the Edo Period the practices of "dropping a child" (abortion) and "thinning out" (infanticide) were so common as to suggest that they were widely accepted social practice. After the Second World War a new constitution was enacted, but no one called for the abolition of the criminalization of abortion. In the midst of the hardship of the immediate postwar period, legal abortions were not available because of the continued existence of this law. There was a marked increase in the number of women who rushed into illegal, backyard abortions and died as a result. More and more women who couldn't afford illegal abortions resorted to infanticide. Many of these women were pregnant with the children of American servicemen.

During the war the government passed the National Eugenics Law (1940) as a simple form of population control and as a wartime measure for mass eugenic screening for handicaps and genetic disease. The law was revised in 1948 to allow abortions in the interest of the mother's welfare, with a physician's approval. This version was fundamentally revised in 1952 and has remained unchanged to the present. Section 14 of the current Eugenics Protection Law reads:

1. When a woman or her spouse suffers from mental illness or mental deterioration, or exhibits traits of retardation, hereditary disease, or hereditary handicap;
2. When a woman or her spouse has a family member of direct blood lineage within the last four generations who suffered from hereditary mental illness, hereditary mental deterioration, hereditary traits of retardation, hereditary disease, or a hereditary handicap;
3. When a woman or her spouse suffers from a recurring disease;
4. When the continuation of a pregnancy to full term poses a serious threat to the health of the mother for either physical or economic reasons;
5. When pregnancy results from intercourse under circumstances of violence or menace or other situations in which the woman was unable to reject or refuse;

In the above circumstances it is acceptable for a registered medical practitioner, with the agreement of the woman or her spouse, to induce an abortion.

Section 2, Paragraph 2, of the Eugenics Protection Law states that for the purposes of this law the term "induced abortion" refers to the evacuation of a fetus and other birth matter from the body of the mother within a period prior to the extra-uterine viability of the fetus. It can be said that the Eugenics Protection Law does permit limited access to abortion; however, the Japanese law presumes the criminal status of abortion. Approval is given only in those circumstances that satisfy the conditions of the law and this constitutes the legal restriction of a woman's right to choose. Moreover, traditionally the Ministry of Health and Welfare has defined the period of "extra-uterine viability." The standard period has been reduced three times over the life of the law. As of 1991 the legal limit was twenty-two weeks.

Over 95 percent of the abortions performed in Japan today are approved under Section 14, Paragraph 4, clause 4, of the Eugenics Protection Law (the "Economic Reasons Clause"). Access to abortion can be limited by narrowing the interpretation of this clause and shortening the legal period of abortion.

2. It goes without saying that the right to the self-determination of one's body is at the heart of any new notion of human rights. However, sexual difference, which is at the core of gender discrimination (the fact that only women have the physical functions necessary for pregnancy and birth), must be reconceptualized in such a way that this difference will never again become the basis for discrimination. I am presently writing a book on this issue.

3. There are still no works published in Japanese that seriously explore this new approach to gender equality. I am interested to know if the *Roe v. Wade* decision led to a new notion of human rights in the United States.

4. A member of the Group for Women's Sexuality and Human Rights, Yumiko Janson, introduced this concept to me. There is the risk, however, that "reproductive health" will be narrowly interpreted to mean only women's capacity to give birth. We should take note of the worrisome fact that at about the same time that group was beginning to use the term "reproductive health," the Japanese government was rushing to launch a research group focusing on the same concept. Janson has reported that a controversy that developed around the issue of reproductive rights at the recent International Women's Forum in India. This controversy emphasized the need to develop a terminology that can accommodate a notion of women's health that extends beyond the reproductive role to include women's sexuality and the right to choose not to give birth.

5. I have given an example to this conference of my own experience in the capacity of divorce counselor. During an extended period of treatment for infertility, the husband was reduced to a stud and the wife to a birth machine.

Faced with a declining chance of success, they were driven into a state of mental stress. The backdrop to all of this was the fact that the husband was the eldest son in a household that was still under the influence of the continuing Japanese tradition of the *ie* and the belief that a wife who cannot bear an heir for the *ie* line should be thrown out. The wife was too "weak" to fight against a sense of the inevitability of her situation. A further example is the kidnapping of a newborn infant in May of 1992. The baby was returned unharmed about one month later, but the kidnappers were a husband and a wife who had been undergoing a protracted "infertility treatment." It was disclosed that this couple had been pushed to the point where the husband spread the lie that his wife was pregnant in order to make the kidnapping plot plausible. The case set off a warning alarm of the potential risks associated with a continued, unmonitored escalation of "infertility treatments" in Japan.

6. In our contemporary society, where a sexual culture that discriminates against and scorns women continues to grow, the notion of valuing sex as an opportunity to discover love will inevitably be considered mere idealism. And yet we cannot deny the increasing importance of gestures of cooperation to end the sexual culture of discrimination and replace it with a sexual practice grounded in equality.

7. The philosophy underlying Nazi Germany's racial eugenics, the policy at the heart of its extermination and oppression of Jews and its sterilization law, was thoroughly criticized and rejected by the world in the aftermath of the war. And every country eliminated laws containing the term "eugenic" with the exception of Japan, where the Eugenics Protection Law still remains. Behind the escalation of reproductive technologies in Japan there remains a strong philosophy of eugenics. It is the difficulty of eliminating this lingering acceptance of the principles of eugenics that has hindered any movement to ban this law, despite its continued use of such an offensive term. The name of the law reflects the fact that it is essentially the same wartime National Eugenics Law, passed five years prior to the defeat, with a mere revision added in 1948 to accommodate abortion in cases where the mother's health is at risk.

What distinguishes this law from the Nazi sterilization law is that it restricts sterilization to processes that sterilize without the complete removal of the reproductive organs. The problem is that the "eugenics" of the title is present in more than name only. This law can be, and is, utilized in the following circumstances: The state (physicians working with the Eugenics Commission) approves of eugenic surgery in the "interest of the public good" in order to "prevent the reproduction of genetic defects"; the elderly, mentally retarded, or mentally impaired undergo eugenic surgery in the absence of approval from the individual undergoing the procedure or their spouse; to further eugenic selection (the current abortion law clearly designates this as an appropriate criterion). There are also many cases of eugenic surgery that have no apparent medical justification among patients in long-term institutional care. It would appear the procedure is used as a means of reducing the workload of the staff by eliminating the menstruation cycles of women patients. All of the above indicate that there are serious problems to be considered here.

Using only statistics for cases officially processed by the Ministry of Health and Welfare, we find that more than one hundred eugenic surgical procedures are performed every year and that the rate for women undergoing these operations is 4–5 times higher than that for men. Recently, handicapped people have led the movement to eliminate the Eugenics Protection Law. But because they are not campaigning directly for the decriminalization of abortion, this issue must remain an important concern for all women.

8. The attribution of legal motherhood to the woman who physically gave birth to the child is a traditional underpinning of laws of parentage. At the point of issuing the birth registration, it is standard for the attending physician to verify the proof of parentage and produce the necessary documents. In the absence of the attending physician's attestation, the mother-child relationship must, as in the case of the father-child, be established by mutual agreement of the parties. Of course, if the claim to motherhood is contested, it is possible to seek a legal nullification of the other party's claim.

9. There had only been one adoption regulation in Japan, but in Shōwa 62 (1987) the Special Adoption Law was enacted, and consequently the preexisting legislation came to be known as the Standard Adoption Law. Under the Standard Adoption Law the adopted "child" can be older than the adoptive parent(s) so long as they are not of the same direct blood lineage. The adoptive parents themselves must be legally of age. (These last points are meant to accommodate the adoption of a husband into the family register of the wife — a common practice, particularly if the wife's family has no male heir.) The courts must give permission for the adoption of a minor. In the case of a child of fifteen and over, the person(s) holding parental or legal guardianship of the child can act on behalf of the child in the adoption procedure. The Standard Adoption Law is intended as a process for the legal adoption of the child of another person or persons. It is not a system that allows the non-birth parent(s) to establish a child as their own from the moment of registration of birth.

10. The Special Adoption Law came into being against the backdrop of a

new population policy developed in response to a recent decline in birth rates. The policy aimed at reducing the number of abortions and encouraging as many "healthy" pregnancies as possible to be carried to full term. By allowing prospective adoptive parents to register and raise as their own the unwanted child that a woman was forced to carry to term, this new regulation created a solution to the "we want a child of our own" syndrome of modern Japan.

It is generally a condition of adoption that the child be under the age of six. The adoptive parent should be married, and the household should be legally registered. If the procedure is completed under the Special Adoption Law, then the child's birth origin (biological parent-child relation) is legally terminated. However, if the status of the original (biological) parents changes so that they feel able to raise the child themselves or if the police or courts rule that the child is suffering under the care of the adoptive parents, then either the police or the original parent(s) may apply to the family court for the adoptive agreement to be annulled.

11. In her book *Women, Law, Sexuality, and Knowledge* (Nihon Hyōron-sha, 1991), Kanejiro Seiko writes critically of *A Dangerous Reproductive Revolution*. "Most women are arguing for a rejection of reproductive technologies. And that tone is strangely linked to a traditional way of thinking that insists that all children should be born within the limits of marriage and by natural means 'blessed by the gods'. . . . If we consider that one of the sources of the present state of gender inequity is the fact that, following industrialization, women stayed, or were forced to stay, within the traditional [preindustrialized] structure of the household, then isn't there a risk in a total rejection of all technology?" And then she writes by way of her own argument, "What needs to be problematized is not the reproductive technologies themselves but the social conditions within which the technologies are utilized, the results these conditions produce, and the surrounding context of power relations." Kanejiro thus limits women's point of view to an emphasis on political power and participation. As is evident here, Kanejiro's epoch-making work is unsatisfactory because it deals only vaguely with the task of building an essential theory of human rights that can establish women's human rights through genuine equity between men and women. Instead Kanejiro invests everything in political action — the critique of power.

12. Public inquiries in Japan are usually conducted by either a ministerial or a prime ministerial committee of inquiry, whose members are not elected but appointed. For the most part they are not open to the public. Therefore, they are far from functioning as a democratic process.

13. In Japan the only public poll that occurs other than the usual elections

is the popular ballot to select judges to the Supreme Court. It is held at the same time as general elections for the Upper House, and public referendums on questions of constitutional reform. In the first instance, the lack of adequate information makes it virtually impossible for the public to make any real selection. In the second, as we saw in the case of the PKO Reform Bill, even if the public votes against a proposed reform, the law can be modified by resorting to a process known as "interpretative constitutional reform." This has become the conventional method by which the government can circumvent the results of an unfavorable public referendum.

Selected Works

Abunai seishoku kakumei (A Dangerous Reproductive Revolution). Yūhikaku, 1989.
Fujin hogo jigyō kondankai repōto (Projects for the Protection of Women). Fujin Hogo Jigyō Kondankai, 1992.
Kazokuhō kaisei no shiten (Concerning the Revision of Family Law). *Jurisuto*, no. 1019. Yūhikaku, 1993.
Kodomo no tame no rikon kōza (Lectures on Divorce for Children). Yūhikaku, 1993.
Onna no jinken to sei (Women's Rights and Sexuality). Komichi Shobō, 1984.
Sabetsu to jinken, vol. 3: *Josei* (Discrimination and Human Rights, vol. 3: Women). Yūzankaku, 1985.

KŌRA RUMIKO
Poet and Critic

» » » » » » » » » » » »

THE WELL-KNOWN POET AND FEMINIST Kōra Rumiko has collaborated on several collections of feminist writings and published her own books on the subject of female sexuality and identity. Kōra's work demonstrates a particular concern with the concept of motherhood and its role in defining female identity in the context of Japanese society. She uses both her poetry and her theoretical writings to explore these issues of identity. Her status as a major contemporary poet has been recognized by her inclusion in such collections as the *Shichō-sha Anthology of Modern Poetry* and by the recent publication of a six-volume collection of her poetry and prose. In 1988 she won the National Modern Poet's Prize.

As a poet, Kōra is deeply concerned with the role of language in shaping the options for self-expression available to women. Her poetry is often an explicit exploration of the relationship of women to the language with which they speak themselves. She has written extensively of her experience as a poet and a woman working to construct a voice that can adequately describe female experience. Kōra's poetry is very much about the body of woman, the desiring body, the pregnant body, the mothering body. Describing her own life's work she states, "The question of 'Woman' is the major obsession of my life . . . and like the 'Asia' question it won't be solved in the modern age, and yet it is only [by looking] in that direction that we might catch sight of the horizon of the future of human civilization." For Kōra race and gender issues are inseparable, and much of her life has been committed to the politics of race. As one step toward reducing the distance between peoples of color, she has promoted and translated the works of Asian and African poets. She, like Matsui Yayori and Aoki Yayoi, has sought to complicate the relationship of Japanese women to the women of the third world both in her poetry and in her critical writings. Kōra traces her commitment to the politics of peace to her childhood experiences of the Pacific War and the Occupation. Political corruption and the need to remember the war as a deterrent to remilitarization are frequent themes in her work.

Kōra supports the concept of biological difference and the active reclamation of the maternal and nurturing role of the feminine. She is often in disagreement with feminists who reject the maternal as too essentialist a site on which to construct an alternative female identity. As the title of one of her collections of feminist essays, *Woman's Choice: Birth, Nurturing, Work,* suggests, she sees motherhood as a primary dimension of a woman's life but not to the exclusion of non-domestic work in the paid labor force. Kōra's emphasis on the multiple roles that women occupy over their lifetime, and even at one moment in their life, leads her to a strong political interest in issues such as welfare, childcare, employment equity, and pensions, in recognition of the need for adequate support systems for women's work, both paid and unpaid.

Unlike many other literary traditions, Japanese literature, with its golden age of women's writing, the Heian* Period, offers a rich heritage to contemporary women writers and poets. But from that period all the way to the present, women poets have been concerned with the implications of the firm boundaries drawn between women's and men's language in both daily life and artistic production. Kōra's strategy has been to retrieve or redefine certain qualities of women's language rather than to reject that language out of hand. She actively seeks out the richness and potential of women's forms while also experimenting with new voices and styles. Her poems seldom follow a simple forward narrative progression; instead, they fold and unfold, line on line, as she plays with such traditional forms as pivot words, double entendres, and "pillow words" (*makura kotoba*, or stock epithets). A movement forward into a poem or sentence often carries the reader back into what has already been read, disrupting or undoing the surface of the first reading. Kōra is one of only a small number of poets in Japan who have sought a dialogue beyond either an Anglo-European or a Chinese-Japanese axis of influence. Many of the echos and traces in her poems flow in and out of Africa, Southeast Asia, and South Asia. In this way her work creates a meeting place — a new ground. Her style is of the tradition she writes out of at the same time that it is already located elsewhere and working against the grain of familiar forms. The voices of the tradition are the palimpsest discernable still beneath the experimental surface of her poems.

Interview

SB: The thing that struck me first when reading your poetry was the exploration of feminine identity and language within the poems.

KR: From the time I was a small child, I was intensely aware of language. I felt even as a child that language was not mine, that I existed outside the language that surrounded me, like a foreigner. The warmth and familiarity of a language that was my own, wrapped gently around me, remained a dream, unknown. In the absence of a language that I could wear comfortably, I took the sounds and words around me and played with them. Language was one of my favorite toys as a child. Yes, it's true that I have always been aware of language as something outside myself and have written about it, and within it, in a very self-conscious way.

SB: In a short essay included in the Shichōsha publication of your collected poems, you write of the frustration of trying to describe your life in a language that excludes your experience.

KR: In my own experience there has been confrontation, even war, and yet when I try to communicate these experiences, as I remember them, I find only an empty language that cannot accommodate me. I began reading foreign verse and found escape there, especially in French poetry. I came back to Japanese and began to experiment with words, breaking down the boundaries between language and self, allowing words to disappear into me, and me into words, in moments of struggle and confusion.

SB: *A special issue of the poetry journal* La Mer *(Ra mēru) was devoted to questions of sexuality and language. I believe you wrote an article for that issue.*

KR: Yes, but let me ask you about your work on Kawabata. It seems to be related.

SB: *In that particular article I look at Kawabata's representation of the feminine. He is renowned for his depictions of female characters. Several critics argue that his greatest skill is his ability to capture the essence of his female characters. I try to argue that Kawabata's women are the constructions of a male imagination and in no way reflect the reality of individual female experience.*

KR: This, too, is very much a question of sexuality and language. The woman that is created in the texts of Japan's male writers is a stranger to me. These novels make me angry. There is a difference between prose and poetry, but maybe we can come back to that later. Mori Ōgai, Tayama Katai, Kawabata Yasunari, all the greats, are men. In their time, the gap or barrier between male and female was so great that the two constituted separate social classes. There was no opportunity for these men to interact with women who would meet them on an equal footing. For example, in Kawabata Yasunari's *Snow Country,* Yukiko lives in a comparatively free environment, and yet her relationship with the protagonist never transcends the inequality of "patron" and "geisha." Contemporary male writers are possibly even worse. They are not mature enough to be able to represent adequately the individual experience of a woman. I can only wonder at the fact that they're so popular. It's frightening. As a Japanese I'm embarrassed at the thought of these male writers being translated and read outside Japan. What does it say about this society? Perhaps it's better that it's all out in the open. Japan has always been most sensitive to pressure from the outside. Certainly no amount of pressure from within has seemed to make any difference. They write on unashamedly.

When I first began writing, I was so troubled by the overt masculinity of the language of so many male writers that I was determined to try and write in a language that was not bound to my identity as a woman. I had to break away from the "femininity" or emotiveness that is so much a part of the traditional Japanese literary language. I suppose that at the time I equated this with women's speech. I was aiming at some sort of neutral voice while still trying to express the many levels of eroticism that surfaced in my poetry. I wasn't writing specifically about sex, but sexuality was always just below the surface of the poems. Perhaps at this time I still hadn't made a clear link between the two, language and sexuality. With time I came to want to write quite specifically about female sexuality and desire. As a woman, that's only natural, I suppose. I began to speak my own experience as the subject and consciousness of the poems. I was not as concerned with sex as with those other moments in a woman's life when she is deeply aware of her own sexuality and her identity as a woman. I wrote about birth and the experience of mothering. The most deeply erotic moments of feminine experience may be those that occur not in sexual contact but in realizing the eroticism of the female body within the context of nature. This is a much more universal concept of the erotic than anything that is bound to physical sexuality. The source of this pleasure is a woman's experience of her own body. This experience is not achieved through a correspondence between the conscious and the universe, but falls in that space between the universe and nature and can be discovered through the woman's own body as she comes to know herself. This is my understanding of eroticism or a female sexuality.

SB: *You seem to be moving freely between the words eroticism, sexuality, and sex.*

KR: I'm using "sex" to describe the physical relationship. "Sexuality" is something very clinical. When I try to imagine a female sexuality, I find myself moving toward an eroticism of the female body that is not clinical, which cannot be diagnosed or described but only experienced.

SB: *What you're describing seems to exclude the male from this erotic space.*

KR: There is the potential for men to take part in this space, but in this "civilized" society, the only way open to men is for them to forget their bodies, for them to leave the body behind. It's so much easier to forget your body and move on unburdened. A man may perhaps be able to live inside his head, cut free from the memory of his body, but how can a woman do that? Our bodies are constantly shifting, changing, reminding us of our whole selves. A woman's body is a world in miniature. Within this frame that is visible from the outside, there is another world that cannot be seen, a world that can only be experienced in the living of that body. There is a cave within the female body that is the only world known to a new life as it forms and grows. Within this cave-world, there is a sea of life and from that sea a pathway out into the visible world. The first world we know is that other world, and yet it is beyond our memory. As soon as the infant passes through the pathway into the outer world, the inner world of that sea is gone forever. As a fetus grows within a woman, she draws close to her own body, knows herself, knows that she is not the same as men. She is a woman.

SB: *Some feminists would argue that such a strong emphasis on biological difference can work against women.*

KR: Difference does not have to be negatively defined. The challenge is to redefine female identity positively, to affirm a woman's experience of her body. It is very sad if women lose the right to celebrate their difference.

SB: How does this relate back to literature or poetry?

KR: I suppose that one sensitive area is the categorization of women's writing under such labels as "women's literature" and "women's poetry." Some argue that these categories are a strategy to marginalize women's writing and that the entire canon of literature should be reevaluated to reflect the role women have played in literature in Japan. You have to remember that it was women who dominated the golden age of Japanese literature in the Heian Period. In that sense, Japanese women writers and poets have a strong tradition of women's literature to draw on. I don't know that I agree with people who argue that these categories are discriminatory. If they exclude women from the mainstream of literature, they also create an exclusive territory of women's writing and language. This might be one situation where separate and different can be redefined positively as a creative space within which women can work free of obstacles. I must admit though that I have felt very strange on those occasions when I was introduced at public functions as "Kōra Rumiko, the woman poet." As more and more women are published, I suspect that the distinction will begin to break down unless women choose to maintain it for their own reasons.

SB: You mentioned earlier that you thought there was a distinction between the poetic language and prose of male and female writers.

KR: Yes. I think that in Japan it is true to say that poetic language is generally marked as feminine. There are some poetic forms that cultivate the Chinese style, which has traditionally been associated with public affairs and marked as more masculine. However, most poetic language, regardless of whether the poet is male or female, is feminine in that it draws on the *kana* tradition, which is generally associated with feminine language and the women's literature of the Heian Period. It is designated as a language of the private and not the public world. It is often impossible when reading a Japanese poem to identify whether the poet is a man or a woman. This is compounded by the avoidance of pronouns.

SB: In some recent French feminist theory a link has been drawn between poetic language and the possibilities of a feminine language.

KR: I recently took part in a roundtable discussion on just that subject. I think the situation is slightly different in the case of English and French. These languages are deeply patriarchal. Until the emphasis on unified language and universal education began with the modernization process in the last century, the Japanese spoken language was arguably more feminine than masculine. The trend over the last century has been to disguise the masculinization of the language under the rubric of standardization. The clearly feminine quality of Japanese poetic language poses problems for any translation into English, for that quality is almost inevitably lost because there is no equivalent level of distinction. It is my sense that in English the patriarchal dominance of language is so pervasive that feminists would have to create a whole new space for feminine language. In Japanese we already have a feminine language in place, which is also the language of poetry. You could even argue that poetic language is more immediate and familiar in a society where it is so close to the language of over half the speaking population.

It took me a long time to come to the realization that the language women speak in daily conversation can also be empowered as a language of women's poetry if it is recontextualized, redefined, to speak its own meanings. As with the categorization of women's writing, women's speech need not be negative. It is a beautiful language. Why shouldn't it be a language of liberation and flight instead of one of constraint and limitation?

SB: The feminine quality in poetic language in Japan applies not only to syntax and sound but also to the visual surface of the poem on the page, doesn't it?

KR: Japanese poems are seldom read out loud for that very reason. The visual quality of the calligraphy and the effect of the presence or absence of Chinese graphs and Japanese *kana* are crucial to the meaning of the poem. They are a part of the construction. This distinction only strengthens further the sense of two distinct styles, masculine and feminine.

SB: Dale Spender has argued that the qualities of softness, emotiveness, gentleness, and so forth, which are frequently associated with feminine forms in language are negative markers of weakness. She sees such distinctions as limiting women's language to the private domain.

KR: Why throw out the baby with the bath water? Why not take all these qualities of women's language and work with them on the assumption that they can be something other than negative. In Japan there is a long and deep heritage of women's culture. Within that culture women are not bound only to such qualities as softness, gentleness, emotiveness, but are also often angry, laughing, fighting. This diversity is apparent when you look at the actions attributed to the goddesses in Japanese mythology. It would be a mistake to define the feminine too narrowly. When I think of feminine qualities, I don't think of softness and emotiveness; I think of vitality, synthesism, continuity, and egalitarianism. These are not qualities that are negatively marked. They are the very basis for the future development of society.

SB: You've mentioned the Heian Period as the source of a mother language for Japanese women writers, and yet the Heian Period was followed by a long period of silence for women, which was broken only very occasionally. Why do you think that we are only now seeing a new wave of women's writing in Japan?

KR: The new wave of women's writing you speak of dates from the Meiji Period, with women like Higuchi Ichiyō and Yosano Akiko. I think that certain periods have a cultural potential to generate particular forms of literary production. The Edo Period saw a blossoming of *haiku* and *waka* verse, theater, and certain forms of popular fiction. No matter how rich the culture of that period may have been, it was not a period conducive to women's writing. It was a period of oppression for women. The neo-Confucian morals of the period constrained women at every level of their daily lives. My own grandmother was born in 1871, the fourth year of Meiji. She and her husband would regularly hold poetry circles in their house in the southwest of Japan. Women have written, especially short poems, throughout Japanese history, but there have only been two periods that were conducive to the circulation of women's writing in the public domain — the Nara-Heian Period and the modern period. The external conditions affecting women's lives have only allowed for the possibility of a public voice for women at these two times. That women go on writing, even without an audience, should not be forgotten.

SB: *More and more women writers have been published by the major publishing houses since the 1980s. Do you see any potential for this process of mainstreaming to affect women's writing?*

KR: It's true that more women writers are being published, but I don't know that it's as true for poetry as it is for fiction. We all risk falling into the trap of believing that an increase in the number of women writers published is a sign of success. If what is being published is of poor quality, then what is gained? I would argue that the very best writing is not taken up by the publishing houses and that what we are seeing on the shelves of bookstores today reflects only what the publishers believe will sell. I seriously question whether the recent wave of women's books marks any progress in women's writing in Japan. Anyone who wants to sell a book today puts the word "woman" in the title. What is this book of yours going to be called?

SB: *"Broken Silence: Voices of Japanese Feminism."*

KR: "Feminism" is quite a different thing. Publishers feel much less comfortable with that than with "woman." Let me just say a little more about the question of women and publishing. There have been some journals established specifically to publish women writers or poets. *La Mer* is a good example. These journals are important as a focus and stimulus for women's writing, but there is also a risk involved. It is the problem of marginalization again. While these journals can offer an important focus and stimulus for women's writing, they should not develop into a ghetto to which all women's writing is confined. Choice is the real issue. If a woman wants to publish in non-women-specific publications, there should be the freedom to do so with equal access. I think the mass communications industry has been actively encouraging the marginalization of women's writing and other cultural production through the establishment of the *karuchāa sentā* (culture centers) throughout urban Japan. It's no accident that these are concentrated in the cities and not rural areas. Once it was perceived that women had too much free time on their hands and might begin thinking about the quality of their lives, the establishment devised a scheme to divert their creative energies through endless hours of adult education courses. Most of the courses are on culture — flower arrangement, tea ceremony, French cooking, etc. — or related to their children's education — refresher courses in English, mathematics, etc. Some courses are even on writing and poetry, but these institutions are places of containment and refinement. They are not going to generate politicized creative production that might begin to break down the artificial exclusion of women from the public domain. What is needed is a women's writing that challenges and disrupts the dominant male-female roles. That eroticism I spoke of before is not restricted to the individual woman's experience. It is a stream of shared consciousness that flows between women, across boundaries. This feminine eroticism and vitality is a potential political force.

SB: When you speak of disruption or a challenge to the dominant politics of gender, what alternative(s) do you envisage?

KR: A major problem is the extent to which men have been totally drawn into their role as loyal employees. Work has ceased to be one part of their lives and has become the organizing principle of their entire existence. This is the first thing that needs to change if there are to be any significant developments. Look at the popular political movements in Japan, and you'll find that the majority of the activists are women and the elderly — the two groups excluded from the permanent workforce. There is no time left in men's lives to even begin

to think about the conditions under which they're working and living, let alone take any political action for change. As a consequence,
it is women in Japanese society who are politically and culturally
more astute and aware. This gets back to the strategy of organizing
women's free time through *karuchā sentā* activities. Even so, women
are currently outpacing men in many intellectual areas, and it is
women who seem most likely to lead any major political movement
for change in Japan. There is no doubt that there is an awareness of
this; otherwise, there would be no necessity to monitor women's activities and time so closely.

One problem, however, is that thus far women have chosen to express themselves in the form of literature, in poetry and fiction. A serious female presence in the area of criticism has been missing. The
role of *hyōronka* remains male in Japan today. A high priority seems
to be for women to come out into the public domain and develop a
feminist critique of Japanese society. Even our most radical social
critics always fail to expand their analysis or critique of a problem
into the area of gender. It is up to women to do this. An effective pattern would be first to establish this critical space for women's voices
and then to move into the domain of literature. The reverse process
seems to have gone nowhere. If the space you speak into remains
deaf to the issues you are writing about in your poetry and fiction,
then what do you achieve? At the very least the two should be developed hand in hand.

*SB: These aren't just empty words for you. In addition to your poetry
you've written many articles on women's issues for a wide range of
publications. Your poetry collections are frequently accompanied by
essays on questions of women and language or the role of women's
writing.*

KR: There are other women doing the same thing. It would not be
fair to say women are not trying to move in this direction. The ongoing problem is how women are to achieve a place in the public space
of the media. The handful of women who have been allowed entry
into that predominantly male domain are often there only because of

the relatively unchallenging style of their critique and their willingness to compromise. This is obviously not enough. Women must win
their own ground in that public space and speak uncompromisingly.

*SB: You have devoted considerable effort to introducing the poetry of
African and Asian countries into Japan through translation. Is there
any link between your own experience of life as a woman and your
concern for the poetry of these countries?*

KR: Oh yes! When I was twenty-three, I took a ship to France. This
was right at the time of France's withdrawal from Vietnam. Traveling
through Southeast Asia at that time, I was exposed to a Europe that
was very different from the fairytale land Japan so envied then. From
the perspective of Southeast Asia, Europe was a beast of a different
color. I was also forced to recognize the atrocity of Japan's own war
crimes in the region. After this experience I felt a deep affinity with
the countries of Southeast Asia. As a woman living in Japan, as a
mother, I came to recognize increasingly the parallels between the status of women in a male-dominated society and the status of the so-
called third world in relation to the industrialized capitalist nations.

*SB: I think it is Hélène Cixous who speaks of the colonization of the
female body.*

KR: Exactly. Territory, identity, language are all appropriated. The
irony is that most of the poems I have translated are by male poets
and not by women. It was much more difficult to find poems by
women in the 1970s when I was translating.

*SB: Perhaps there are boxes within boxes, colonies within
colonies . . .*

KR: You mean that the women of a colonized country are already the
victims of another form of gender-based colonization within their
own society? Yes, I suppose the silence was being generated even before the Europeans arrived. In that sense, the colonization of these regions intensified the level of oppression experienced by the women.
The sense that one's own body has been colonized is one more reason

why women are potentially more politicized than men. The issue is how that personal experience is translated into political action.

SB: *In what ways, as a Japanese woman, have you experienced a sense of colonization or possibly appropriation?*

KR: The most obvious answer is language. I described before my sense from childhood that language and experience were incompatible. The struggle was to find ways of playing with language to fit it to me, instead of me to it. I don't know if appropriation is the right word for the devaluation of women's speech, but this is the other strong memory I have from my youth. The language that I spoke was women's speech, but it was as if that language could only be heard in certain contexts. Outside those private contexts a woman's voice couldn't be heard. It was like speaking into a void. Things have improved in the wake of the women's movement of the 1970s and 1980s, but there is still a long way to go.

SB: *This goes back to what you were saying about the negative marking of women's language and the possibility of redefining that language positively. In terms of colonization, women's language is like land that is renamed or redistributed along new borders.*

KR: The land itself doesn't change. It has to be won back.

SB: *What of the theories of women's language that argue that it is a space to which women are confined, a space allocated to them? That approach seems to deny that language was ever the property of women.*

KR: It appears to deny any autonomy to women. It may be that the language women came to speak has been historically defined in certain ways. It may even be true that its boundaries were externally determined, but the language itself developed among women and in that sense is the property of women. It is now up to women to defy the boundaries and make this language work for them. To speak the language rather than be spoken. I still believe that women's language is a place of departure and not something to be escaped.

Another important thing to keep in mind is that what we call women's speech began to be spoken beyond the aristocracy only from the fifteenth century. The spread of women's speech into the merchant class came in the eighteenth and nineteenth centuries. The widespread use of honorifics is something we can only trace back over the last two centuries or so. The deep historical roots of women's language, the idea that it is part of the tradition or heritage of Japanese language and society, all this is a well-constructed and well-maintained myth. Put in perspective, the task of dismantling the present status of women's language is much less daunting.

SB: To move back to your own writing, how are your poems received by male critics?

KR: Critics often talk about women's poetry as flowery or emotional, but I frequently get comments such as "Her poems are unusually intellectual for a woman." Of course, when you think about it, the two approaches amount to the same thing in terms of categorizing women's poetry. I must say, however, that male critics have become more sensitized to questions of gender in recent years. It is less common these days to read overtly sexist or discriminatory remarks by the better critics. This doesn't represent any significant conversion of men. What it represents is the lack of any firm intellectual commitment on the part of Japanese male intellectuals, or all Japanese men for that matter. I think this is a fundamental difference between Japanese men and Western men. This lack of commitment means that a phenomenon such as *tenkō* (turncoating) is widespread and easy among Japanese intellectuals. Some of Japan's most prominent intellectuals shifted intellectual and political alliances two, even three times, in their lifetime. If they just say something often enough — women are emotional, women are there to bear children, etc. — they start to believe it, but it has no roots. If the tide starts to flow in the other direction, they have no particular personal commitment to that view of women and begin to shift again. The motivation for sustaining this construction of gender roles is not rooted in the personal belief system of individual males. It is an external social construction that is internalized by the individual. The whole structure is very fragile in this sense, and that is why there are so many subtle mechanisms of reinforcement in place. That's where your interest in the relationship between culture and ideology comes in.

SB: Yes. To pursue that direction further, let me ask what potential you see in the realm of cultural production, specifically poetry, to disrupt or alter the present constructions of gender? In other words, how can culture be used to subvert rather than support oppressive ideologies?

KR: That's a huge question. We could write a book on it. There has been a tendency over the last ten to twenty years for critics in Japan to argue for the separation of culture or art and politics. This approach defined as political only what was radical or anti-establishment. It failed to acknowledge the pervasive presence of establishment politics across the arts. To put it differently, art that did nothing to disrupt the status quo was considered nonpolitical, while art that was disruptive or challenged the status quo was denounced for mixing art with politics. Of course, the distinction is ridiculous. All art is political; all poetry is political. It's just a question of which politics. To strip politics out of poetry would amount to taking the life out of the poem. Poems don't come from some ephemeral place. Both poetry and politics are the territory of human experience. They should both smell of the bodies that have made them, that inhabit them. That's good poetry. I sometimes try to write such poems. It may be difficult to find anything poetic in a speech by Nakasone, or any other politician for that matter, but there was theater and poetry in the AMPO riots. To say this is not to try to romanticize that very violent period of confrontation, but to try to politicize artistic production.

SB: What's your opinion of the present political situation in Japan? Several of the feminists whom I've interviewed have expressed their concern at what they perceive as a significant conservative swing among women.

KR: I think the situation is dreadful. The most frightening thing is that everyone seems content just to express their concern and to take

no action. It is shocking that the recent attack on the union movement in Japan was allowed to proceed with almost no public outcry.
The systematic dismantling of the nationalized railways and the fragmentation, or dissolution, of their unions amounted to a dismantling
of democracy. The demise of the unions also represents a significant
weakening of the Japanese Socialist Party. It is no coincidence that
the unions that came under attack first were those with the closest
links to the left, and to the JSP in particular. The whole consensus approach camouflages processes intended to expand the profits of the
largest corporations and set in place the political structures necessary
to secure the future of the right, regardless of the specific party con-
figuration the conservative alliance takes in the wake of the breakup
of the LDP. The nationalization of certain key industries guaranteed
at least some degree of redistribution of profits. What we are seeing
now is a new differentiation of classes. The victims of this process are
the poor, single-parent families, the elderly, the handicapped, illegal
immigrant workers, and farmers. If the process continues unchecked,
we will see the gradual atrophy of both culture and politics. Living in
Tokyo today I sense a listlessness among writers. An entirely new vitality is needed in the face of the current political situation. There are
signs of a revival in poetry, but a different, new literature is required
in this environment.

*SB: What do you think accounts for the extent of the conservative
swing in recent elections and this general atmosphere of
complacency?*

KR: There are still people in Japan committed to political causes.
There are members of the women's movement, environmentalists,
unionists, and so on, but when it comes to the real test at election
time, the conservatives always win hands down. The mistake is to
think that this represents popular support for conservative politics.
Only about a third of eligible voters actually vote regularly. What
these election results represent is the level of complacency or disin-
terest among the Japanese public. Any form of external pressure will
always mobilize the Japanese. Look at the way Japan has rallied in

the face of criticism over the strength of the yen. In the absence of external pressure, however, there is a general inertia. Complacency is not the same thing as satisfaction. This is an important distinction.

I think that there are historical factors operating here. With few exceptions, there is no tradition of popular intervention in government in Japan. Traditionally the "commoner" has been distanced from the political process. There have been isolated instances of democratic movements in Japanese history, but, for the most part, any call for democratic practice was suppressed by the government of the day. Some would argue that the lack of any continuous tradition of popular participation in politics compounds the failure of the modern democratic process in Japan. If I thought that election results reflected a genuine level of satisfaction among the majority of Japanese, I suppose I would have to reconsider my position, but I don't believe this is the case. I think the fundamental problem is that individuals in Japan don't have any real sense of their own worth. They don't value their life as independent from the whole — the society. This is something Japanese have not learned despite more than a century of modernization. If one has no sense of one's own value, then how can one value the life of another individual? Look at welfare for the elderly in Japan. The pension is a mere pittance, just a few hundred dollars a month. In Japan today that is nothing. People start planning their saving for retirement from the time they enter the workforce. There is no sense that welfare is a state issue, that the elderly have a right to support. The same problem flows over into Japan's attitude toward the rest of Asia. There is no sense of responsibility either at the individual level or at the national level. The traditional structures are based on social obligations and contracts, not individual commitment and responsibility. These same traditional structures obscure the exploitation of individuals behind a rhetoric of group cohesiveness. Women raise children. They are located, not necessarily by choice, at the center of the household and the family. This is one place where change can begin. Women's writing — poetry, fiction, and criticism — can create an essential framework of support for that change.

Selected Poems and Prose

THE PAINTING THAT DISAPPEARED ME

First the artist painted me into an ocher landscape. Next he drew in a white roadway behind me. The supple stem of the paintbrush. Paints squeezed fresh from tubes shine elastic on the pallet. The artist rests his brush briefly and stares off into the sky, lifts the pallet knife from the edge of the paint box, and runs it across my throat. With each stroke I am whittled away. I hear strange sounds below my lip and armpit. My body is falling to the floor in neat, red clumps. In the dark space over my head a myriad of colors gather as houses, trees, even a sun, take their place. I wasn't too worried about the house, but surprised when the gleeful face of a large sun began shining overhead. It didn't compare in heat to the South Pacific sun. I spoke in a soft, displeased voice, "This isn't your place. How about moving over there?" but to no avail. Suddenly the sensation in my arms changes and my right arm has turned into a freight train. My left is a jet black furnace. A terrible heat. My body begins to fade in the sweat of the combined heat of furnace and sun. I may disappear at any moment. I might have been able to escape down that white roadway stretching out behind me. I should have been able to flee into the background of the painting. No choice but to slide myself away in a drawer somewhere. And yet. I meekly accept each of the objects that piles its way into the canvas. I'm as thin as paper now. Stuck to the canvas, am I the canvas or is the canvas me? I blend in with the paint beneath me to become a complex color, shining like a phosphorescent bug. Like mud splashed against a wall. I look at the face of the artist. He is deep in thought as he paints (what a politician!). He pushes me further into the background. I am a failure. What can I do? My life is over. Rather than take flight in fright and hide myself in a drawer, better to go on existing as an unseen particle within the canvas. No matter what, I can never have a life that has any form of its own.

Translated with the permission of the author by Sandra Buckley.

WAVES

The flowing moonlight washing over their backs
like a snake sliding across treeshade
the waves follow the ocean face,
a cool breeze blows.
Facing the distant shore
the waves roll silently.

Shining like fishscales
almost a fragment of light itself,
yet, it is water — verdant, distant,
something shorelike visible.

What is there, where the wave glistens
is unknown to me, but still,
the waves flickering in the cool breeze are beautiful.
Knowing that they flow toward somewhere
I am washed with a feeling that is almost calm.

When the waves beat upon the shore
in rhythm with the drumming of my heart
I know what it is, there within the wave.
I think of living.

IN OUR COUNTRY

In our country they waved as they sent off the last of the fighter pilots
  then sank the mothership that should have made the return voyage.

In our country they waved the flag at the children as they sent them
   to the villages
  then burnt the cities together with the mothers and fathers.

In our country they exchanged firm handshakes with the youths
  then loaded them onto special weapons of death.

In our country they sent the young boys and girls to work in the
   factories
  then slowly made them over into machines.

In our country they had them lay down their arms
   then shot them in the back.
In our country they ask, a smile on their face, to shake our hand
   then slip a gun in it.

THE MEETING

I slip on the stairs and there's a room
I enter the room and there you all are
(I don't need you, let's get rid of you)

I turn into a sword and run through the streets

The air faces me
and shrivels around me like a burst balloon
as I slash
between the gazes, my body writhing
at the folds in the air
at the invisible wall of words

Tomorrow
another person who is me and is not me
will exchange warm greetings with you
slip on the stairs
and break down the door.

IN THE DARKNESS OF A COINLOCKER

Baby, thrown away, locked in a coinlocker,
   your birth robes —
your first robe of steel,
was it cold, was it warm, against your skin, too soft?
When those men in uniform lifted you out
was the blue eye of the sky gentle to you?

Inside the coinlocker
around the coinlocker
our darkness only deepens.
Inside the coinlocker
around the coinlocker
our ruin only deepens.
That's why there was no one to save you —
traded for a hundred yen coin, your life will never return.

That's why you don't have to forgive us,
why you don't have to forgive the woman
who suffered to give you birth,
why you don't have to forgive the man
who amounted to no more than a single sperm.
You don't have to forgive each and every one of us.
In the name of all the gentleness denied you,
in the name of all the joy you never knew,
you should denounce us again and again.

Until our darkness has reached its depths
you should stay there in the coinlocker.
Until our ruin has reached its depths
you should stay there
inside that steel birth robe
inside your cold grave
where darkness gathers on darkness
becoming a new, unseen nucleus —
until our civilization falls.

Baby, thrown away, locked in a coinlocker
    your birth robes —
your first robe of steel,
was it cold, was it warm, against your skin, too soft?
When those men in uniform lifted you out
was the blue eye of the sky gentle to you?

TREE

Within a tree
another tree that is not yet,
and now the upper branches shift in the wind.

Within the blue sky
another blue sky that is not yet,
and now the horizon is rent by a bird in flight.

Within a body
another body that is not yet,
and now the shrine gathers blood.

Within a road
another road that is not yet,
and now that space is shaken by my destination.

LIKE THE MOTHER IN THE SEA

If only my heart were
vaster
deeper
like the sea,
like the mother in the sea,
then, perhaps, it could carry some part of
the grief of a grieving child.

   The grief of a grieving child
   should not be in this world.
   I want to take that child in my
   arms in a deep embrace.

If only my heart were
richer
softer
like the sea,
like the mother in the sea
then, perhaps, it could melt away the frozen tear streak
of a wounded child.

The frozen tear streak
of a wounded child
should not be in this world.
I want to save that child
and melt away the tears.

If only my heart were
harsher
raging
like the sea
like the mother in the sea
then, perhaps, it could rage together
with the anger of a grieving child.

The cold anger
of a grieving child
should not be in this world.
I want to let it rage
endlessly.

Is there a mother in the sea?
Is there a sea in the mother?
If only my heart were
vaster
deeper.

I CAN'T SAY HELLO TO THAT PERSON

When I meet that person
I can't say hello.
The exhaustion of last night
permeates my body,
I can't say hello.
Though I can smell the sweat that runs down me
I can't say hello.
Though the touch of the breeze burns my forehead
I can't say hello.

I can't say hello to that person
like all the others I meet along the way.

If there's something to be done
we see someone.
If we make an appointment
we meet someone.
If it's convenient for them
we meet someone.
Sometimes we can't meet
but eventually we do.
Except, I have no reason to meet with that person.

There is no business
and there is no favor.
There is no gift
and there is no letter.

There is nothing to be minded
and there is no message
(the message I carry is too heavy to bear).

I can't say hello,
I can't even ask "How are you?"
If I asked there'd be no answer.
Even if I had the need I couldn't meet.
I have no need for that person.

ELEGY TO A POLITICIAN

He stands,
a dim shadow cast across his back
that shadow shrouds our country

His head has two faces,
he has a thousand hands
and ten thousand legs

With some of these hands he binds a friendship,
with his other hands he nurtures the friend's enemy

With some of these hands he supports his colleagues,
with his other hands he pushes them over the edge into Hell

With some of these hands he creates order,
with his other hands he evades the law

He rules from the shadows,
and in those shadows countless people die

The shadows move on with the passage of history,
while he keeps his dirty hands hidden in his pockets

He disappears into the sunset,
and from behind he looks just like all of us.

WHEN THE WAR ENDED

When the war ended
the men came home.
At last, the cry of babies
was heard abundant throughout our cities and villages,
the stream of life of the young children
promised to fill the dreadful void left by the dead.
But in this country there are some women who will never mother
    children,
the women who lost the men they were to marry,
the women who lost the men who were to be their lovers
before they even knew their names.
And in this country there are some men who will never father
    children,
the men whose white bones lie rotting in the South Seas,
the men who lie not beside the warm flesh of their wife
but in the cold earth of a foreign land.
Those who ordered them to die
father children, carry on the bloodline,
surrounded by the warmth of family, they smile.
But the dead look on
in the spaces between the highrises

they reflect on the meaning of their death.
Why did we kill and why did we die?
A wind blows down from the heights of futility
an infinite anger.

WAR DEAD

They say the nation will celebrate the war dead,
they say the nation will pray for the war dead at Yasukuni Shrine.
What would they have us celebrate?
There are no war dead there,
only empty wooden coffins, parched,
cry out,
blown by winter winds.
It is to their birthplace,
the mountain peaks and river banks,
the family hearth, familiar lanes,
street corners, close to those who remember them,
that the war dead return.
This nation supplied no ships or fuel for their return.
This nation abandoned them to the mud and blood
on the far shores of the South Seas.

WORDS AND OBJECTS (EXCERPT)

For a long time I existed outside language. Words were like objects to
me. To enter inside an object, to open it from within, to be spoken by
the object; this was the same process for me as language — to enter
inside language, to open it from within, to be spoken by language.
One could say that I declared my own revolution in the face of language and objects. Words were dead. Objects were dead. My own
death was implicit in language as it was in objects. Yet at the same
time, my future, the possibility of life, lay hidden there. If my life
held any possibilities, they were only to be found in these two. I was
trapped by words and objects. I was seduced by words and objects —

they spoke the unknown, the language of men. I tried to understand. I tried to grasp my death and my life within that language.

I felt I couldn't speak myself in normal language. Perhaps what I was reacting against was the language of the powerful, or the language of intellectuals, language separated from daily life, or perhaps it was the language that pretended to be the everyday language of everybody. I hated language. That is to say, the language of others. The language of men. And aren't the objects also their objects? They merely lend them to me. Those who can put them into motion are others, not me. It is not I who benefit from the depth and richness bound to the spirit of these objects. I cannot use these objects. All I can do is pretend to use them; a solitary and senseless magic act that inscribes them into the proper order.

My life sat there before me like one more object. It was like an unspeakable word. To speak it, I had only the language of others. To speak my life, I chose my words paradoxically. This was an act of treason against their language — the language of men.

Selected Works

POEMS

Basho (Place). Shichōsha, 1962.
Kamen no koe (Voices of a Mask). Doyōbijutsusha, 1987.
Koibito-tachi (Lovers). Yamanashi Shiruku Sentā Shuppan, 1973.
Kōra Rumiko shishū (Collected Poems of Kōra Rumiko). Gendaishi Bunko. Shichōsha, 1971.
Kōra Rumiko shishū (Collected Poems of Kōra Rumiko). Nihon Gendaishi Bunko. Doyōbijutsusha, 1987.
Mienai chijo no ue de (On Invisible Ground). Shichōsha, 1970
Seito to tori (A Student and a Bird). Yuriika, 1958
Shirakashi no mori (Forest of White Oaks). Doyōbijutsusha, 1981.

ESSAYS

Ajia Afurika bungaku nyūmon (Introduction to Asian and African Literature). Orijin Shuppan Sentā, 1983.

Bosei no kaihō (Liberation of Motherhood). Aki Shobō, 1985.
Bungaku to mugen na mono (Literature and Infinity). Chikuma Shobō, 1972.
Kōra Rumiko no shisō no sekai zen shū (Collected Essays of Kōra Rumiko: The World of Kōra Rumiko). 6 Vols. Ochanomizu Shobō, 1992.
Mono to kotoba—shi no kōi to yume (Things and Words—the Dream and Action of Poems). Serika Shobō, 1968.
Onna no sentaku: Umu, sodateru, hataraku (Women's Choice: Birth, Nurturing, Work). Rōdō Kyōiku Sentā, 1984.

NOVELS

Ijime no gin no sekai (Silver World of Torment). Sairyūsha, 1992.
Tatsutoki wa ima (The Time to Leave Is Now). Sairyūsha, 1988.
Tokino meiro. Umi wa toikakeru (The Maze of Time. The Sea Beckons). Orijin Shuppan Sentā, 1988.

MATSUI YAYORI
Senior Staff Editor, Asahi shinbun

» » » » » » » » » » » »

MATSUI IS A SENIOR STAFF WRITER at the major Japanese daily *Asahi shinbun*. As a journalist she has traveled extensively in Asia, focusing particularly on issues related to women and development, the sex trade, grass-roots politics, human rights, and the environment. In 1981–85 she was based in Singapore as Asia correspondent for the *Asahi shinbun*. Matsui is well known for her books and articles, both in English and Japanese, dealing with the politico-economic relationship between Japan and the other nations of the Pacific region. She has undertaken extensive research on the impact of Japanese capital on the lives of women in those nations. A central theme of Matsui's writings and public lectures in recent years has been the traffic in prostitution between Japan and Southeast Asia. She has done a great deal to draw attention to Japan's complicity in the continued growth of the sex industry in the region. She unhesitatingly links the structure of the current sexual politics of Japanese marriage and the family with both the continued increase in illegal Southeast Asian women workers seeking jobs in Japan's sex industry and the flow of Japanese men on organized sex tours to the brothels of Thailand and the Philippines. Matsui has also done much to publicly expose the practice of importing Filipino brides for marriage into Japanese rural households.

Matsui's concern with recognizing the responsibility of Japanese women for the impact of Japan's economic growth and regional investment on the lives of Southeast Asian women has significantly influenced the agenda for feminist research in this area. In 1977 she, in conjunction with friends, founded the Asian Women's Association, and she has remained an active participant in the organization's activities to the present. The focus of the AWA's specific campaigns has shifted over the past two decades, but its primary concern has remained the creation of stronger links between Japanese women and the women of the rest of Asia. Japan's relationship to the countries and peoples of Asia remains highly contentious. A not-so-distant history of Japanese military expansionism and a continuing history of official Japanese attitudes that reflect, at best, indifference and, at worst, prejudice and aggression, combine to cast a shadow over Japan's contemporary relations with the countries and peoples of Asia. Matsui and the AWA have done much to refocus the attention of Japanese feminism on Asia. In addition to opposing Japanese sex tours to the countries of Southeast Asia, the AWA has actively supported Asian immigrant workers in Japan. The Drop-in Center for Filipinas and the Thai Women's Support Fund, both established under the umbrella of the AWA, provide essential support services to illegal women immigrants working in the sex industry in Japan. Filipino brides "imported" into Japanese rural villages also frequently seek some form of community or support network through the AWA and its affiliated groups. While the AWA has on occasion been criticized for its fairly conservative antiprostitution platform, in recent years a desire to protect the rights and welfare of illegal women working in the prostitution industry has overshadowed the organization's history of moral opposition to prostitution. While the AWA remains committed to dismantling the sex industry, it clearly identifies the protection of the women within the industry as a key dimension of its role.

As one of a very small number of senior women in the media, Matsui is aware of her importance as a potential mentor for other women. She has openly criticized the token gestures that television, radio, and the print media have made to mainstreaming women. Recent increases in the number of women in visible or key positions in the media (anchor women, interviewers, international correspondents, etc.) have received much publicity. But Matsui wonders whether these women will still be employed ten years from now, and if so, how far they will have progressed through the organization in comparison with their male cohort. Matsui is uniquely placed to develop an insider analysis of the predominantly male media industry.

Matsui's criticisms of the representation of women in the media and the processes of selection and exclusion which continue to marginalize women and certain issues such as the environment and human rights extend beyond Japan. Her analysis extends to the interactive levels of racism and economic exploitation that she considers characteristic of Japan's relations with the third world. This capacity to identify the continuities between the local and the global is characteristic of all of Matsui's work. She breaks through the smooth surfaces of media representations to expose the complex relations of dependency and responsibility that underpin the prosperity of contemporary Japan.

Interview

SB: When I was speaking with Saitō Chiyo of Agora, she mentioned that 99 percent of the employees in the mass media are male. That makes you something of a rarity.

MY: Just look around you in this office. There are several hundred people working on this editorial level but not another woman in sight.

SB: Why did you choose journalism for a career?

MY: It was really a question of options, or the lack thereof, at the time I was looking for work. Very few companies gave equal access to female and male applicants, but the Asahi's employment tests were open to both sexes. I took the tests and passed.

SB: Has the number of women in the media been increasing?

MY: Yes, there are more women in the media these days, but the total number is still very small. One of the biggest problems with working my way up through the machinery has been a kind of professional "loneliness." This is not only a question of gender but also my personal preference: I might be described as people-oriented, and so I missed the opportunity for more contact. Gender is never such an issue when I'm on assignment out of Japan and moving in the international press environment, but here in Japan the media, especially newspaper journalism, is a man's world. You can't network alone! All too often as I was coming up through the ranks, there was no one there when I needed support.

There are definitely more women coming into the media. This is partly a result of the impact of the United Nations Decade of the Woman. Only time will tell, however, what effect these younger women will have. *Asahi* has a policy of hiring women in each incoming group these days. It's my feeling that if they perform well, they will have more equal access to promotion, but there are still so many other prejudices operating outside the work environment that can act to disrupt a Japanese woman's career.

SB: In North America I believe the first wave of women entering the media were frustrated by the limited access they had to promotion and jobs that were considered "serious." For example, a woman could be weather girl but not news anchor.

MY: There has been something of the same problem here, I think. Women have tended to be placed within a predictable range of jobs—for example, the "women's page" of the newspaper. It's only recently that women reporters have been accepted in other fields, such as political or economic reporting or even the editorial section. I see more women on television at prime news time these days, but usually they just smile and nod at the male newscaster. I wonder whether women have an impact on the definition of what constitutes "news." Are the women entering the media allowing themselves to be subsumed into the existing order of things as a way of being accepted into the male-dominated world, or are they actively working to change that order?

It has been a constant struggle to get the news printed as I report it. The "news" as I write it reflects the world seen from a feminist point of view, and that often doesn't fit what the editorial board wants. I've found, though, that with persistence and accurate reporting I have somehow managed to gain the print space I want. When I was assigned the post of Asia correspondent in Singapore, the stories I sent back were not about the international politics of the region or the economic policies of governments. I tried to send reports on the grass-roots issues affecting the lives of ordinary people. I was particularly concerned with Asian women, for they are the ones who suffer the most from the poverty and exploitation created by Japanese economic expansion. I visited eighteen countries in Asia and everywhere I went I saw sex tours of Japanese men and the appalling working conditions of women employed by Japanese multi-national companies. Many of my articles dealt with environmental destruction and human rights issues. I was eager to describe the struggles of the people who were victimized.

News is created by the media through the choices it makes about what is and isn't newsworthy. The media constructs the external reality of the Japanese through the stories and images it selects for its audience. The picture has been too coherent, too clean, too homogeneous. We need a more diverse range of information, which will better reflect the complexity of the "real world" and Japan's relationship to that world.

SB: *In both your books and your journalism, you emphasize Japan's relationship to the rest of Asia and, in particular, the position Japanese women occupy in relation to other Asian women.*

MY: I think an awareness of these issues is essential to Japanese feminism. Feminism goes beyond national issues. It may take different forms and grow out of different circumstances in each country, but any movement that focuses only on internal, national issues is not what I consider feminism. It is crucial for feminism to recognize and trace the complexity of the multiple contexts that generate gender politics. It is true that Japanese women are oppressed within their own society; it is also true that some Japanese women occupy positions of relative power, from which they oppress, or are implicated in the oppression of, other Japanese women. But this is not enough. We need to go one step further and look at the relationship of Japanese women to the women of countries that are economically dominated by Japan. What price do other Asian women pay for the prosperity and daily comfort of so many Japanese women? How do we as Japanese women stand in relation to the thousands of Filipino hostesses working in Japanese bars? Then there is the whole question of the Filipino, Korean, and Sri Lankan brides who are imported to Japan to overcome the shortage of women.

SB: Immigrant labor has become a "hot" topic in the press lately.

MY: With the number of immigrant workers increasing as it has, it was inevitable that the question of their legal status would eventually arise. If you look at who is doing the dirty work, the underpaid and undesirable jobs, you find Filipinos, Thais, Bangladeshis, Pakistanis, Chinese, and Koreans. Most of these people are working illegally, and many are in the country without visas. Legally, they are very vulnerable. But it would not be easy for the government to round up and deport all the illegal immigrants. They are performing the tasks that Japanese workers are no longer prepared to undertake, but the government is not willing to grant any legal status to them.

SB: You don't think that the sheer numbers involved will eventually force the government's hand?

MY: The difficulty for the government lies with the female illegal workers. So many of these women come to Japan to work in the sex industry, centered around the bars, clubs, and restaurants. Most of these women are forced into prostitution. Half of the 150,000 immigrant workers are women. To legalize unskilled, immigrant labor would, in the eyes of the government, amount to publicly condoning the current "market" for overseas prostitutes. Of course, this is hypocritical, for by taking no legal action to prevent the traffic in young Filipinas, they are condoning the practice. Given that it is not possible to legalize the status of male, unskilled, immigrant labor without extending the same privilege to females, I don't see how this situation is to be resolved. I expect it will get a lot worse before anything concrete is done to protect these workers.

SB: When I arrived at Narita this summer there was a line of about thirty Filipino girls standing at immigration. They were traveling with an older Japanese woman. It seemed clear that she was a mama-san *escorting a group of recruits to work in Japanese bars.*

MY: Many of the Filipino girls who come into Japan in this way have been working in bars or brothels in the Philippines. They come here on a contract basis, but some try to stay beyond the period of their sponsored visa and end up working illegally. The reason they come to Japan is simple. If you ask, they'll explain that they can support an entire extended family on what they send back home from Japan. Many of them hold down daytime jobs as well and economize by living in groups in small apartments. In addition, the working conditions here are better than in the Philippines.

SB: At least two other feminists I've spoken to since coming to Japan this time have commented that they disagree with your opinion that Japanese women have a responsibility toward these Filipinas. One of them suggested that your approach denied the self-determination or autonomy of these women.

MY: They just don't know how the Filipinas are abused and exploited. These women don't come to Japan of their own free will or at their own expense. They are recruited and sold into the Japanese sex industry. In other words, they are victims of international trafficking in women.

I don't think I am guilty of denying the self-determination of these women. I do, however, insist that Japanese women recognize their own complicity in the economic and political structures that create the poverty underlying the limited range of options available to these women. When you stop to ask how Japan maintains its present level of prosperity, you are confronted with the reality of the lives of the peoples of the Asian region. The economic hardships faced by Filipino women are intimately linked with the profits Japanese corporations send back to their head offices from their overseas operations. Japanese women both support and benefit from this economic system.

Japanese women are themselves captive within late-capitalist, consumer society. But any liberation movement that is concerned only with the lives of Japanese women is doomed to failure. What is needed is a liberation movement that includes the position of unskilled Filipino women workers in Japan and in the Philippines. These kinds of links are essential. Such a movement is only possible if Japanese women are prepared to recognize the extent to which they are implicated in the current economic and political structures and actively work to dismantle those unjust structures.

One Japanese feminist commented on this position of mine in a recent article. She argued that it was not realistic for me to expect Japanese women to deal with the liberation of the women of Asia when so many of us still don't have even the most basic understanding of our own status and rights. This is the old "help those in your own backyard first" approach, and I cannot accept it. The problem arises from a willingness to separate the lack of politicization and self-awareness among Japanese women and Japan's role in the Asian region. The existing patriarchal structures have colonized women's bodies, Japanese and Filipino alike, just as they have colonized this entire geographic region.

SB: In my interview with her, Aoki Yayoi was critical of such actions as the Blankets for Africa campaign. She felt that this approach avoided the issue of responsibility.

MY: I agree with her. While it shows some sign of concern or a level of awareness of the conditions in which others live, it is a Band-Aid approach. It doesn't come close to analyzing the direct role Japanese women have in creating and sustaining these conditions. This is not the level at which action is required. Look at the two of us sitting here, sipping our coffee during this interview. The hypocrisy is constantly with us. We grumble about the price of a cup of coffee, but we don't think of the horrifying working and living conditions of coffee plantation workers in the countries where it is grown. We must be able to at least begin to make connections between our daily lives and the lives of other women. There has been a noticeable and worrying trend among Japanese feminists lately toward focusing on the issues that are immediate to our own lives. The growing concern with what it means to be a Japanese woman denies the complexity of the international political and economic reality.

SB: Let's come back to the question of prostitution. Would you see the legalization of prostitution as an option given the size of the industry (and it is an industry in Japan)?

MY: I don't know if I can comment either way yet on that question. It's a very complicated issue. It would certainly clarify the status of the women themselves. There are countries in the north now where the prostitutes have organized themselves into unions, I believe. It might also reduce the stigma attached to an industry that has been a source of employment for poor women. I think it's unlikely, though, that we'll see a move in this direction. The whole process would be formidable given the numbers involved, and many women in the industry would not be willing to participate in, or support, legalization because of the stigma attached to prostitution. For many women it is the current anonymity of the work that makes it a viable source of income, and they would resist any attempt to document their form of employment.

Prostitution may be illegal in Japan today, but I don't know any other country where the prostitution industry has flourished as it has in Japan. There have been attempts at licensing procedures at different times, but, legal or not, the government has actively colluded with the prostitution industry. Look at the Edo Period. It was very convenient for the government that the prostitution district thrived the way that it did — it kept a lot of people out of political mischief and a lot of money in circulation. With modernization and expansion came increased contact with the rest of Asia. The *karayuki-san* were young girls, often from poor rural families, who were sold into prostitution by their parents for an advance payment. From the late nineteenth century on, these girls were sent out to work in brothels across Southeast Asia and as far afield as Siberia and Africa. Their arrival was usually one stage in the development of a trade link. The brothel owners followed the trade ships, and the government turned a blind eye. In the twentieth century, when Japan sent its soldiers out to prove how modern and powerful it had become, it also sent prostitutes to "service" the troops. It's ironic that Japan is now importing women from the same region it once exported its own women to. Japan has been called a prostitution culture, and I think that is a very accurate description. Prostitution is a central characteristic not only of Japanese society but also of Japan's relations with other countries.

SB: Why is prostitution the major industry that it is today in Japan?

MY: I'd be interested in hearing your own answer to that as a foreign woman in Japan.

SB: I think there are many contributing factors, but if I had to choose just one it would be the denial of the sexual identity of married women in this culture. When you look at recent survey results, it's clear that there has been little change in the attitude that marriage is primarily an economic and social unit of reproduction. The wife is not treated as a sexually active person with her own desires and pleasures. The man is free to pursue his sexual desire outside the family, either in his work environment or within the water-trade [mizu-shōbai]. In North America and Europe since the early nineteenth century, sexual activity has been primarily focused on the marital relationship — that is, in the private or domestic sphere — with the degree of denial of the wife's sexuality varying considerably across time and also, significantly, across class. In the Japanese case the sexuality of the married female (where sexuality is distinct from her reproductive role) is denied, and the male articulates his sexuality in the semi-

public domain of the sex industry. The result is the virtual institu-
tionalization of both motherhood and prostitution.

MY: Before I go on, let me say that I prefer not to use the term *mizu-
shōbai*; I prefer a noneuphemistic term such as "sex industry" or "sex
trade." I think this is an important point, and you are right to say
there has been little change. In this sense, the fundamental problems
in the traditional husband-wife relationship — for that matter, the
very nature of the Japanese family — contribute directly to the existence and vastness of the sex industry. It is not possible to discuss the
status of Filipino prostitutes in Japan or the nature of the sex industry without looking at questions of sexuality and gender in the Japanese family.

*SB: I've seen various feminist articles in Japan recently that have em-
phasized the need to feminize the Japanese male. It is suggested that
it is not enough for women to strive for the right to equal employment access; men should also be liberated from their role of bread-
winner. This approach argues that the status of Japanese women
cannot be addressed without equal attention to the status of Japanese
men. It comes down to the the right of any man to play an equal role
in the domestic, nurturing role.*

MY: Do you think they're serious or just having us on?

SB: I think they're serious.

MY: It would be lovely if every Japanese man and woman was free to
choose how much of their life they would spend in the workplace
and how much in the home, but really, what kind of feminist utopia
is this? Where is the reality of class difference? How many Japanese
women actually do not work? We know that close to 40 percent of
the workforce is female, but more and more women are employed
part-time. This growing category of workers is both invisible and un-
protected. Part-time work is unstable and disadvantageous. How
many households could afford to have the father at home sharing the
nurturing role? We know that women don't have access to the same

jobs or the same wages, so how is this supposed to work financially? What Japanese men and women are we talking about? It sounds like an incredibly naïve or elitist theory to me. It must have come from an academic! No offense meant to you, I could tell from the way you asked the question that you were just too polite to say the obvious yourself, so now I've said it for both of us.

SB: The rhetoric appears radical, but then recently I was reading the LDP's agenda for "strengthening the family base" and it is eerily similar. I think that any time feminists find themselves in agreement with the strategies of the far right, it's time to regroup. Elements of the antipornography movement in the United States have shown signs of converging with the Moral Majority in a similar fashion.

MY: This kind of theory is one more example of a feminism that is focused on individual experience. I would never dispute that the personal is also political, but it shouldn't blind us to the experience of other women, the majority of women. I'm not arguing that there is some universal experience of womanhood. Actually, I'm arguing just the opposite: that we have to recognize the diversity and complexity of female experience and not fall into the trap of universalizing individual experience into the experience of some mythical, holistic category of Woman. Too many Japanese feminists are more comfortable writing of a fantasy domestic world that fits their own theoretical utopia than facing the political and economic reality of sexual exploitation and the lives of the women in it. As you said, this is a huge industry in Japan that exploits millions of women, Japanese and non-Japanese. The feminist silence is particularly ironic when you consider how many Japanese marriages remain stable only because of the husband's relationships with women working in the sex industry. Some things are just too personal. It is a cop-out to argue that we feminists shouldn't take a critical stand on the sex industry because we would somehow be denying the autonomy of the women workers in the industry. We have to start making connections at the most fundamental level. Any move toward a change in the status of Japanese women has to take into account how the question of sexuality in the family is linked to that line of Filipino bargirls in Narita airport.

Asian Migrant Women in Japan

I am here to make heard the painful cries of victimized Asian women.

I come from Japan, the country that grew rapidly into an economic giant only four decades after the devastation of World War II. On the surface, such rapid economic growth really does look like a miracle. It is little known, however, that this "miracle" was achieved at the expense of countless women both inside and outside Japan. One of Japan's most serious social problems is an expanding sex industry — this is the other, less publicized side of economic prosperity.

In the 1970s, Japan was known as the country that sent men on sex tours to neighboring Asian countries; today it has become the country that receives the largest number of Asian migrant women working as entertainers in the booming sex industry. Some estimate that nearly 100,000 such women come to Japan every year, including both legal female workers with entertainer visas and those who work illegally on tourist visas.

More than 90 percent of these female migrant workers come from only three countries: the Philippines, Thailand, and Taiwan. The number of Filipinas now accounts for 80 percent of that total, although the number of Thai women coming to Japan is also increasing at an alarming rate. Their jobs are concentrated in the sex industry, with most of them working as prostitutes, hostesses, striptease dancers and other sex-service–related entertainers.

Almost without exception these Asian women are the victims of exploitation. First of all, they are brought into Japan as objects of the international traffic in women, and then, more often than not, they

Opening address given at the Conference on International Trafficking in Women held in New York, October 22–23, 1988. Translated with the permission of the author by Sandra Buckley.

are forced into prostitution. Most of these women neither raise their own travel expenses to Japan, nor do they find jobs in Japan by themselves. Usually they are picked up by recruiters in their own countries and sent to Japan with the promise that they will work as waitresses, models, or ordinary hostesses (not engaging in prostitution). However, in reality, they are sold by the recruiters to promoters in Japan, many of whom are related to organized crime gangs, better known as *yakuza*. For each woman, the recruiter receives between $2,400 and $8,000. The women are then sold again, by the Japanese promoters, to clubs or other sex business owners, at double the price. Sometimes they are simply rented at a monthly charge of $1,600 to $6,400. In order to cover such expenses, the owners force the women into prostitution, taking advantage of their vulnerability, the prime cause of which is their illegal visa status. Without the protection of a visa, there is no limit to the abuse and exploitation that these women may have to face. Besides, they are usually young—under thirty, with many in their late teens or early twenties. Not surprisingly, they cannot speak Japanese, and in the case of Thai women, they often cannot speak English either. Furthermore, they have little idea of how to cope with life in a foreign country with a completely different culture and climate. On top of all that, they carry with them a sense of obligation to earn and send money to their poor families back home. Obviously, they are in no position whatsoever to resist their employers or fight for their rights.

Usually they are deliberately kept ignorant of the names of their employers or the owners of their workplace. Moreover, they are forced to live under the close supervision of these anonymous "masters," often in shabby, cramped houses. The women are virtually kept prisoners, locked systematically in "cells." In addition to all this, their passports and air tickets are confiscated, and they are not paid the wage fixed by the contract (which they probably cannot read anyway). Nor are they given holidays. Prostitution is clearly a most effective means of exploiting these Asian victims of the international flesh-trade.

A number of tragic cases of victimized migrant women have been reported over the last few years. Here is a sample:

— A Filipino hostess was beaten by her employer because she refused to sleep with customers; she subsequently died of brain damage.

— A Filipina was abandoned, nearly unconscious, near the gate of the Philippine Embassy in Tokyo; she died of tuberculosis in the hospital five days later.

— A Filipino snack bar waitress was found dead in her apartment in Shizuoka City, more than ten days after she died; the cause of death — malnutrition.

— When a fire broke out in a club in Okinawa, two Filipino dancers burned to death after being confined to their room on the second floor.

— A Filipino stripper in Nagoya tried to commit suicide after one of her customers forced her to perform a sadistic sexual act.

— A young hostess was forced to go out with an extremely drunk customer; her face was severely injured during an accident in his car.

— A Filipino hostess refused to sleep with a customer and jumped from the second floor of a club in Awajishima; with both legs broken, she was sent back to Manila in a wheelchair.

— A Filipino woman had her face badly slashed by her pimp; with bleeding cuts all over her head, she ran into a shelter.

The growing number of migrant women who find their way to shelters all over the country also indicates the scope of human rights violations, inhuman humiliating treatment, and sexual abuse. Over the last three years, 1,200 women have sought refuge and assistance after being subjected to physical violence, psychological threats, non-payment of wages, or forced prostitution. While migrant women suffer from this gross exploitation, traders — including recruiters, promoters, club owners, and pimps — make enormous profits at their expense; the returns from forced prostitution are particularly high.

Exactly why is it, then, that such huge numbers of Asian women are flooding into Japan? Essentially, this phenomenon results from the unjust economic imbalance between the north and the south. In other words, it is a symptom of deep-rooted economic problems on a global scale.

The countries that send out these women are all facing deteriorating economic conditions. In the the Philippines, even after Marcos's dictatorial regime was overthrown by a movement of people's power and Cory Aquino became president, the economy did not improve; on the contrary, it actually worsened. The burden of the country's huge foreign debt, the failure of land reform, continued corruption, intensified militarization, and other problems make people's lives even harder than before. Unemployment and unlivable wages force both men and women to emigrate to survive and support their families. The Aquino government could not give up Marcos's policy of exporting workers for the purpose of providing employment and earning foreign currency.

In the country that receives these women, Japan, the shortage of young workers in the sex industry is filled by imported foreign labor. Usually, young Japanese women high school graduates get jobs in offices, factories, or stores. The women who work in the so-called night industry — bars, nightclubs and snack bars that cater to men — are mostly middle-aged. Some are even over fifty, and many are married with children. They mask their age by wearing heavy makeup. This situation reflects the low status of women in Japan. It is difficult for women to get ordinary jobs with an adequate salary to support their families. If something happens to their husbands — sickness, death, or an accident — wives are forced to work in the night industry to earn money. The gap in the average income of men and women is larger than in any other industrialized country, with women earning only half as much as men.

But why does the sex industry flourish in Japan, creating such a high demand for female workers? The answer to this question is an inseparable part of Japan's economic system and reflects the situation of women and men in Japan. Japanese men are forced to work very hard and are virtually enslaved by the companies that employ them. Under the "Japanese-style management system," which is supported by the three pillars of life-long employment, seniority, and cooperative management-labor relations, employees are treated as members of the company family. In return, they are expected to be loyal and to devote their life to the company.

Employees average more than 2,000 working hours per year, compared to 1,600–1,700 hours in Western European countries; they take only nine days of paid holidays. They will even work on Sundays. Seeking relief from these extremely tense work patterns, Japanese business "warriors" frequent entertainment facilities with their colleagues or business customers. The companies themselves often provide their employees and customers opportunities to drink and enjoy entertainment with women. Sometimes the companies organize sex tours abroad for their employees as a reward for hard work or successful business deals.

In the context of such business practices, the role of Japanese women is either, as hostesses, to extend sexual services to men or, as wives and mothers, to take care of husbands and teach children to be future business warriors. Temporary work is another option, yet this is low-paid and unstable.

It cannot be overemphasized that the sharp increase in Asian female migrant workers coming to Japan is fundamentally linked to the very economic system that has brought about Japan's unprecedented rapid economic development. Based on the dehumanization of both Japanese men and women and on imported cheap labor, that development supports a growing sex industry in Japan, estimated at ¥10 trillion.

In addition, there are historically formed cultural and ideological factors that are vitally important in exposing the origins of the incomparable prosperity of Japan's sex industry. Japan has a long history of prostitution culture, based on deeply rooted sexist and patriarchal attitudes that show the influence of Confucian ideology. Within Japanese traditional values, prostitution has long been socially accepted. After Japan's feudal rulers established the public prostitution system in 1528, the *kuruwa*, or officially authorized prostitution areas, increased. There were twenty-five such areas throughout Japan in 1720.

During the feudal period, Japan was ruled by the warrior [*samurai*] class, which followed a strict Confucian ethic. It was considered unethical for a married couple to enjoy sexual pleasure. Women were supposed to follow the Confucian rule of the three obediences: as a daughter, obey the father; as a wife, the husband; and as a mother, the son. The essential role of women was to give birth to a son, a successor to the head of the feudal family [*ie*]. In other words, they were expected only to be breeding machines.

However, there was another type of woman as well. Men were provided with facilities, the *kuruwa*, where they could enjoy sexual pleasure outside the home. In these areas, prostitutes called *yūjo* (later, *geisha*) were indentured from poor families to serve men sexually. They were used as tools of pleasure for men. We can say that women were divided into those with wombs and those with sexual organs. Both types of women were treated as mere objects, not as human beings or persons with human dignity.

This dichotomy has been carried over into the present day. Women are divided into "good women," or housewives, and "bad women," or prostitutes. It is common thinking in this society that "bad women" are necessary in order to protect the "good women." Men buying prostitutes are never socially condemned, nor is women's acceptance of this behavior condemned. Women often say: "If my husband goes to a 'professional' woman, it's not a problem, but if he is attracted to an ordinary woman, I get hurt and jealous." Such a double standard is still deep-rooted; the Japanese consider prostitutes as a special category of woman and fail to treat them as human beings or to accord them their human rights.

This dichotomy is also applied to Asian migrant women. In addition to the increasing importation of entertainers, brides have also been imported systematically from Asian countries for the last two or three years. This is arranged by marriage agents or even by local authorities. Only women who have never been to Japan and who cannot speak Japanese are qualified to be candidates for these arranged international marriages. This is because brides should be "good women" and different from entertainers — the "bad women." In brief, the background explanation of the increasing numbers of Asian female migrants is both economic and cultural.

Trafficking in women for prostitution is a common social issue that is becoming more conspicuous in most Asian countries. The recent expansion of international tourism is the primary contributing factor toward the flourishing sex industries that exist in many countries. At present, Manila, Bangkok, and other Asian capitals are known as international sex cities with a vast number of entertainment facilities for tourists. In addition to these, a number of tourist resorts have been newly developed in third world countries to sell the three Ss — sun, sea, and sex — to male tourists from affluent countries.

One of those resorts, Phuket Island in southern Thailand, which was advertised as "Paradise," turned into Hell in late January 1984, when a fire destroyed a brothel there and five girls perished in the flames. They were young prostitutes, aged nine to twelve, who had been locked in the basement and were unable to escape. They had been sold to the brothel by poor peasants from depressed rural villages in northern Thailand.

Yawarat, in Bangkok's Chinatown, is also known for child prostitution. In the brothel called "Teahouse," I saw girls in their early teens waiting for both local and foreign customers. They had to offer sexual services to several men every day.

In Taiwan young aboriginal girls from mountain villages are sold out to red-light districts in Taipei. The number of aboriginal people is less than 2 percent of the entire population, but 40 percent of the prostitutes in Taipei are tribal mountain girls, according to a survey done by Rainbow Project, an organization which aids these girls. Uhlai is an aboriginal village not far from Taipei and a famous tourist spot. Many women in this village work as prostitutes for the tourists.

Most third world countries suffer from heavy foreign debts, and their governments, which promote tourism to attract foreign currency, perceive a need for fresh young girls to attract tourists. That is why prostitution tourism continues to expand and the traffic in women is growing. But before prostitution tourism, military base prostitution flourished in the form of the R and R industry (rest and recreation for U.S. servicemen) in Thailand and Taiwan until the end of the Vietnam War. Even today this kind of prostitution is a serious problem in several locations in Asia—for example, in Okinawa, Japan; Osan, South Korea; and most notably in Olongapo and Angeles in the Philippines.

Olongapo used to be a quiet fishing village and is now a city of 200,000 people, who depend on the sex industry and base employment for their livelihood. There are more than three hundred R and R establishments where nearly twenty thousand women work. In the summer of 1982, twelve girls between the ages of nine and fourteen were hospitalized with severe venereal diseases. According to an Irish Catholic priest, these young victims were forced into prostitution by a criminal syndicate and contracted VD from U.S. military men in the base.

Filipino girls are imported into Okinawa to extend sexual services to U.S. soldiers. Until the 1970s the bars and clubs in Okinawa employed primarily Japanese girls, but the changes in the economic situation of the two countries—particularly the rise in the value of the yen—meant that GIs could not afford Japanese girls and therefore cheaper Filipinas were in demand.

Another type of prostitution that deserves attention exists primarily in South Asian countries and takes a more traditional form. Narayanganj, about 20 kilometers from Dacca, the capital of Bangladesh, has one of the oldest brothel areas in the Indian subcontinent. There, about half of the 3,000 working prostitutes are under the age of sixteen.

Bombay has one of the biggest red-light districts in the world. It is said that 100,000–300,000 prostitutes work there. Called "cage girls," they are literally slaves, without freedom of movement. It is estimated that about half of them are Nepalese girls. According to a woman journalist working for the abused women in this area, there have periodically been cases of women who were beaten to death by the madam for refusing to take customers. A VD doctor in the area told me, "Two or three days ago a thirteen-year-old Nepalese girl was brought to my clinic. She had served 2,000 customers last year. About 80 percent of the women here suffer from VD, and 10 percent from tuberculosis."

Agents brought these women from mountain villages in Nepal all the way to Bombay; they made no payments to the parents, but simply deceived them with false promises of good marriages or jobs in India. In Thailand poor peasant parents do receive some money, 5,000–10,000 baht for the sale of their daughters, but in Nepal parents aren't even paid. In other words, the girls are kidnapped.

I heard that in Kathmandu, the capital of Nepal, trafficking in women had become such an important social issue that the Nepalese government had to intervene. According to the Nepalese Ministry of Welfare, about 3,000 women were sent to India in 1975, but the number has increased every year. The estimate may now be as high as 50,000. Girls are easily taken out of Nepal, because life in the villages is so poor and oppressive. It is natural that they dream of escaping from despair and hardship. In Nepal the average lifespan of women is only just over forty — shorter than men's — and 90 percent of the women are illiterate. Lucky girls who could escape the hell of Bombay were accommodated in a newly established women's welfare home in the suburbs of Kathmandu.

After visiting most of the red-light districts in Asia and talking with prostitutes, I can sum up several characteristics of the traffic in women in our times. First, women involved in prostitution are getting younger and younger in most countries. In some places, virgin girls who have not yet menstruated are traded. Because trafficking in women is such a profitable business, many want to engage in it. As a result, competition is becoming fiercer among traders, who want to have fresh, easy-to-control girls in their early teens. In other words, they seek attractive commodities. AIDS is another factor in the demand for virgin girls. Child prostitution in third world countries, which is linked with tourism, is considered the most urgent issue to be tackled.

Second, it is an entirely new phenomenon since the 1970s that trafficking in women has become a multi-national business on a global scale. Thai women are sent to Western Europe, Japan, and many other countries. For example, in Singapore, there used to be hundreds of Thai prostitutes near the Clifford Pier. But Prime Minister Lee Kuan Yew decided to clean up the area in order to present the image of a "clean, green garden city." At the end of 1983 as many as three thousand prostitutes were deported back to Thailand within a mere six months. Most of them were young girls brought into Singapore along the western coast of the Malay Peninsula by a Thai "vice operator." At Johor Baharu they were handed over to a Singapore operator, who said to me: "I buy about twenty girls at a time for a few hundred dollars and let them do business." He repeatedly used the words "buy" and "sell." To him these girls were nothing but commodities.

Filipino women also migrate as entertainers to countries on all continents, and, as I mentioned earlier, Japan is the largest receiving country of Filipinas. In any situation involving the traffic of women, there are close links between the underground crime syndicates of the sending and the receiving country.

Third, trafficking in women is part of a consumer culture created by transnational corporations, which strongly influences third world countries. Everything is utilized as a commodity to be sold. Even women are commodified and traded to satisfy men's desires, which are stimulated by all forms of mass media. In this context, Asian women are favorite goods because of the "Oriental charm" and exoticism that Western and Japanese men see in them. Thus, countless women in the third world are victimized by racism, colonialism, commercialism, and sexism.

The tidal wave of such sexual exploitation should be stemmed by all available means. What kind of actions should we take? Here I would like to present a brief history of our campaign against sex tours since the mid-1970s. Japanese women were shocked when Korean women protested against Japanese male sex tours in 1973. First, Korean Christian women's groups published a very strong statement condemning the wealthy Japanese men who were dehumanizing their country's women. Then a handful of Korean women students went to Kimpo airport carrying placards stating: "We are against prostitution tourism!" "Don't make our motherland a brothel for Japanese men!" Some of these women were arrested because the dictatorship didn't like such protests.

Responding to the courageous action of these Korean women, we Japanese feminists organized demonstrations at Haneda Airport, distributing leaflets to tourists bound for Seoul. We used strong language, such as "Shame on you!" "Stop your shameful behavior!" and "We will never allow you to repeat your sexual aggression!" During the war, the Japanese Imperial Army forced young Korean women to serve as prostitutes. Hundreds of thousands of them were sent to the battlefields of China and Southeast Asia, and they were abandoned in the jungle when Japanese troops had to withdraw in defeat.

It was during this demonstration against "*Kisaeng* tourism" that I coined a new word for prostitution. In Japanese, prostitution is called *baishun*, written with two Chinese characters meaning "sell spring." I changed the characters so that it meant "buy spring." I wanted to change attitudes toward and concepts of prostitution. Traditionally, women who sold their bodies were blamed, while men who bought their sex were not condemned. Therefore, the word had to be changed. It may seem a rather small thing, but it is revolutionary to shift the responsibility from women to men. Those who buy sex are to be condemned more than those who sell.

We should not look at prostitution from a perspective of moral judgment but rather analyze the problem within the context of the global economic structure.

Another example of our efforts against sex tours was a united action by Filipino and Japanese women in 1981. A large protest rally was held in the heart of the tourist area in Manila on the occasion of the visit of former prime minister Suzuki Zenkō. About one thousand participants adopted a resolution condemning sex tours as a form of economic exploitation of women in poor countries by men of rich countries and also as a form of sexual exploitation.

It was the first mass protest action jointly organized by Filipino and Japanese women. It drew much attention from the media in the Philippines and discredited the image of Japanese men. As a result, Japanese travel agents refrained from sending tourists to Manila, and the number of Japanese visitors decreased 25 percent after the spring of 1981.

An anti–sex-tour campaign was also launched in Bangkok when Mr. Suzuki visited there following his Manila trip. Thai women and students presented a protest letter to the Japanese embassy, performed street dramas, and held placards reading "No More Sex Tours!"

Even though our campaign achieved some results, the root causes — poverty and sexism — were left unchanged, and Filipino women began to come to work in Japan as entertainers. The rapid and ongoing growth of trafficking in women is a worldwide phenomenon. Therefore, concerned women urgently need to create linkages and global solidarity.

Let's make this conference the arena in which to work out a strategy and a plan of action to stop the sexual exploitation of women of any country. We need both a long-term strategy and short-term plans of action. We must form a strategy that will attack the root causes. We must change the unjust international and national economic systems that impose poverty and misery on millions of women. It is our task to check transnational corporations of the first world and monitor official development aid. We need to work out development alternatives that terminate trafficking in women for sexual exploitation and abuse. As a beginning, we need to reconsider our own lifestyles. We also need to change the sexist culture that commodifies and dehumanizes women as sex objects. We have to change our consciousness and create a new feminist culture based on independent human relationships between women and men.

However, we cannot just sit and wait for the structural change — it will take a long time. Consequently, we should start by taking action now to protect the human rights of victimized women. We need shelters, drop-in centers, telephone counseling, legal aid, medical care, information for women before they leave their own countries, and many other support activities in both the receiving and sending countries. Detailed proposals and suggestions will be discussed at the conference.

In order to respond to the frightening realities of international trafficking in women, it is vitally important to create networks of concerned women, especially between the receiving and sending countries. How to establish such a network is also a subject to be discussed here.

Finally, I would like to appeal to you to listen to the cry of victimized women and share their pain and agony. Only then will you be driven to take action, in one form or another, to humanize yourselves and your society.

Selected Works

Ajia onna minshū (Asia, Women, and the People). Shinkansha, 1987.
Asian Children for Survival. N.p., 1991. *Ajia kara kita dekasegi rōdōsha-tachi* (Asian Migrant Women in Japan). Co-edited. Akashi Shoten, 1987.
Gendai o toinaosu tabi: Kaigai no shimin undō (My Journey to Question Our Time: Reports on Environmental Movements in the World). Asahi Shinbunsha, 1973.
Jinmen no chinmoku: Watashi no Chūgokuki (Silence of the People: My Days in China). Suzusawa Shoten, 1980.
Josei kaihō to wa nani ka: Onna-tachi no danketsu wa tsuyoku kokkyō o koeru (What is Women's Liberation: Sisterhood is Powerful and Global). Miraisha, 1975. Korean ed., 1981.
Onna-tachi no ajia (Women's Asia). Iwanami Shoten, 1987. English ed., London: Zed Books, 1989.
Shimin to enjo: Ima nani ga dekiru ka (Citizens and Aid: What Can We Do Now?). Iwanami Shōten, 1990.
Tamashii ni fureru Ajia (Asia That Touched My Heart). Asahi Shinbunsha, 1985.

MIYA YOSHIKO
Freelance Writer and Critic

» » » » » » » » » » » »

IN HER RESEARCH AND WRITING, Miya Yoshiko explores questions of female sexuality and institutional responses to the female body in crisis. She has written books and articles on rape, anorexia, physical and mental handicaps, sexual violence and harrassment, and the cultural construction of gender and sexuality. Miya's insistence on the need for clear theoretical distinctions between gender and sexuality is an important component in the ongoing "nature-nurture" debate within Japanese feminism. In Japanese feminist writing and translations of the 1980s it was not unusual to find a lack of distinction among the concepts of sex, sexuality, and gender. Miya was quick to state that this blurring of terms must stop if Japanese feminists were ever to be in a position to develop theories of the construction of gendered identity that could go beyond essentialist biological arguments. She identified the collapse of sex, sexuality, and gender into one another as an effective traditional technique for the containment of women's bodies and female desire within the dominant ideological construction of "the feminine." Miya's writings are always carefully grounded in a thorough critique of the translation of ideology into everyday practice through popular culture. While the terms *sex, sex-*

uality, and *gender* are still often used inconsistently in some Japanese feminist texts, Miya has done much to consolidate an understanding of the potential advantages to Japanese feminism(s) of moving beyond the conflation of the three that characterizes a tradition that prescribes traditional notions of "the feminine" onto all bodies biologically marked as female.

Miya is particularly concerned with the role of certain key institutions — the law, medicine, and the family — in framing women's relationships to their bodies and the relationships of those individuated bodies to the body politic. She frequently develops her analyses by examining the institutional treatment of "disfunctional" bodies. She implicates the supposedly objective science of "diagnostics" in the complex mechanisms of the gendering and medicalization of the female body. Miya describes the process of identification or diagnosis blurring with the production of new categories of disease in the recent "discovery" of a proliferation of "women's diseases" among urban middle-class housewives and a new generation of young career women. Miya consistently returns to "disfunctional" individuals to listen to their own narration of the experience of their bodies. This attentiveness to the voices of disempowered or marginalized people (e.g., the elderly, the handicapped, the chronically ill), which are usually drowned out by institutional static, explores the silences in the official story/diagnosis.

Miya's books have done much to break down the taboos that have traditionally surrounded such issues as rape and incest. Her work is often built around interviews with patients and victims collected over an extended period of time. She is also careful to incorporate the institutional position through interviews with relevant "authorities." Her study of anorexia was particularly controversial because of its criticism of the Japanese medical profession's inflexibility in dealing with these predominantly female teenage cases.

In much of her work, Miya poses a challenge to the practices of such established and influential elites as the medical and legal professions. This, as well as her critique of the role of language in maintaining particular gendered relations of power, overlaps extensively with the issues explored in Nakanishi Toyoko's interview. Nakanishi's initiative in translating *Our Bodies, Ourselves* was based on a similar concern for women's lack of access to a language in which they could speak the experience of their own bodies. Kōra Rumiko is also describing this same lack when she writes of the dominant language as the "language of others" and women's perception of "existing outside language." In all of her work Miya carves out a space where women can try to speak their own meanings even as they speak the "language of others." For Miya, though, there is no possibility of an existence outside language; rather, she strives to make language work for women. She is deeply concerned with the narratives that weave the "real" conditions of women's lives and with the mechanisms for the appropriation of those narratives that women do tell/write for one another. An example is her criticism of the film version of Ochiai Keiko's novel, *The Rape*. When Miya examines contemporary rituals for memorializing aborted fetuses, she disentangles the multiple voices that converge in this newly constructed social space of guilt and appeasement. She complicates and destabilizes this ritual space with a feminist retelling of the story of its making.

At the time of her university graduation, Miya was determined to make a career in journalism. This was a field in which she felt she would be able to explore her commitment to feminist politics and to write about and work with questions of language and meaning. However, opportunities for women in journalism were scarce in the 1960s, and at the age of twenty-three she married and took up life as a full-time housewife. She describes her experience of marriage and divorce, together with her memories of childhood in the conservative and intensely patriarchal environment of a Japanese provincial city, as two key factors in her eventual move into feminist activism and a career as a social critic and writer.

The pieces by Miya translated in this volume are all concerned in one way or another with the relationship between power, the body, and language. The breadth of issues dealt with, from pornographic film to abortion temples, is typical of Miya's commitment to exploring as widely as possible the sexual politics of the everyday lives of women.

Interview

SB: So many of the feminists I've spoken to in Japan trace their political activities back to the AMPO crisis.

MY: At the time of the AMPO demonstrations, I was a housewife. I think my main concern then was looking for a career that would give me some personal satisfaction and take me out of the domestic role. I was motivated less by feminism than by boredom and frustration. My awareness of questions relating to the status of women, of a feminist politics, only developed after I entered the workforce.

SB: What was the career you chose?

MY: In 1975 I joined the staff of a small women's newspaper. Even though I date my active feminism from this time, I would have to say that from childhood I was aware of a constant sense of difference. This was not a difference I identified in myself but one that I saw in the ways others treated male children and me. My own family was quite large. I can recall that from about middle high school age, I realized from observing my mother and grandmother, both of whom were professional housewives, that this was not the life I wanted for myself. That is not to say I didn't respect them, but I was intensely aware that they had not had any serious options other than the roles of wife and mother. I determined that I would create and explore as many options as possible.

SB: What newspaper was it that you joined in 1975?

MY: It was *The Democratic Woman* (*Fujin minshu shinbun*), a newspaper established by General Headquarters of the Occupation forces.

SB: You could say that The Democratic Woman *represents an older feminist voice that straddles the pre- and postwar periods. Over the years the gap separating what are almost two distinct generations of feminists seems to be widening.*

MY: This is true. Although we would like to deny that there are such gaps, there is no question that the older generation and the younger generation — and it is usually an age split — are finding it increasingly difficult to communicate with each other. Their objectives and priorities, as well as their methods, are so different. At the risk of oversimplifying, feminists of the older generation have focused their demands on legal reforms dealing mainly with equal opportunity legislation. The so-called new feminists have refocused attention on male-female interpersonal relations. In other words, the primary distinction can be identified as the location of discrimination. Legal reforms have focused on discrimination in the public domain, in particular in the workplace, and issues of equal access. The new feminism has shifted attention back to the private domain of male-female relations. What we are already beginning to see is that laws alone are not enough to make a significant change in the status of women. To begin with, the new laws do not change the fact that many women don't want equal access to the workforce. They may be satisfied with their domestic role — this raises all sorts of questions about internalization — or they may find the workplace, as currently constituted, something they would rather be out of. If legal reform only guarantees women the right to be like men, then it hasn't fundamentally changed the system. The recent emphasis on the private domain and male-female relations has introduced a new concept into the gender debates: sexuality. In recent feminist writing it is finally being recognized that the absence of any discussion of the relationship between gender and sexuality can only distort the reality of gender politics.

SB: How do you respond to the suggestion that the new feminism is "selfish" in the sense that it focuses on the micro level?

MY: I neither understand nor agree with such accusations. If we can't achieve a process of liberation at the level of the individual woman and her personal relations, then how are we going to achieve a political movement? Any feminism that aims at solving the entire global condition, without first dealing with the status of the individual woman in this society, is doomed to failure.

SB: *Why do you think there has been such a resistance to the topic of sexuality?*

MY: There is a significant difference in both the education and the experience of feminists who were born in the prewar period. I'm very aware that I am overgeneralizing here, and there is a risk of denying that there are older feminists who don't fit this mold; but for simplicity's sake let's maintain the distinction. I think that older feminists strongly feel the need to liberate women's lives, but this does not extend to their bodies. There is a confusion of sexuality and sexual practice. The sexual identity of a woman is constructed within the context of her sexual relationship with a male rather than as an integral part of her own being or self.

Public attitudes have been an important factor as well. There was what amounted to a taboo that prevented any public discussion of women's sexuality beyond the reproductive function. The exception is the "after-eleven" television shows, which specialize in bare breasts and suggestive jokes, but this is a negative sexuality that is the product of male fantasies. What has always been denied and silenced is women's right to express their self-determined sexuality.

There has been some minor improvement in the media, but on the whole we still live in a society largely determined by male sexuality.

SB: *How is your own work received then, given that you write almost exclusively on questions of female sexuality?*

MY: People often ask me why I want to work on such strange things. You probably get the same type of response to your work on pornography. People ask if I've been raped or abused. They think that I must be working through some deep personal trauma to want to write about something like rape. The other reaction is just as predictable; men in particular assume that if I haven't been raped, then I must secretly want to be. Rape is like pornography in our society. It is something that women aren't supposed to talk about. Men participate in it, enjoy it or are disgusted by it, talk about it, joke about it, fantasize about it, but "good" women should pretend it's not there.

SB: How did you become so aware of the issue of female sexuality?

MY: Partly, I think I was reacting against the taboo. At another level I think I became intensely aware of my own inability to express or act on my own desires during my marriage. Over time I became increasingly conscious of the power relation in place between my husband and me. I was not "empowered" to say "no." Even the possibility of saying no was excluded from the "husband-wife" script. At first I saw it as an individual problem, my own shortcoming. With time I became more aware of the extent of the social structures operating to keep both my husband and me in our "place."

SB: A major issue in Anglo-American and European feminist theory in the 1980s was the clarification of the differences between the terms sex, sexuality, and gender. I've noticed in reading recent Japanese feminist works dealing with female sexuality that there is often not a clear distinction drawn between the three terms.

MY: I agree that there has been quite a bit of confusion in the application of these three expressions. It's really only been since the late 1980s that we have started to grapple with the need to make the distinctions, and, as is clear from the ongoing debate between Aoki and Ueno, there is still no real agreement on the question of gender. I believe that it is not fundamental biological and bodily differences but culturally enforced differences that create the gender gap. Sexuality is the individual's sense of a self-identity that extends to one's body and links that body to one's sexual drives. This sense of self is not limited to a heterosexual model.

SB: Homosexuality is another area in which there has been a noticeable silence in Japanese feminist writing.

MY: I think this is yet another taboo but one that few feminists have turned their attention to yet. Part of the problem may be a reaction against the type of labeling that goes on: feminist = man hater = lesbian. This may be an explanation, but it is not a justification. There is a serious need for feminists in Japan to take a more open attitude toward homosexuality, whether it is gay or lesbian. Ironically, the negative status of homosexuality is not a problem of traditional values. It would appear that there was traditionally no particularly negative stigma attached to homosexual love in certain approved contexts. The shift to the public condemnation of homosexuality is a modern phenomenon. Even in the modern period there has been a fairly high tolerance of a homosexual subculture so long as it did not "flaunt" itself. What is new in the last few years is the movement for gay rights. I would say that the public is more tolerant toward male homosexuality than toward lesbianism. There is a lingering sense that if a lesbian could just meet the "right man" she would "get well." Traditionally, there was a greater freedom of movement across heterosexual and homosexual boundaries. They were not mutually exclusive. The modern tendency to insist on a clear demarcation, a line that distinguishes normative from aberrant, is a result of our having bought the psychoanalytic package on psychosexual development and all its implicit homophobia.

SB: Your own book on rape was one in a series of attacks on the traditional taboo against women discussing rape in the public domain.

MY: Rape is an expression of the obstruction of the rights of the individual female. There are many social expressions of rape other than the physical rape of an individual. The rape victim blames herself because she is blamed by society. Traditionally, women had no way to counter the social construction of the identity of the rape victim. With feminism, women are beginning for the first time in Japan to find ways to express their own experience as victims of rape and their anger at a society that has turned a blind eye to such a widespread problem for so long.

SB: Are there any rape statistics available for Japan?

MY: The police and the government will argue that the incidence is very low; however, the number of distress calls coming in to the Tokyo Rape Crisis Center contradicts this. The official attitude that there is no rape problem means that there is also no financial support for the Rape Crisis Center. It's entirely dependent on volunteers and donations. In North America and Europe governments actively fund such centers and shelters. The center accepts reverse charge calls from anywhere in Japan, but one center, nationwide, is not enough. It is very difficult when a call comes in from a remote area for the person taking the call to have immediate access to the necessary information on medical, legal, or other regional support facilities. In a society where women have for so long accepted silence as the only response to rape, it is extremely difficult even to guess at the real figures from the level of calls received by the Rape Crisis Center. We are beginning to recognize that rape is not something that happens out on the street, but, in the Japanese case, it is located within the family. This only adds to the problem of silence.

SB: *The myth that the rapist is a stranger is also being broken down in North America. What you're saying, though, undermines the image of Japan as a nonviolent society.*

MY: First, there is the question of what we mean by violence. In a society where women's sexuality is constantly denied while men are free to indulge their desire as much as they can afford, I would argue, there is a high level of psychological violence against women. There has been a lot of attention paid lately to the new array of "women's diseases," ranging from the increased occurrence of menopausal symptoms to a host of new syndromes — there are syndromes associated with open spaces, closed spaces, department stores, subways, and the list goes on. Some feminists here suggest that these "women's diseases" are being manufactured by members of the medical profession to line their purses. I think that this may be the case in part, but after doing the research for the *anorexia nervosa* book, I am convinced that the pain and distress of these "diseases" are real to the women who suffer the symptoms. The medical profession may be making money out of the ways it chooses to treat the symptoms, but I think that in questioning the reality of the condition itself, we do an injustice to the individual woman who is undergoing the trauma. In our zest for critiquing the medical profession, we can lose sight of the identity of the individual woman who is striving to articulate the symptoms of her condition.

All of this, I think, is intimately linked with the psychological violence against women that so permeates Japanese society that we too
frequently lose sight of it. We have to do all we can to support women
who are attempting to name and define the conditions of their lives,
conditions whose expression they may sometimes find in the body before they can be articulated in words. I think that the project to translate *Our Bodies, Ourselves* constituted a major step toward creating
a language of the body that will give women a far greater level of self-
determination. The question is not the legitimacy of the diagnosis but
its negative connotations. It is the woman who is declared sick, rather
than her environment. Her condition is read as a set of symptoms
rather than articulations.

SB: *Your book on* anorexia nervosa *combines your own exhaustive
research with patient and doctor interviews. In reading the interviews, I was struck by the consistent link between language and the
body in both the development and recovery stages. There is a passage
where one doctor admits to his own process of learning—or more
correctly, unlearning—through his experience of treating an*
anorexia nervosa *patient. He recognized the inadequacy of both
medical language and dominant psychoanalytic methods of dealing
with this condition.*

MY: Yes, I know the comment you're referring to. I think this was
not an easy thing for the doctor to admit. In fact, he is really saying
that by refusing to question his medical practices even when they
were clearly inadequate, possibly even detrimental, he compounded
the girl's condition.

   He had to allow her to develop unthreatening channels of communication with her own body that would allow her to both recognize her body's form (an anorexic usually can't see her own thinness)
and then use those channels to explore and accept her own sexuality.

SB: *In what ways was the treatment inadequate?*

MY: To begin with, by working largely within a psychoanalytic
framework he was constantly frustrated in his attempts to get the pa-

tient to talk or narrate, and these acts are fundamental to analysis. He did not recognize that her condition itself was her self-narrative and that she was incapable of any other form of communication that could be of assistance to him in his analysis of her. The problem was not that she wouldn't talk to him but that he was only listening with his ears. The other obstacle was his emphasis on transference. It was impossible to achieve the patriarchal blend of power and trust that is fundamental to successful transference. This began to raise serious questions about the traditional association of this condition with the mother-daughter relationship. In fact, there appears to be good reason to suspect that anorexics may respond better to a female therapist. A final problem arose out of a Japanese style of psychoanalytic practice, which emphasizes the creation of a nurturing environment for the patient. In the case of the anorexic, this can be salt in the wound.

SB: In your preparatory research, you read widely on the treatment of anorexics outside of Japan. Do you feel that there are any differences in the conditions of the disease or the profile of the anorexic in Japan?

MY: The media took up the subject of anorexia and turned it into something of a media event in the 1980s, tending to treat it as one aspect of a "diet culture." The theory went that young girls were constantly exposed to images of thin, streamlined bodies in advertising and the media, and strove through overzealous dieting to achieve the pencil-thin look. This explanation is totally simplistic, but I believe it has had some currency in the Western popular media as well. There seems to be a pattern in reports of anorexia in the West for the patient to be a daughter of an upper-middle-class family. I don't know if the pattern is accurate or part of an emerging mythology. When I first began my research, I knew very little about anorexia. I was surprised to find how closely related the condition was to teenage sexuality. I hadn't realized that there was such a strong link. I was also struck by the fact that the more I read, the clearer it was that anorexia is not an illness in the generally accepted sense of the word. What I am trying to say is difficult to put into words, but the closest I can come is to say that it is neither a psychological problem nor a physical illness. Anorexia is a physical expression of a psychological condition, but it is not psychosomatic. It is about sexuality. If sexuality is located at the point of interface between the physical and the nonphysical dimensions of the self, then anorexia is the physical expression of a dislocation. At this level I think there is no difference between cases in Japan and in the West.

In fact, I think that any differences there are occur in the area of treatment rather than in the condition itself. A major factor is the extent to which the Japanese medical profession has bought into Western psychoanalytic theory. This is not to suggest that psychoanalysis has nothing to offer in the Japanese context; rather, that along with all its insights, it brings the same patriarchal baggage that feminists have criticized it for in the West.

It is unfortunate that the androcentric nature of psychoanalytic theory feeds into the extreme forms of gender differentiation in Japan. For this reason the treatment of anorexia here has focused on the mother-child relationship and in a sense laid the blame on the mother. In many of the cases I looked at, however, it seemed that the mother also was a victim, either within the family or within the context of the treatment process itself. More recently, there has been a shift among some doctors toward treating the entire family of an anorexic patient. It is claimed that this approach better reflects the "nature" of Japanese society and family structure, but I reject this. I believe the new focus on the family as a unit of treatment is just another import from American medical practice. All of these approaches fail to focus on the needs of the individual patient. All too often, the goal is the restoration of a "happy family," which can usually be achieved only by totally denying the anorexic's right to self-determination. In order to be declared "well," she is required to return to the family structure, either in its original or in some altered and "improved" form, and act "normally."

In the area of "school refusal syndrome," there has been some experimentation with alternative approaches to education. Open space schools have been established to accommodate children who refuse to attend "normal" schools. This step represents a shift in attitude away from the diagnosis and cure of an illness — either in the child, the family, or the school system — and toward the concept of the right of self-determination, even among minors.

It is in the nature of the medical profession to want to intervene, to diagnose and to cure. In the treatment of anorexia, there is still a strong tendency to try and cure the patient, despite the mass of documented evidence that in most cases the crisis that triggers the first stage of the reversal of the condition is generated by the patient herself. In cases where the reversal is forced by external intervention, the likelihood of a recurrence is high. A member of the medical profession can prevent or treat malnutrition or other dietary complications that can cause basic bodily functions to fail. A therapist can work with the anorexic to help her discover a way of creating a symbolic system that will allow her to speak her experience of her body in a language coherent to herself. The way out is often a monologue, not a dialogue.

SB: Let me change the topic and ask you about the pornography debate in Japan. Working on questions of sexuality and gender differentiation, you must have to deal with this aspect of the media in Japan.

MY: It's inescapable. Feminists have dubbed Japan a prostitution society, but I think it is more accurate to call it a pornographic society. The problem with pornography is the same as with rape or prostitution; most women are not concerned, because they don't perceive that it touches their own lives in any direct way. I was at a recent meeting at the Adachi Women's Center in Tokyo, where the discussion focused on pornography. What was most striking was the difficulty many of the women had even talking about it. There was considerable interest in the lecture, but very few women seemed able to articulate their reactions or to connect the images shown to their own life. I think many of the women present were shocked, but that is good. The only way there will ever be any consciousness raising in relation to pornography is through such shock exposures. Feminists are gradually recognizing that the distinction between pornography and nonpornography in this culture is artificial. The Lesbian Feminist Center has a collection of slides, which they make available to anyone who wants to give a talk on the subject.

SB: At a conference at Cornell University in the United States a couple of years ago, Ueno Chizuko questioned a graduate student who showed slides of Japanese pornographic comicbooks. Ueno expressed concern that showing the slides out of context would create a false impression for a Western audience.

MY: I don't know how you could talk about Japanese pornographic comicbooks without slides. How would a non-Japanese audience begin to imagine what the images are like without seeing them. I also think that this attitude denies the international dimension of pornography today. There is no doubt that there are certain differences in images and focus from culture to culture, but what seems more important is looking at the transfer of images across cultures and the implications this has for feminism. A good example is the predominance of images of Western women in Japanese pornography. It is often in pornography that we are best able to identify the connections that are usually obscured: the link, for example, between racial and sexual discrimination. It was Gloria Steinem who said that feminism is antinationalism. There is only a thin line separating cultural relativism and nationalism. To me, all feminist issues are essentially human rights issues, and human rights are not relative, they are fundamental. I think that all other forms of discrimination will be eliminated before gender discrimination is overturned. All discriminatory practices are linked, but to eliminate gender discrimination would require the undoing of the entire fabric of society, and that probably won't happen in our lifetime.

Excerpts from *Sexuality*
WHAT IS THE ECONOMIC REASONS CLAUSE?

It is written in the Eugenics Protection Law that "in cases where the continuation of a pregnancy to full term poses a serious threat to the health of the mother for either physical or economic reasons," an abortion may be performed on the recommendation of a doctor (Article 14, Paragraph 4).

The Economic Reasons Clause is the primary explanation for the hands-off attitude toward abortion in Japan. However, Japan's GNP is now thirty-two times higher and its national income twenty-four times higher than in 1953, when the law was promulgated. The original rationale for this clause is thus no longer valid, and it should be eliminated. . . . At least, this is the argument made by the leader of the reformists, Diet member Murakami Masakuni (a Liberal Democratic Party candidate from Seichō no Ie — "House of Growth," a right-wing religious group).

A communiqué from the assistant minister of welfare explains the economic criterion as "conditions of hardship already qualifying for protection under the Standard of Living Law or clearly deserving such protection." The decision, however, rests entirely with the surgeon who is to perform the abortion, and so there are no means of checking for deviations from the legal definition of cause. The reformers would really like to demand the withdrawal of this unmonitorable clause. But let's put this particular argument aside for the moment. In a pamphlet entitled "Why Rapid Reform to the Eugenics Protection Law Is Needed: Saving the Japanese Race from Extinction," Murakami posits another argument, which can only be described as displaying a strikingly superficial understanding of the real state of affairs. He writes, "In this flourishing Japan of ours, where we are so prosperous that we even joke about the beggars of Ginza eating well enough to get diabetes, the very fact that we have a law on the books condoning abortion for economic reasons is truly strange."

Translated with the permission of the author by Sandra Buckley.

It is certainly true that our standard of living has reached a level of prosperity consistent with Japan's status as one of the great economic powers. However, if a woman opts to bear and raise a child alone, she is soon overwhelmed just trying to keep food on the table. How many jobs are there where one can confidently place a child in daycare? It is not unheard of for a mother — even knowing there are no nurseries, no daycare, and no parental leave and ignoring the risk to her own well-being — to hesitate to "kill her inutero child" (legal abortion), only to resort to taking its life soon after birth (illegal infanticide). The underside of this prosperity is that women and children cannot share in it as long as they have no guarantee of at least a minimum standard of living. A society that cannot guarantee this level of prosperity for women and children, a society that does not protect the newborn, no matter how financially well-off it may be, is a society that can only be described as impoverished.

Nowadays, even people who are married are forced to limit the number of children they have to one or two in order to guarantee a minimum standard of living. A Kyūshū woman named A-*san* became the focus of considerable media attention. She boasted proudly of her miraculous record of fourteen births, only to have her own life cut short by cancer. The fight to protect her lucrative media status as "Japan's Most Prolific Mother" became her raison d'être and her only hold on a philandering husband who otherwise spared her no thought. While she may have found a means of securing her children's welfare, one is struck by the sadness of this woman's life.

If the Economic Reasons Clause is to be abolished, the government must provide funds to enable women to give birth with peace of mind and to raise their children comfortably as single mothers if they so choose.

MIZUKO JIZŌ

"What is that small jizō (an effigy of the guardian deity of children) over there?" If one erects a *jizō*, is one freed from feelings of guilt?" asked Alice, glancing at me with a rather odd expression. Alice was a reporter for the local newspaper of a small American town called Quakertown (Pennsylvania). She had come to Nagasaki and Hiroshima for a month's summer visit on a grant from a foundation promoting international understanding of the atom bomb. Not long before she was due to leave Japan, she saw some *mizuko jizō* in an old temple in Kyoto and appeared at my doorstep, wanting to know all she could about these objects. There are dramatic differences between the belief of the predominantly Buddhist Japanese that after death one can become a bodhisattva and the belief of the predominantly Christian Americans that after death one is called to heaven by God. Such issues lead into the whole question of cultural difference.

Why is it that *jizō* have come to memorialize the souls of fetuses? Perhaps there is no other way of answering but to turn to a story in the Buddhist canon. Infants whose link to their parents is weak, those who died soon after birth, and those who died in the womb, never having seen the sunlight, come to the bank of the River of Death. "One stone for mother, two stones for father," they chant, as they pile little stones on top of the other on the riverbank and clasp their small hands together in prayer for their parents and siblings in this world. Demons appear at the river bank and viciously knock down the stone mounds and torment the children. No matter how much the children cry out, there is no one to come to their aid. They cry themselves to sleep and then, there by their side, a *jizō* appears and draws them to him beneath his robes. As he rescues them, he says, "From this day forth, you should think of me as your parent in the Land of the Dead." That's the story I'm thinking of.

Alice was intensely attracted by this story. "Do the women who have abortions erect *jizō* because they believe in this story and believe that this is how they can escape guilt?" she asks. "Well, not really," I respond. "For those who don't believe in an afterworld or a spirit world, this is no more than a fictional tale. And yet, even so, people in a Buddhist environment have learned the custom of invoking the Buddha just as people in a Christian context worship the Cross. However, whether or not prayer will free the individual from guilt will depend on that person's own feelings." "I suppose so." Alice nodded in agreement. She went on to ask if women in Japan resort to psychoanalysis as a means of resolving their sense of guilt after an abortion, as is sometimes the case in America?

On the one hand, we have America, where one seeks to unburden oneself through one-on-one "treatment." On the other hand, we have Japan, where women, terrorized by people who circulate stories of vengeful spirits, are coerced into memorializing their aborted fetuses. I explained that plastic *mizuko jizō* cost ¥5,000 each, while a stone effigy can cost as much as ¥40,000–50,000. "The commercial motivation of the temples is blatantly clear. The obstetricians make money from women's abortions, and then the temples cash in on them as well," concluded Alice for herself. From the perspective of someone from a different culture, such as Alice, the temple advertisements for *mizuko* memorial services that were so prominent in the newspapers around the time of Obon (the Buddhist festival of the dead) appeared especially questionable.

THE MAKING OF A *MIZUKO* TEMPLE BOOM (PART 1)

The car climbs slowly up the slope, and as we pass into the mountains, we find ourselves in a long deep hollow. The cedar forest has been cut back from the foot of the mountains stretching up both slopes of the valley, and the fields that mark the land development are densely lined with *jizō*. The troops of small stone figures stand, orderly and polite, as if ready to overpower all who enter the valley. Their eyes stare right at us.

This is the *jizō* Temple of Shiun, deep in the mountains of Chichibu. The temple, which specializes in *mizuko jizō*, stands near a sign marking Chichibu Sacred Site, No. 31. Among the temples that have jumped on the bandwagon of the recent *mizuko* boom and are now enshrining effigies, there are many that, in the interest of cheap mass production, are now using plastic *jizō*. However, this particular temple uses effigies made from sacred stone. A 55 cm model costs ¥80,000. An 85 cm model costs ¥150,000. Today, because there is no domestic industry in memorial stone carving, orders are imported from Southeast Asia and Korea. Even so, these prices seem exceptionally high.

The temple was built in 1971. The prime minister of the day, Satō Eisaku, drove into the Chichibu mountains to attend the commemoration ceremonies for the new temple along with an impressive array of other dignitaries of the conservative party. Prime Minister Satō had such a keen interest in the building of this temple because of his own political goals. "Since the promulgation of the current Eugenics Protection Law, the number of abortions has risen and large numbers of fetuses have been killed. As someone who holds a position of responsibility for the care of this nation, I find this most regrettable. However, as nothing can be done in the short term about the existence of the Eugenics Protection Law, we risk being ruined by the weight of our guilt." Given these sentiments, we might surmise that Satō was drawn to this project by its clear stand against abortion.

The chief priest of the temple at the time was a man named Hashimoto. He was also the head of a local political party organization and was manifestly right-wing. Hashimoto continued to maintain close ties with the ruling Liberal Democrats after taking up his position at the temple. "We live in a time when we do not memorialize aborted fetuses. We originally built this temple as a site for memorializing these souls and for offering expressions of regret and grief. However, we later found that many people came to the temple when it became known that we are blessed with the favor of a deity that can miraculously heal illnesses that cannot be cured by a doctor," the temple official explained. In his publication, *A List of Spiritual Experiences at the* Mizuko *Temple*, the head priest cites the miraculous cures of such varied complaints as teenage neurosis, aggressive behavior of children toward their parents, weak eyesight in children, epilepsy, bed wetting, chronic nasal inflammation, assorted gynecological conditions, sexual rejection, marital breakdown, breast cancer, lower back pain, heart disease, and shoulder and arm pain. He claims that these conditions are all related in some way to the presence of the spirit of an aborted fetus and are therefore curable through the act of memorialization. The individual who did the most to circulate stories of vengeful fetal spirits and to fuel the current *mizuko* temple boom was Head Priest Hashimoto.

I wonder if you are aware that *mizuko* temples can be divided into three categories. The first includes temples built with a particular moral or political objective, such as the Shiun Temple. The second contains temples that already had an established tradition of being connected to particular mother or child deities, which found themselves inundated with new supporters during the boom. The third category contains temples built by developers who have taken up a religious office for the sole purpose of profit. These are often funded by "syndicate" money. While it is generally still considered inappropriate to describe the memorializing of aborted fetuses as nothing more than a "money maker," it remains truly sad that there are women who, experiencing an emotional state of contrition toward their lost child, cannot see through the sham of this black market in guilt.

THE MAKING OF A *MIZUKO* TEMPLE BOOM (PART 2)

Not every temple is involved in memorializing fetuses. Some religious sects flatly reject the practice as heresy. According to Ochiai Seiko, a spokeswoman for the Ōtani sect within the Jōdōshū school of Buddhism, the goal of Buddhism is to save the living. She considers "funereal Buddhism," as some refer to the practice of memorializing the dead, a contradiction of the basic tenets of Buddhism. "The Guatama Buddha teaches, 'Draw on the Buddhist doctrine, and draw on your inner self in living your life.' This philosophy dissociates itself from the world of spirits and sentiment and insists instead on a more realistic doctrine in which the individual who has borne the scars and inequities of life faces them head on and determines how to constitute his or her own subjectivity."

Ochiai explains that the trend toward circulating stories of vengeful spirits of fetuses and the widespread increase in temples offering memorial services aimed at purification or release from a spirit is evidence that much contemporary Buddhism has become no more than a form of spiritualism; it is Buddhism in name only. Spiritualism, with its belief in vengeful spirits, is a characteristic of primitive religions worldwide. This form of religious doctrine can enshrine a certain principle of human equality, but only for the period that a society's modes of production are at the most primitive level. As the complexity of the modes of production increases and creates different levels of wealth and poverty, the earlier spiritualism rapidly becomes the basis for a caste system.

In the India of the time of the Guatama Buddha the Brahman caste prospered. Using the Brahmanic code as a point of departure, the Buddha crafted a theory of equality and freedom for the liberation of humankind that went beyond the principles of caste. This was Buddhism, a universal religion that transcended national interests and was thus transmitted to both East and West. It reached Japan, via China, in the sixth century, and there it merged with Shintoism. The emperor, himself a Shinto shaman, was also a Buddhist, and thus Japan's state Buddhism was realized. The previous universal nature of Buddhism was done away with, and it was drawn within the framework of state sovereignty. With the Kamakura Period and the emergence of such new sects as those of Dōgen and Nichiren, there was a gradual shift back toward the more universal qualities of Buddhism, but to the present the two distinct streams exist side by side in Japan.

"By blaming the likes of vengeful spirits, those in power have avoided dealing with the despair and hardship of the people, and have thus been able to continue to rule the country and manipulate the populace. A world that is believed to result from the work of vengeful spirits is not going to produce conditions where people live self-motivated or autonomous lives. The women who go to *mizuko* temples live unhappy lives. It is not just that they suffer feelings of remorse for having aborted their child. Living is difficult for them. Along with problems at the individual level, they can resort to a causal explanation for their situation. As long as the individual is tricked into thinking that this is all the work of a vengeful spirit, she won't be able to see the contradictions that are right in front of her."

Ochiai exhorts everyone to see through the deceits of spiritualism.

The *mizuko* temple boom has brought to light for me just how frightening the risks are if, living in this country of Japan, one remains ignorant of the influence of religious matters.

THE MAKING OF A *MIZUKO* TEMPLE BOOM (PART 3)

In 1961 Seichō no Ie, a major religious sect that has demanded the reform of the Eugenics Protection Law, built a pagoda for the "adoption" of aborted fetuses at the site of its head temple in Uji. It now holds somber monthly memorialization ceremonies at that location as well as an annual festival of the dead. Before the reading of the sutras at the memorialization ceremonies, the following passage is read out to the gathering: "This sutra is not the property of one sect or one school of Buddhism. It is the translation into modern Japanese of the religious truths codified by our ancestors. From this creed we can comprehend the true nature of life. Listen to these words so as to achieve a still higher level of enlightenment in the spirit world and to move yet further along the path of advancement."

The organization was founded in 1929 by Taniguchi Masaharu with the religious motto, "Know the Truth of Life." He insisted that the "truth" he spoke of was universal and transcended the differences between sects. We can better understand this concept when we see how it was in tune with its times. During the Second World War the organization ingratiated itself to state Shinto, which itself accrued remarkable power and influence at that time by propagating the notion of the emperor's divine descent. After the war, with the emergence of the LDP's political power base, Seichō no Ie was well placed as a mouthpiece for the right. Taniguchi's two central prayers for his country were for ratification of the "legitimate constitution" (the Meiji Constitution) and reform of the Eugenics Protection Law.

Ochiai describes Seichō no Ie as the civil arm of state Shinto. "According to Taniguchi, the main idol of Seichō no Ie is the great deity of Sumiyoshi, the herald of Amaterasu. The goal of this deity was the purification not only of Japan but of the whole universe." When one recognizes that this organization, which calls for the reform of the Eugenics Protection Law with such emotion-laden expressions as "the sanctity of life," is the same organization that promotes the expansion of military, reactionary, constitutional reform, state funding for the Yasukuni Shrine, and other, similar fascist trends, then one begins to see the real purpose of its proposed reform of the Economic Reasons Clause: the transformation of all women into patriotic mothers who are willing to bear many children for the sake of the nation.

After one has exposed Seichō no Ie for what it is, and after one has seen through the motives behind the memorialization boom, the question still remains of the "life" of the fetus. As a Buddhist adherent, how does Ochiai view this? "From a Buddhist perspective, a fetus has life from the moment of conception. An abortion is clearly a wrongful act. However, according to Buddhism, all life is equal. Grass, trees, animals, and so on — every form of life is equal with the rest. Humankind lives with the guilt that we take life but go on living ourselves. The necessity to kill a fetus occurs only unexpectedly, but if that is our karma, then we may have to experience it and survive. Understanding this, the Gautama Buddha tried to reduce the sense of guilt associated with this particular wrongful act. The memorial service was intended in this light."

The memorialization boom of the *mizuko* temples is an extension of the impoverishment of the modern condition. It is only about money. Interestingly, Ochiai criticizes the use of the concept of "mothers' rights" as a counterstrategy to the "sanctity of life" platform. She argues that the concept of "rights" is itself the product of an impoverished modernism and therefore cannot function as a source of power for the cause of women. Women perhaps still have a lot to learn when it comes to moving beyond the strategies of the "enemy."

THE TAMING OF *THE RAPE*

"Read the book, then see the movie," or "See the movie, then read the book"? Since the first financial successes of joint film and book productions, there have been numerous such cooperative ventures. However, the film is not always true to the book. In fact, there are times when it is better to think of the film as a separate production, a vehicle of the director's images. For example, Ochiai Keiko's novel about rape, an act of violent aggression against a woman's body and soul, was made into a movie by the Tōei Group.

In the novel, a graphic designer, Yahagi Michiko, is attacked by a male passerby late at night, close to her apartment. For the sake of her own self-esteem, she does not choose silence as many women do, but sets out to report the crime. At the police station she is bombarded with questions about her own past, which have nothing to do with the attack: Is she a virgin? Has she had an abortion? What about the details of her relationship with her lover? The lawyer for the young woman emerges as the representative of women's myths, fantasies, stereotypes of women. A central theme of the novel is the "logic of the powerful," which causes rape victims, who cannot begin to verbalize the depth of their wounds, to be raped over and over again within the legal system, to be repeatedly assaulted by words, looks, and thoughts. By contrast, the film director reduces the story to the sexual relationship of a couple. "I have no intention of representing this as a social problem. I want to enter deep into the emotions of a man and a woman who experience rape."

In the book Yahagi, the female protagonist, is represented as a character of intelligence and strong will, who files charges with the police to protect her self-esteem. Tōei gave this role to the popular actress Tanaka Yūko and played up the sex appeal she exudes. The scene of a woman being raped in a dark, empty lot, her hands tied behind her back with a belt, was transformed into a bedroom scene. The scene of the rape victim showering immediately after the attack and other, similar scenes were rendered as sexual as possible. Even the rape scene was transformed into something closer to a mildly violent love scene between consenting adults. Another aspect of the book that is totally lacking in the film is the rape victim's sense of anger. In the book the author has a female police detective act as a mouthpiece for the victim's anger. She declares, "A society that cannot recognize rape as a crime is a society that treats lightly the character of women, one half of the human race."

The sound of women's voices shouting out in the courtroom is cut from the film. Instead, to achieve a sense of realism in the court scenes, the director recruited a real judge and real lawyers. But the result, which never went beyond the level of amateur theatrics, was a complete failure. The motives of the author and the motives of the film studio were just too far apart. Perhaps it was a difference in genres. Perhaps it was a difference in the way men and women see things.

The studio targeted the movie at young women and billed it as a film made for a female audience. At the meeting to launch the film's production, the head of Tōei described it as "pornography for women office workers." One by one, the studio stripped away the intentions of the author. Surely this, too, is part of the structure of rape. In the context of Japan's impoverished culture, the word *rape* may have indeed come to be synonymous with pornography.

THE AGE OF SOFT SEX

From the age of hard sex ("to be touched, to be masturbated") to the age of soft sex ("not to be touched, not to be masturbated)" — the sex trade is subject to its own trends. The latest trend in the "industry" could be described as masturbation stimulation cubicles. Even though the young female models take off their clothes, they never lay so much as a finger on the customer.

The "F Club," which stands in front of the central exit of the Shinjuku station in Tokyo is representative of the soft sex trade. Let us have "Ms. A," a fourth-year student at a private university who worked as a waitress in the F Club for some three months, sketch out an insider's story of the sex trade. "It's a place where the experience begins with masturbation and ends with masturbation with the help of various devices. But the models and customers are just ordinary folks; there's nothing perverted about it at all."

According to "Ms. A," the "F Club" is designed around a series of five rooms. The first room is a spacious lounge where, every thirty minutes, there is either an auction of underwear or a pornographic video show. The second room is made up of private booths. Each booth is no more than a square meter and contains porno videos and photo magazines. They are essentially masturbation rooms. These rooms also function as nude studios. The customer enters with one of the models and a polaroid camera and can take nude shots of the model. The third room is set up for telephone sex. Once again, the customer enters a booth with a model, but they enter through separate doorways into compartments separated by "magic" glass — one-way glass, so the customer can see the model but not the other way around. The customer and model speak via telephone. The model strips at the request of the customer (but not her panties); she strikes various poses; and they maintain a lewd conversation by phone. The fourth room is the adult toy store. The fifth room is the information center. Every detail of the Shinjuku area sex trade is entered on the computer here, and it is very easy for a customer to identify the next "watering hole."

"Ms. A" worked as a waitress in the lounge, where she could wear ordinary T-shirts and slacks. She was paid ¥800 an hour and worked a six-hour shift (the early shift was from 12:00 noon to 6:00 P.M., and the late shift was from 5:00 P.M. to 11:00 P.M.). She was easily drawn by a friend's suggestion of an interesting job. However, she was quickly put off on the day she went to inspect the club and saw the mountains of pornographic photo magazines and the young men who sat huddled over them. As any average young woman would have done, she made a quick U-turn out the door. "But then with time I started to feel that I wanted to go back and look more closely at this human trap. I had just split up with an older man at about that time. He was someone who had wanted to control me, so perhaps I was also reacting against him."

In the lounge area after clients paid the entry fee and a cover charge, the coffee, tea, soda, juice, and other soft drinks were free. It was the job of "Ms. A" to carry drinks to them, but she was also responsible for going out to buy the panties to be auctioned. It was left to her discretion what kind of panties to buy and how much to pay. "I would buy panties for ¥310 apiece in the lingerie section of a nearby department store. These very cheap panties would sell at auction for more than ¥1,000 each. On average, between ¥3,000 and ¥4,000. One pair went as high as ¥17,000, but the boss stepped in and said the price couldn't go higher than ¥10,000. Can you believe it? These are ¥300 panties we're talking about!"

The panties they bid for have been worn only once, by a model who climbs naked inside a silhouetted box placed middle-stage before the auction. How deficient must be the daily lives of the men who put out such large amounts of money for these panties! With the exception of a handful of flashy customers, most of the men are average office workers (25 percent are bachelors) and some elderly men and students. "You'd think that they'd be able to masturbate for themselves without any help. Can't they even control their own bodies?" I find myself reacting to her description. "The number of young men who want help masturbating in a mechanical and controlled way certainly seems to be increasing. They aren't capable of seeking out a full relationship or a full sex life with a woman. Because there are so many young men who are afraid of sex, I guess the soft sex trade will stay in fashion."

In order for there to be trade in soft sex, there has to be a confused customer (the consumer), a service provider (the worker), and an entrepreneur who makes money off the sweat of the other two. The effect of this industry is to take the sexual desire that is usually released in a natural relationship between a man and a woman and sequester it in an unnatural space, in the illusion that it can be gratified there. Yamamoto Shinya, a well-known reporter of cultural trends, wrote in an attempt at a humorous mode, "They're all sick. It's as simple as that!" But, this is no laughing matter.

RORIKON

The slight swelling of newly formed breasts. Tight, flat, boyish buttocks. A hairless crotch. A teenage girl, too young to know shame, exposes her maiden flesh and strikes a captivating pose. It must have been around 1981 that collections of such images of young girls first began to sell wildly, and the "*rorikon* boom" still shows no sign of subsiding. *Rorikon* is a Japanized abbreviation of the English expression "Lolita complex." In more familiar language, one might call it a sexual preference for young girls. The term originated with Vladimir Nabokov's novel *Lolita* (1955), the story of a fifty-year-old university professor whose life is destroyed when he succumbs to the seductive ways of a twelve-year-old girl.

For this middle-aged man, his eyeglasses resting on his nose, the pursuit of a young girl is one means of rejuvenation. In a magnanimous moment I might be able to see how, with creeping old age, the desire for young girls in sailor suits is a "reasonable" response to impotency. But no, it's not that simple. Today, *rorikon* are widely popular among young university students around twenty years of age. According to a young reporter who is a friend of mine, this fascination among young men for *rorikon* is the natural outcome of "young men who can't make the step to adulthood" and "young men who can't act like men." This generation has survived a life of "examination hell" with their mothers waiting on them hand and foot. They were raised with one goal in mind, taking their exams. Needless to say, any sexual diversions were taboo. This is a generation of innocent virgins. For these young men, who are incapable of psychologically separating themselves from their mother's breasts, a mature female is a terrifying she-devil. One can see how they might turn their attention to "unwomanly women," or pre-pubescent girls, rather than frightening "older women." The symptoms of the *rorikon* generation, the average profile of the "patient," includes (1) no sexual experience with women; (2) feminine character traits; (3) timid and incapable of wrongdoing; and (4) academically at the top of their class. Put simply, the children of the *mazākon* (mother complex) generation graduate into the *rorikon* generation.

The psychologist Sasaki Kikoji wrote, "In a country where the principle of motherhood is as strong as it is in Japan, it is extremely difficult for a young man to mature into manhood." Even after these under-matured men have physically moved away from their mothers, it remains difficult for the women who share their beds to acquire

their own sexual identity as women. The existence of the *rorita* generation has some serious implications for women. And it is important to
remember that this *rorita* generation of young men is having an undesirable impact on a still younger generation of girls. No matter how
much of a mix of innocence and coquettishness the consumer might
perceive in the photos of these young girls, they are still far from an
age where they are sexually mature (many don't even have pubic hair
yet). Who can say with certainty that they won't increasingly fall
victim to violent sexual abuse if they continue to be treated as objects
of desire in this way? Above all, it is frightening to think that the
rorikon boom threatens to play a perpetual prelude to abuse.

Selected Works

Bi no kusari (Chain of Beauty). Sekibunsha, 1991.
Daietto tte nan darō (What is Dieting?). Iwasaki Shoten, 1991.
Dokyumento seibōryoku (Document on Sexual Assault). San Maku Shup-
    pan, 1984.
Funin to mukiau (Facing Infertility). Kyōiku Shiryō Shuppankai, 1992.
Kussetsu shita shōjo no sei (Distorted Girls' Sex). Ushio Shuppan, 1981.
Onna. Ikiru. Manabu (Living and Learning for Women). San'ichi Shobō,
    1983.
Onna nante iya! Shishunki yasesho o ou (I Don't Wanna Be a Woman! Report
    on Anorexia in Puberty). Asahi Shinbunsha, 1988.
Sekushuariti (Sexuality). Gendai Shokan, 1984
Sekushuaru harasumento (Sexual Harassment). Kyōiku Shoryō Shuppankai,
    1989.

NAKANISHI TOYOKO
Owner-Manager, Shōkadō Women's Bookstore, Osaka

» » » » » » » » » » » »

NAKANISHI IS BEST KNOWN for her role as the founder of the Japan Women's Bookstore (Shōkadō) first established in Kyoto and now located in Osaka. The bookstore has served as an important focus of feminist activity in the Kansai (Kyoto-Osaka) region. In addition to its permanent stock of Japanese feminist writings, fiction and nonfiction, the store also carries a wide range of foreign feminist works in translation. Nakanishi and the feminist circle that has developed around the store have done a great deal to promote specific translation projects, of which the most challenging was the translation and publication of the Japanese edition of *Our Bodies, Ourselves*. The project took several years to complete from the first initiatives in the mid-1980s. A team of women from a wide range of backgrounds and specializations managed the mammoth undertaking. They hoped that the availability of a Japanese edition of *Our Bodies, Ourselves* would eliminate the feeling that doctors had a monopoly on knowledge about the female body, as the original English version had done years before when it was released in North America. There was concern from the outset that the medical profession would react strongly to the final publication.

The translators saw the negatively marked and highly specialized vocabulary that had been traditionally used to describe and diagnose the female body as a major factor in the widely perceived inability of women to articulate their individual experience of their own bodies. On this basis it was decided to create a new Japanese vocabulary that would be more accessible and less alienating for women seeking a language in which to speak their physical pain or pleasure. Nakanishi clearly links the development of such a new language of the female body with the need described by Kanazumi, from her perspective as a lawyer, for women to be better able to negotiate their relationship to the institutions of power. The process of creating a new language of the female body involved extensive consultation with women from a wide range of specializations including medicine, law, language, psychology, social work, and so on. The rejection of the traditional medical vocabulary was a provocative strategy for the reclaiming of women's bodies.

The Japanese version of *Our Bodies, Ourselves* was published with an extensive amount of material developed specifically for Japanese readers. Statistics, historical background, and regional information on services and medical alternatives were researched and added to the volume. Some of this material, together with sections of the Japanese preface, is translated in this collection. It was Nakanishi's suggestion that I translate excerpts from the Japanese edition rather than an original piece of her own writing. This gesture is characteristic of the commitment Nakanishi has to cooperative feminist strategies. As is clear from her interview, Nakanishi is herself a provocative and challenging feminist. However, in this case she said she preferred to make some of the specific details of the Japanese edition accessible to English readers. Nakanishi identified this as one more stage in an ongoing process of translation and transmission of feminism between Japan and North America.

The Japanese edition of *Our Bodies, Ourselves* dovetails with many of the concerns explored by the other nine feminists in the volume. For example, information on services offered in Japanese obstetrics clinics and brief accounts of abortion policy in Japan offer an interesting context for Miya's short essays on the *mizuko* temple boom. The detailed documentation about such areas as maternity clinics and abortion facilities and procedures is an indication of the level of existing feminist information networks in Japan. In some areas the Japanese edition of *Our Bodies, Ourselves* is able to offer more specific local information than the authors of the original U.S. version could.

As a publisher and distributor, Nakanishi brings her own concerns and experience to questions of the treatment of women writers and feminist researchers in the media and the publishing industries. She has on various occasions publicly rejected the procensorship strategies of the antipornography movement in Japan. Nakanishi attributes her resistance to any suggestion that censorship laws should be extended or strengthened to her memory of not only prewar and wartime censorship but also the strict censorship measures of the Occupation. Nakanishi describes the need for feminists who lived through Japan's period of imperialism and the Allied Occupation to find ways of communicating their experiences of that time to the younger generation of postwar feminists.

The bookstore stocks a backlist of the more substantial publications of the informal *minikomi* (mini-communication system) that is discussed in several of the interviews. Nakanishi supports the *minikomi* as a network for transmitting information among the many, diverse women's groups across Japan. Although in their interviews both Aoki Yayoi and Saitō Chiyo express some reservations regarding the continuing role of the *minikomi*, Nakanishi is convinced that there is still a vital role for this style of informal and accessible communication within the larger framework of feminist publishing in Japan. The supporters of the *minikomi* consider it essential to maintaining the diversity of Japanese feminism(s) in the wake of recent trends toward the mainstreaming of feminism in the media. There is a concern that the new status afforded feminism in both the print and electronic media comes at the price of a reduction of its multiplicity to images and soundbites from the same few high-profile feminists, thus mediating difference into a false representation of homogeneity.

Nakanishi promotes many other feminist activities in the region
under the auspices of the bookstore, including lectures, workshops,
and other educational forums for the dissemination of feminist knowledge. The bookstore offers a valuable point of intersection for the
activities of grass-roots feminists as well as feminists from the academic community of the Kansai region. Nakanishi has been an influential figure in the formation of a cohesive and active feminist network in the area. The wide range of backgrounds and expertise of the
women who gather around the activities of Shōkadō reflects her own
commitment to the need to address what is often perceived to be the
growing gap separating academic and nonacademic feminists in Japan
today. For Nakanishi books remain an important bridge beyond such
differences.

Interview

SB: When did you first open the Women's Bookstore?

NT: It's been over a decade now.

SB: And you run the bookstore alone?

NT: I own the bookstore, so in that sense it is my business. But there
are other women involved who are committed to the future of the
store as much as I am, and their assistance is invaluable. I couldn't do
this alone.

SB: How many other women's bookstores are there in Japan?

NT: As far as I know we are the only full-fledged women's bookstore
in the country. I started this store to fill the gap that existed. I think it
would be a real loss to the women's movement if this store were ever
forced to shut down. It's not easy, though. We stock a lot of titles and
try to keep up with all the new materials coming out, but there is so
much these days. As you probably know, there has been a real publishing boom lately in feminist literature in Japan. There are also a lot
of books on women's issues that you might not necessarily call feminist in the stand they take, but we try as much as possible to stock

these as well. In addition, there are all the works in translation from overseas. The problem is that the books often stay on the shelves. We have a lot of names on our mailing list and a lot of women come in and out — we used to be just down the road from St. Agnes' College — but they don't always buy. Many feminist titles are expensive because they come out in small runs for the first edition. Our overall turnover is not that high.

SB: What explains the recent increase in feminist literature?

NT: I think at one level there has been a genuine increase in the number of women interested in feminist issues, and this has led to more women both writing and reading in the field. Of course, it's not just the book industry that has changed but the media in general. At another level I think one has to be realistic and recognize that the media has caught onto something it believes will sell and is trying to cash in on it as much as possible. You just have to look at the titles to get a sense of this.

SB: Coming to Japan this time, I've been struck by the extent that the media has warmed to feminism and, at the same time, the extent that some feminists have warmed to the media.

NT: I think it's particularly obvious in the area of literature. There is no question now but that women writers and poets have been recognized by the publishing industry and the critics. Women writers are now published by the major publishing houses. The ground gained is quite remarkable compared to even ten years ago.

SB: Is what you're describing a process of mainstreaming?

NT: Yes. The general public — male and female — has a much better sense now of what feminism is. Of course, there is still a long way to go. However, there is a far better representation of women's issues in the media, and the publishing industry is just one example of this.

SB: The other side of the coin is the impact this contact with the mass media will have, has already had, on Japanese feminism.

NT: I'm not sure that I know what you mean.

SB: In English you can pun on the word media and talk about the process of "media-tion" when a topic is taken up by the mass media. One of the early feminist strategies in Japan was the development of alternative media through the minikomi, *but there seems to be a new trend now toward accessing the mainstream media. The problem of "media-tion" is not unique to feminism, of course. There is a risk that the end result is a peripheralization of radical positions and a process of selection that favors a position or range of positions that is most easily recuperated into the dominant value system.*

NT: I suppose there is a price to pay for the wider currency feminism is achieving. Some compromises are made along the way, but the overall effect seems to be positive — far more people are aware today that there are issues to be considered even if they are not always sure what they are or how to deal with them. There has been a general improvement in the public consciousness in Japan, where the situation of women was so dreadful compared with other developed countries even into the 1970s. I think this is a major step. We keep a lot of *minikomi* materials here in addition to books and journals. The *minikomi* still plays an important role in the movement, and I see this continuing; but it is a medium through which women communicate with other women, and I believe the time has come in Japan for feminists to develop strategies for influencing the whole structure of the society. We can't do that if we just go on talking to one another. By its very nature, the *minikomi* is not an appropriate medium for such a goal.

SB: I believe the women's bookstore is involved in various other projects in addition to the book shop itself.

NT: Yes. We are the representative office here in Kansai for various national women's groups and act as a meeting place for them. We have also recently started to host symposia on feminist issues. We sponsored a conference on ecological feminism in 1987 and then published the contents of the proceedings. That was just one of various activities along those lines. Another project that has been centered around the bookstore is the translation of the American book *Our Bodies, Ourselves.* The translation was undertaken as a group project, and we've put a lot of time and energy into it. We see it as very timely. If you look at the titles of the books being published lately, say over the last two or three years, and the kinds of works that are being chosen for translation into Japanese from American, French, English, and other feminist writers, you'll see a proliferation of works dealing with the question of female sexuality. Much of the theoretical debate in Japan today among feminists centers on questions of the construction of a sexual identity. There is a major problem here, however. While feminists are debating the theoretical distinctions between sex, sexuality, and gender, far too many Japanese women are still struggling with the most basic problems of their own physical experience.

It was not that long ago that we had a major scandal here over a hospital where more than a thousand women were operated on unnecessarily. On the advice of the doctor, the women agreed to hysterectomies. Most of them simply didn't know enough about their own bodies to question the diagnosis, and of course, they had grown up in a culture that places great trust in the medical profession. A major difficulty for women has always been the lack of a vocabulary that even allows them to express their experience of their own bodies. Various studies have shown that a large proportion of Japanese women cannot even adequately locate or describe the complaint they come to receive treatment for when it is in any way related to their reproductive system. This has given the medical profession a great deal of power over female patients. Of course, there are medical terms for all the body parts, symptoms, and treatments, but they are all usually gibberish to the patient, who sits and listens to her own body and her own pain translated into words that are foreign to her. So much of this comes down to a very basic question of language. There has been an increasing amount of work done on the effect this problem of language has had upon the treatment of female patients suffering from "women's diseases," such as anorexia among young teenage girls, complications related to menstruation and pregnancy, postnatal depression, and menopause. The social definition of these experiences has overridden the physical reality, creating a virtual taboo that has silenced women and rendered the conditions nonexistent.

SB: *How does one explain, then, the recent increases in surgery and other interventions related to reproduction — for example, induced births, cesarean births, hysterectomies, and so forth?*

NT: Well, the medical profession is an industry that sells services for profit. This is possibly most true for obstetrics and gynecology. These are simple surgical procedures, comparatively speaking. It's very convenient for the medical profession to suddenly recognize and name those conditions that it's denied until recently. It's quick income. The difficulty is how to educate Japanese women about their own bodies so that they can question the diagnosis when it is handed to them. The problem again is language. Much of the medical vocabulary related to the female body is itself negatively marked. A good example of this is the large number of words used to describe female bodily functions or conditions that include the character for "blood" with all the negative connotations that character carries in Japanese. It may be hard for Western women to understand, but for many Japanese women these words are very difficult to utter. So to start with, there is the problem that many women may not know the medical words in the first place, and even if they do know them, they may find it very difficult to speak them. The tradition in Japan is that women accept the discomforts or even extreme pain that may relate to their female bodily functions. It is important that women overcome the sense of taboo that this has created if they are to defend themselves against the aggressive practices of the medical profession.

SB: *And the translation of* Our Bodies, Ourselves *is a step toward dealing with the problems of naming and the right to self-expression and self-determination.*

NT: Yes. It may seem like we are a bit slow on the uptake given how long the book has been available in English, but in a sense the time wasn't right before now. More and more women in Japan today are aware of their right to express their own experience of their bodies, free of any social or cultural taboos, and yet come up against the problem of how to express themselves without resorting to a medical vocabulary that tends only to confound the situation further. Even the women who have done research in this area have found this a major problem. By collecting their survey information anonymously, they have helped overcome the women respondents' sense of inhibition, but they are still left with the problem of how to ask questions about the body in a way that makes it possible for the women to reply accurately.

SB: I saw a recent survey on the sexual development of women and found the approach innovative. The surveyors had abandoned a multiple-choice format whenever possible, opting instead for something like a short essay answer. There was no medical terminology, and some questions came with sketches of the body to allow the women to locate specific sensations, rather than calling them symptoms. The women were left to explore and express for themselves their experience of the various stages of sexual development.

NT: Yes, that kind of thing is necessary if women are to feel free to speak. What we have done in the translation of *Our Bodies, Ourselves* is to develop a new vocabulary to replace the medical language. We give both the medical term and the new word the first time it occurs and then drop the medical word after that. For example, we frequently opted to replace the character for "blood" with the character for "sexuality" in words describing a female bodily function. We were aiming at positively redefining these functions as sexual, rather than negatively marking them as polluted.

We anticipated a strong reaction from the medical profession and were well prepared. We worked closely with a respected female gynecologist to be sure that we made no factual errors, and she is committed to defending the project against any onslaught from her male colleagues. Others will inevitably be bothered by the explicitness of many of the photographs. We've used Japanese photographs and changed some illustration techniques throughout, so that the content is translated into the Japanese context not just by language but also by images. This is important if the book is to be well received among a general female readership here. I expect that conservatives will see it as promiscuous because of the information it offers on birth control and abortion, in addition to basic sex education. We've substituted Japanese contact addresses and references for the American information in the original.

A book like this is essential if we are going to prevent the gap from growing between the theoretical debates taking place among feminists and the reality of most Japanese women's experience of their own bodies. I think it is a good sign that an academic feminist like Ueno Chizuko was involved in the translation project. Any controversy is likely to encourage more women to read it. That's the kind of situation where the mass media can work to our advantage.

SB: The last time I was in Japan was two years ago. In all the major bookstores at that time, the family section was expanding most rapidly. Most of the new titles dealt with the crisis of the family (kazoku kiki). Depending on the inclinations of the author, they would either argue for the importance of a reconsideration of the existing family structure or would lament its demise. Authors who preferred to preserve or restore the existing structure were often inclined to blame the symptoms of the family in crisis on the wife/mother. Now there is a whole new wave of literature on "single culture." It seems to be largely positive and often anecdotal.

NT: It is an interesting shift to have occurred in just two years, but you're right, the emphasis has changed. There are still conservative men and women writing eulogies for the family, but on the whole the public attitude has changed gradually toward the possibility of alternatives to the existing structures of marriage and family. It is not only women who are writing these books on single culture or single life. Both men and women are asking serious questions about the costs to the individual of the postwar family structure. Feminists are recognizing that it is not enough to identify men as the enemy. Japanese men are just as exploited within this system. They get very little out of it when you get right down to it. The literature on single life is the beginning of a movement to look for new ways in which men and women can live their lives together or separately.

I think that quite a lot of what is being written now comes out of the personal experience of the authors, partly because we are just beginning to imagine what the alternatives may be and trying them out at a personal level as we go along. These personal accounts are important to others considering alternatives to the accepted structures — young people faced with the pressure to marry, men and women in "normal" marriages who are not satisfied with the direction their life has taken, and so on. The decision to live outside the mainstream is not an easy one. In one sense this is another form of networking, the creation of a support network of single people.

SB: What other shifts have you noted in the last few years?

NT: In the books coming onto the market, there has been an interesting and related development in literature dealing with divorce. At about the same time that the wave of "family in crisis" literature appeared, people began to pay a lot of attention to divorce. A definite link was consistently drawn between the crisis of the family and divorce. Again, it was usually the woman who somehow ended up carrying the blame. The Japanese word for divorce is *rikon*, and a divorcee is called *mikon*, literally "postmarriage." You were either premarriage, married, or postmarriage. A recent pun has been the use of the word *hikon* to replace *mikon*. The character for *hi* means anti-, and so postmarriage is redefined as antimarriage. A much more affirmative statement for the identity of a divorced woman.

SB: The question is one of language again.

NT: I think that Japanese feminists have always had a sense of the importance of language. We are always tackling problems of the negative image and the position of powerlessness that this language creates for women. Often the problem is even more subtle, not a question of what is said but what cannot be said, as with the whole subject of women's sexuality. This has been a problem not just in medicine but also in the law. Rape, incest — these are words that are only now, finally, finding their way into the public domain.

SB: Ochiai Keiko published her novel Rape *in the mid-1980s. The title itself would have been a problem not long ago, not to mention the content.*

NT: Again there has been a shift in public tolerance, a gradual move toward recognizing the reality of women's lives. There have been so many myths blurring a woman's sense of her own identity.

SB: The gap between the myth and her own experience?

NT: Yes. It's that gap that we have to work to reduce, and language has a lot to do with this in both the public and the private lives of women. We have to be able to express our own experience of our bodies and of reality to a lawyer, a policeman, a doctor, without any sense of shame or fear of possible repercussions. We also have to be able to talk to our daughters, our mothers, and one another. A wife has to be able to express to her husband why she isn't sexually satisfied, what she wants him to do to give her pleasure. We can sit here together in this bookstore and talk openly about these things, but many Japanese women don't have a sense of freedom of expression, don't even have the words to speak their experience, their desires, regardless of whether they are in a doctor's surgery, a lawyer's office, or their marriage bed.

SB: Several of the feminists I have talked with have expressed concern, even frustration, over the complacency of the middle-class married woman. National surveys keep showing that the level of satisfaction these women express when asked about the quality of their lives is very high, and they don't seem to want to change things. Feminists and the mass media seem to converge in their discussions of the stereotype of this group of women — freed from domestic toil by their high-tech households, spending their days at culture centers and community colleges or playing tennis. At least, that's the stereotype.

NT: It depends on what kinds of questions you ask, doesn't it? How we measure satisfaction tends to be determined in terms of material prosperity, and these women may indeed be very satisfied with the level of prosperity they've achieved. But there is only so much tennis one person can play, there are just so many culture courses one person can enroll in, just so many temple and garden tours to be taken. I don't believe that any of these women would answer that she is satisfied if you asked her about her husband's long working hours, his drinking habits or golf weekends, his awareness of her sexual needs, the double standard that tolerates his extramarital relations but not hers.

These women are educated university graduates. They are aware, through the media and in some cases through their own travel experiences, of the wider range of options available to women in Europe or the United States. What surprises me is not their level of satisfaction with their present way of life, but the extent to which they must suppress their self-expression in order to sustain that way of life. Their identity is drawn from satisfying other people's needs — their parents', then their husband's and children's, and finally their husband's parents' in their old age (and sometimes their own parents as well).

SB: In my work I'm interested in looking at how women internalize an ideological structure in which they always inhabit the subjected position. I don't accept the argument that Japanese women have power and autonomy in the domestic sphere. I actually see this as one more myth that has worked toward women's internalization of their victim/subject position. However, some feminists react strongly to the use of the word victim.

NT: Women can, at certain moments, enter into a position of power in relation to some other person — a female teacher in relation to a student, a mother in relation to a child, upper-class women in relation to lower-class women or Japanese women in relation to women in third world countries. In this sense, they are not always subjected or victimized, and the victim is not always female.

SB: The problem is that no one is ever located in a single or unique relationship. At any given moment we are directly or indirectly implicated in a myriad of relationships that may or may not be related, and, as you have said, the subjected position is not occupied only by the female. Some feminists have made the distinction between masculine powered and feminine nonpowered positions, emphasizing that both positions can be occupied by either a male or a female.

NT: At the moment in Japan there is a lot of attention being paid to the status of Filipino call girls who come to Japan to work in the bars. They are a good example of how a woman can be in a subjected position within one power structure (the Japanese woman in relation to her husband) while simultaneously being implicated into a power position in another relationship (the Japanese woman in relation to the Filipino call girl). It's so difficult to communicate how all these different levels of exploitation are interrelated. We were talking about the word "rape" before. I think at some level it can be applied to both these power relations.

SB: Introducing a word as charged as "rape" will always generate controversy, but that's not a bad thing. I've heard both Aoki Yayoi and Matsui Yayori describe the economic relationship between Japan and Southeast Asia as a form of rape.

NT: I think Japanese women are finally beginning to recognize these kinds of links. Groups such as the Asian Women's Association had always made these basic associations, but I think we're just starting to see a wider appreciation of these issues. It's not easy though, when there is still so much ground to be covered in terms of the status of Japanese women. If we take our eyes off the Japanese situation for a moment, we always risk having some of the ground we've gained stolen away. There is always the threat of another attack on the abortion law reform front. It's a constant battle, and there never seem to be enough hands, enough time.

Excerpts from *Our Bodies, Ourselves* (Japanese Edition)

PREFACE

Kono Miyoko

The work of revising *Our Bodies, Ourselves* has been both a pleasant and a painful experience. Even while there are social differences between America and Japan, this book elucidates, with great clarity, the various conditions shared by women across the globe — the prejudices and myths associated with the bodies and souls of women and related forms of discrimination. Reading this book, I came to understand that the vague sense of such prejudices and myths experienced by women during routine medical examinations is in no way manufactured by the women themselves, but in fact is socially and historically produced. Working on this book has been a refreshing and pleasing task. I have been struck by the gentleness and compassion of the authors — not just by their warm compassion for those in pain, the destitute who suffer ongoing social discrimination, people of color, and minorities, but also by their open disclosure of the forms of discrimination and their censure of people who discriminate. As a doctor, this work struck me like the blade of a sword. I was led to ask myself, "What have you been doing until now?"

I had been constantly aware during medical examinations that women do not know their own bodies and that they are too all-suffering. For example, there are very few women who are able to clearly name the problem when they experience something abnormal in their sexual organs. There are those who suffer serious bleeding due to a uterine tumor, or the like, but continue to endure until they are faint from blood loss. By the time they finally reach the hospital, they have suffered significant heart damage and yet appear to have learned nothing from the experience. I tell them to learn more about their

Translated with the permission of the authors by Sandra Buckley.

bodies and not to endure so much. However, these situations are in no way the fault of the women themselves. Each individual woman alone cannot hope to confront and overcome the pressures on her to give priority to the day-to-day running of her household over her own well-being. And then there are the taboos that surround a woman looking, touching, and knowing her own sexual body.

This book not only teaches women how to gain more knowledge and self-determination but also strongly encourages networking among women. When women who are suffering can talk together, they realize that the difficulties they endure are not unique, but are shared by other women as well, and they can draw courage from this knowledge. Alone, we are confused, but in our shared power we can find inspiration. As long as Japanese women of all generations share a fear of female sexuality and a complex about their sexual bodies, they will find it extremely difficult to talk about their individual circumstances. Older women continue to have pleasureless sex solely to satisfy their husbands' sexual desire, and younger girls, who cannot even request contraception, still open their bodies to their boyfriends. The same basic things link all these women's lives. What precisely is it that has taught women to live this way? That is what women must talk about together. They need to expand the circle and to talk with women close to them and women of other generations. This is a lesson that *Our Bodies, Ourselves* teaches us very clearly.

I hope this work will be read not only by women but also by men, and most of all by the medical profession — especially by doctors. As I was receiving the text, I often thought, "Well, this will make some doctors spitting mad!" The irate faces of famous doctors decrying the book as malicious floated before me often during the preparation process. To be completely honest, there were some places where I too felt resistance. When I examined these points of resistance closely, I realized that they originated from attitudes I had internalized over years of uncritically pursuing my life as a doctor. Even though it was always my wish to be a conscientious doctor, operating within the present medical system in today's society I found that inevitably frustration, overwork, and self-preservation undermined my best intentions. I must try to be more humble. Working on this project, I came to feel very strongly. This is unmistakably a book for women by women. And it is equally a book for the afflicted by the afflicted. "Let's grow wiser together." "Here's how we'll fight the medical profession together." I think it is important that doctors read this work if only to know it is sending these messages to its readers.

With the conditions for childbirth as they are in Japan, we can expect that women will become an important force in bringing about changes in medical practices—from the concept of birth as "delivery by a doctor" to the concept of "women giving birth for themselves." From a medical practice based on "leaving it up to the doctor" to one of "self-knowledge and informed consent." We doctors tend to treat patients who ask a lot of questions as a nuisance. And yet, if we put ourselves in the patient's shoes, we would consider asking questions to be only natural. We, too, would want to know what is happening to our bodies, and what procedures will be used to achieve a cure. A thorough discussion with an informed patient who has done her research should be a pleasure.

There have been times when speaking with a patient or a pregnant woman that I have wanted to hold my head in my hands. For example, some pregnant woman believe absolutely that they should take no medication whatsoever. They may have a temperature of over 40° centigrade, and yet, despite their understanding of the harmfulness of drugs, they cannot comprehend the harmfulness of a fever. For the baby inside the mother's womb, this is just the same as being left soaking in a hot bath. Even an adult will collapse after an hour in a bath that is too hot. It can be very difficult to get a woman in this situation to understand that medication can be essential in order to discover quickly the cause and bring the fever down. A lack of definitive information is one reason for this ignorance. I have given the problem careful thought. At the same time that women gain a better understanding of their bodies, they should remain flexible in their own thinking. Even those things we believe are good can have their drawbacks when seen from a slightly wider or different perspective.

The American medical profession is hurting these days. With the rapid increase in malpractice suits in that country, the frequency of cesarean sections has increased unbelievably. The individual burden of medical expenses is incomparably high from a Japanese perspective, and they say that access to satisfactory medical care is determined by whether or not one has money. It is also said that Japan is clearly following in America's footsteps. Having completed the revisions for *Our Bodies, Ourselves*, I now hope, with a mixture of anticipation and uncertainty, that we can achieve a new and better medical system through enhanced communication between the doctors who offer medical care and the patients who receive it.

ABOUT THE JAPANESE EDITION
Ogino Miho

The Japanese edition is the product of the faithful translation of the original work. However, the Japanese version of *Our Bodies, Ourselves* has some special characteristics.

   To begin with, there is the problem of language itself. In Japan words that describe the sexual organs frequently incorporate the written characters 恥 (shame, bashfulness, disgrace) and 陰 (negative, shade, secret) with all their negative connotations. We came to resent the fact that these written forms promoted a negative and shameful image of female sexuality and a woman's body and its functions. For example, the word labia has traditionally been written in characters that literally mean "dark [shaded] lips" (陰唇). We replaced the character for dark or secret with the character for sex and renamed the labia "sexual lips" (性唇). Similarly, whereas the vulva had been named the "dark or secret outer organ" (外陰), we renamed it the "outer sexual organ" (外性器). Pubic hair was converted from "shameful hair" to "sexual hair" (性毛), and the pubic bone became the "sexual bone" (性骨) rather than the "shameful bone." These are just a few examples. We supplied the original characters in parenthesis after our positive "reinvention" of the word. However, in the case of the perineum, we were unable to find an alternative designation, and so we retained the traditional form of "dark seam" (会陰) for this edition. We certainly don't consider that the new terms we have developed are the best or necessarily the final forms. But we hope that our reconsideration of the kind of sexual vocabulary that is preferable and comfortable for women to use will offer a useful platform for struggle.

In the case of menstruation, we replaced the euphemistic term designated by the characters for "physiology" (生理), which frequently occurs in medical works written for a female lay audience, with the more straightforward and accurate term "monthly occurrence" (月経). We did all of this in the belief that the first major step toward women's liberation lies in their acceptance of their own bodies as they are and learning to speak out about them openly, without secrecy or whispering. We have translated the word "nurse" using the characters 看護士 (*kangoshi*, person who watches over and cares) rather than 看護婦 (*kangofu*, woman who watches over and cares), because the use of the character for "woman" in the word for "nurse" reinforces the idea that nursing is women's work. This leads to a form of reverse discrimination against men, which we felt can give rise to a range of undesirable effects. (In addition to 士 we considered other gender neutral characters for "person" such as 師, 人, and 者). We have used the gendered form of *kangofu*, however, when the text clearly refers to a past situation that involved only female nurses. We are hopeful that in the future the use of gendered characters to designate the term "nurse" will be reconsidered in the same manner as we described above for words used to describe sexual organs.

In its content, most of what was written in the original book has equal relevance in Japan; however, there are some areas where significant differences exist between the United States and this country. These differences lead to sections that could be difficult for the Japanese reader to comprehend or might easily give rise to misunderstandings. At these places in the text we have inserted a brief explanation of the Japanese circumstances in bold parenthesis or inserted a longer explanatory text in a box placed appropriately in the text. For the lists of food items, we have substituted items that reflect the Japanese context. We very reluctantly gave up the poetry of the English original

TABLE I
SURVEY OF BIRTHING AND ABORTION FACILITIES

	Sekine Obstetrics Clinic	Toho Women's Clinic	Sankyo Hospital
Births			
Lamaze	Yes	Yes	Yes
Delivery options	On back, sitting, other	On back, sitting, other	On back
Labor companions	Husband, family	Husband	Husband, friends
Birth companions	Husband, family	Husband	Husband
Baby in room	Yes	Yes	Yes
Abortion			
Method	D&C, D&E	D&C, D&E	D&C, D&E
Rest period	Admission	Admission	3 hrs–admission[b]
Cost	70,000	70,000	170,000
Method	Curette injection	Not performed	Curette and evaluation
Cost	150,000		300,000–500,000
Prenatal information			
Explanation	Yes	Yes	—
Other present	Husband	None	—
Postnatal information			
Explanation	Yes	Yes	—
Other present	Husband	None	—
Contraception information			
Explanation	Yes	Yes	—
Other present	None	None	—
Advice office	Yes	x[a]	Yes
Women doctors	0	4 (3 part-time)	2

SOURCE: *Our Bodies, Ourselves* (Japan ed.), pp. 572–590.
[a]Data not available.
[b]Rest period from completion of procedure to discharge.

and opted instead to include new sections of the Japanese Eugenics Protection Law and other important problems specific to Japan. In this way we hope that it is possible for the reader not only to learn about conditions in the United States but also to be able to compare them to the Japanese situation as they read and think through issues. Further, AIDS had not become the major problem that it is today at the time the book first appeared in 1984. As a result, the section dealing with AIDS seemed inadequate for the contemporary reader, and we therefore added a section incorporating more recent information.

Toyoshima Obstetrics Clinic	National Medical Hospital	Iwakura Obstetrics and Gynecology Hospital	Tokyo Police Hospital
Yes	x	Yes	
On back, sitting, other	On back	On back, sitting	On back, other
Husband, family, friends	None	None	Husband
Husband, family, friends	None	None	Husband
Yes	x	x	After day 3
D&C	D&C	D&C, D&E	D&C
3 hrs-	Admission	3 hrs-	3 hrs-
80,000	—	40,000	—
Curette	Curette	Curette	Injection medication
120,000–200,000	—	200,000	—
No	Yes	Yes	—
—	None	Husband, children	None
No	Yes	Yes	—
—	No	Husband, children	No
No	Yes	Yes	—
—	None	Husband	None
x	Yes	x	x
0	3	1	0

Last, in the original version there are charts, graphs, lists of American groups and associations, and bibliographic information related to the content of each chapter, which provide a resource for the American reader. We chose to replace these in the Japanese edition with information on the many groups across Japan that are working in areas related to women's health. Whenever possible we have listed relevant groups for each chapter, and in some cases we have also included a description of their activities and contact information. At the end of the volume we have provided a sample bibliography of

TABLE 2

ABORTION PROCEDURES — THE JAPANESE CONTEXT

	Method	Weeks from Last Menstruation	Location of Procedure	Anesthetic	Japanese Case
Suction method	Suction	4–6	Clinic or private practice	None	Pregnancy not verified in Japan before 6th week so method not in use.
Early uterine evacuations	Suction	6–8	Clinic or private practice	None	
Vacuum aspiration[a]	Dilation, suction, and optional curetting	6–11	Clinic or private practice optional	None or local (total optional but rare)	Combines suction & curetting
D&C[a]	Dilation & curetting	6–16	Hospital (clinic and private practice optional but rare)	Local or total	Removal of placenta by forceps optional
D&E[a]	Dilation & evacuation	12; max 16–23	Clinic, private practice, hospital	Local or total	

Induced abortion[b]	The insertion of fluid into the amniotic region via the abdomen. Contractions force expulsion of fetus and placenta	16–23	Hospital	Local anesthetic at time of fluid injection. Painkiller for contractions	Insertion of small inflatable balloon to further stimulate abortion (10–15?)
Prostaglandin[b]	Injection of prostaglandin to stimulate uterine contractions	13?–	Hospital	Painkillers for contraction and expulsion	Used frequently since 1984 in mid-term abortions
Cesarian section[b]	Surgical incision and opening of the womb	16–23, and later in cases of danger to mother's life	Hospital	Total	In rare circumstances only. Expensive

SOURCE: *Our Bodies, Ourselves* (Japan ed.), p. 263.
[a]Used in combination at the discretion of the physician.
[b]Charges for induced abortion are often based on a co-op costing system determined regionally. This leads to regional variation in cost. Public hospitals do not subscribe to such co-op pricing and are therefore generally less.

TABLE 3

STATISTICS RELATED TO HYSTERECTOMY
PROCEDURES IN JAPAN

Hysterectomy procedures in Japan	
Only uterus removed	36.5%
Uterus and both ovaries removed	19.6%
Uterus and one ovary removd	30.7%
Partial uteral extraction	9.7%
Upper vaginal extraction	1.8%
Other	1.7%
Age of woman at time of surgery	
44 years and below	63.3%
45 years and above	35.7%
Unknown	1.0%
Average age at time of surgery	41.6 years

NOTE: The average cost of a hysterectomy without complications with a 14-day hospital stay is approximately 35–40,00 yen. (Health insurance may apply.)

readily available materials published in Japanese. (We have kept an alphabetical list of foreign women's groups at the end of the volume.) As a special feature of the Japanese edition, we undertook a nationwide survey of maternity hospitals and obstetric clinics and included the results in a single comparative chart. We hope this data will be of assistance to women making decisions about abortion and childbirth facilities.

This book is divided into seven sections and twenty-six chapters. It is structured so that one can start reading from any chapter. It can therefore be used as a convenient women's reference book or encyclopedia to answer questions by just opening to the relevant section, whether the question is about contraception, uterine cysts, or menopause. From the young girl anticipating her first menstruation to the aging woman facing the issue of death, women of all generations are represented. In order to make it easier to locate information, we included an index at the back of the volume. However, we would encourage readers to go further than this approach to the book and to allow themselves to be challenged by the less familiar or accessible topics covered; to take time to read Chapters 24 and 26, which ex-

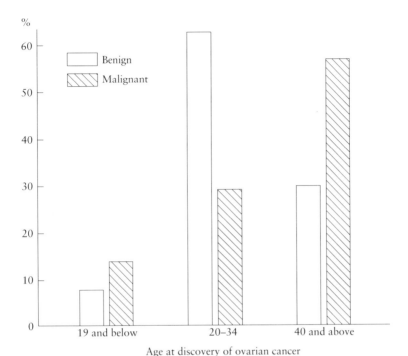

Figure 1.   Ovarian cancer rates in Japan.
SOURCE: Tokyo Mercy Hospital survey (sample of 480 cases of ovarian cancer), in *Our Bodies, Ourselves* (Japan ed.), p. 494.

pand the question of women and medicine into the international fo-rum, Chapter 8 on rape, and Chapter 10 on lesbianism. Doing this will make it much easier to see what kinds of social structures have shaped our sexual awareness and our status as patients and will ex-pose the myriad of attitudes that have deluded us up until now. For me personally, during the period from my first contact with this book until the completion of the translation, I have developed a much greater love for my own body. It is not merely that I have come to know it better but that I feel that I have learned new ways of experi-encing the world differently through my own body. In this sense *Our Bodies, Ourselves* is not just a practical book but in fact a thrilling

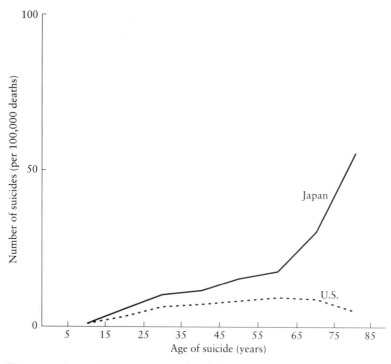

Figure 2.   Japan–U.S. comparative levels for suicides for women according to age.
SOURCE: World Health Statistics Annual, 1986, in *Our Bodies, Ourselves* (Japan ed.), p. 401.

and provocative work that will inevitably change the way of life of the reader.

Throughout the book the first-person plural pronoun appears. This use of the pronoun "we" represents the cooperative writing efforts of the numerous women who worked on the theme of each chapter: for example, the group of middle-aged women who worked on Chapter 22 on aging, the lesbians who revised Chapter 10, and the handicapped women who worked on Chapter 11 on sexuality and the handicapped. The pronoun "we" is also a term of endearment that expresses our affection for all the women readers of this book. It is not the intention of the authors to occupy an elite position as specialists "teaching" the reader but rather to offer an invitation to stand side by

Location of assault

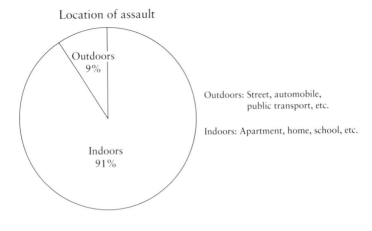

Outdoors
9%

Outdoors: Street, automobile,
public transport, etc.

Indoors: Apartment, home, school, etc.

Indoors
91%

Attacker's relation to victim

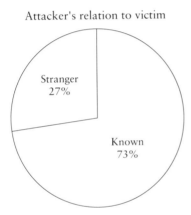

Stranger
27%

Known
73%

Content of calls to rape crisis center
(excludes silent calls)

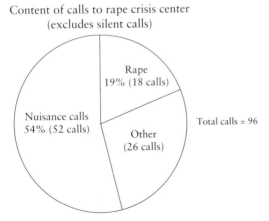

Rape
19% (18 calls)

Nuisance calls
54% (52 calls)

Other
(26 calls)

Total calls = 96

Figure 3. Statistics from calls to Tokyo Rape Crisis Center (March–July 1987), in *Our Bodies, Ourselves* (Japan ed.), p. 104.

side on equal ground and consider the issues together. This is indeed a book by women for women, but I hope that men will read it, too. I definitely want men to hear the sincere messages of the women collected in this volume and to read how we women experience our lives, what women feel, and how all this differs from men's impressions and preoccupations.

Just as the original English edition was the product of a large team of women, so this Japanese version is the result of the solidarity and cooperation of a great number of women. A volunteer team of twenty-three translators and twenty-five editors brought this book to fruition over three years, donating their time and expertise. Fujieda Mioko and Ogino Miho were then responsible for standardization of the style, while Kono Miyoko took responsibility for the medical revisions. Above all, this book is the cooperative labor of this group of almost fifty women. While we used all the graphs and charts exactly as they appear in the English edition, in order to create a sense of familiarity we replaced the original photographs with Japanese images throughout. The photographer Hanabusa Shinzō and many others offered their valuable photos for inclusion in the project. The cover design was the work of Miyasako Chizuru. In addition, there are the people who responded to the survey mentioned above and many others, far too numerous to list, who offered information and support. Through all their efforts this book finally reached fruition. Some of these names are listed at the back of the book, but to all those whose names we couldn't list we want to take one more opportunity to offer our truly heartfelt thanks for lending their hands to the production of this Japanese edition.

One last person who cannot be forgotten is Nakanishi Toyoko of the Shōkadō Women's Bookstore. If it hadn't been for what could be described as the reckless determination and enthusiasm of Nakanishi, who was so committed to bringing out the book no matter what, this network could not have come into being. It is to this woman, who made possible the pleasant experience of shared personal growth and learning as we all worked together on the production of this book, that I offer my final word of thanks.

Selected Texts from Japanese Edition

LESBIANS IN JAPAN

Voices of Japanese Lesbians

I used to live with a man, had children, and held a job. After only having experienced living with a man, I then moved in to live with a woman and discovered to what extent one's sexuality is not just a personal or individual matter. Up until this change there had been a lot of gatherings with other families. People would ask, "How's your husband?" But simply on the basis that my partner is now a woman, the door has slammed shut. There's just total darkness. We're ostracized.

There was a period when I first became a lesbian that I believed I was suffering from some illness. I wondered why I had come to be attracted to women. I realize now that I was forced to think that way about it. Now when I state that I am a lesbian and someone responds by asking, "Why do you like women?" I just ask back, "Why do you like men?" And they can't answer. Why though do I even ask this question? There are conditions under which we live today that we must strive to change regardless of whether one's partner is a man or a woman. It was from the time that I realized this that I made a decision to live my life as a lesbian feminist. It's in my own personal interest, too.

The Present and Future for Lesbians in Japan

In Japan, as in the United States and other countries, the roots of homophobia, prejudice against women, and the distortion of female sexuality run deep. In such an environment how much oppression must be endured by those of us who live our lives as women *and* lesbians? Then again in the face of this very oppression, Japanese lesbians are attempting to live fulfilling lives as women in an independent style, building relationships and living and loving together.

The Japanese Lesbian Community

If we looked at the Japanese lesbian movement, we could identify some of the same situations and conditions as those described by our American sisters in the English edition of this book. In Japan, too, we have lesbian acupuncturists, doctors, and nurses in the medical and health industries. However, because "coming out" can lead to losing one's job, their presence remains largely unknown. Through the lesbian community, at least to some extent, it is gradually becoming possible to speak openly of the existence and status of these women in Japan.

Lesbian Organizations in Japan (pp. 146–48)

(i) Women's Group — Bar and Lodging (Gurūpu Wumenzu Bā Gasshuku)

Our lesbian groups take on the challenge of facing society with the goal of eradicating prejudice and discrimination. One group publishes the poetry and prose of its members. Another focuses on the issue of women's liberation, and still another has developed around the position that our lesbianism takes priority over our identity as women. We are made up of an alliance of diverse elements within the lesbian community. . . .

(ii) Lesbian Group Studio Tokyo (Regumi Sutajio Tōkyō)

With a focus on lesbian liberation, we meet and discuss the possibilities of a way of life for women that incorporates our sexuality. Our basic activities have included the publication of *Regumi tsūshin*, Japan's first lesbian magazine, the running of our organizational office, our regular discussion group, and hiking expeditions. Our membership fee is ¥12,000, and the magazine subscription is ¥5,000. All women are welcome to join us.

Contact: JOKI, Nakazawa Building, 23 Aragi-chō, Shinjuku-ku, Tokyo, 160.

(iii) Lesbian Group Shizuoka (Regumi Shizuoka)

In the provincial areas of Japan there is almost no space available where a lesbian can express herself openly. We are not just pursuing our personal interests and relationships but are seeking to expand the circle of lesbians in order to guarantee that we can acknowledge our sexuality and live our lives to the fullest. Among our activities are the publication of our newsletter *AMIE*, regular meetings, and exchanges with other *minikomi* publication groups. Write us a letter and we'll send you information.

Contact: Regumi Shizuoka, c/o Shizuoka Post Office.

(iv) Sofia Publications (Sofia Shuppan)

We established ourselves as a "circle" and now primarily focus on providing information on activities and meetings in the Kansai* region. Send a self-addressed, stamped envelope and a ¥60 handling fee for information.

Contact: Shijō Nawate Post Office, P.O. Box 20, Nawate, 575.

(v) Gays and Lesbians on the Move (Ugoku Gei to Rezubian no Kai) OCCUR

By bringing gays and lesbians together to support one another, this group aims to eradicate the misunderstandings and prejudices toward homosexuals that are grounded in simple ignorance. Rather than a single shared philosophy or united movement, our goal is for each individual to make his or her own moves. Our membership is open to anyone who shares our approach. Membership is ¥500.

Contact: 4-2-9-13 Chūō, Nakano-ku, Tokyo.

(vi) Hyōkomasha

We publish a journal four times a year that includes essays, criticism, comics, and feminist writings in translation. The annual subscription fee is ¥3,000. We plan to hold regular discussion meetings after the publication of each issue. We welcome all those with an open mind, who do not condone limiting sexuality on the basis of age or gender. Let's promote the pleasure of women madly in love with one another as a new mode of being.

Contact: Takatsu Post Office, P.O. Box 7, Kawasaki-shi

(vii) D.D.

We publish an English newsletter for foreign lesbians living in Japan. Subscription for foreigners is ¥3,500. No fee for Japanese subscribers.

We are presently campaigning for subscriptions. There are still very few bars where a woman can go and pursue her own desires and pleasure with a sense of ease and free of her usual status as a mere sexual object.

Contact: C.T.O. Box 1780, Tokyo, 100-91.

The Lesbian Community in Japan

The lesbian community in Japan functions as a training ground, a place of shared learning. We meet in various groups to discuss issues of concern to lesbians; we sing songs, participate in sports, and hold discos and concerts together. It is nothing short of a celebration of lesbianism. Lesbian weekends are held by different groups across the country in turn. At these weekend gatherings it is possible to meet with many other lesbians, and many participants are able to reaffirm their pride in their identity as women and lesbians during these events.

Lesbian Pride

. . . The lesbian movement is not something that only just got started recently in Japan. In this society, where same-sex love is actively oppressed, it is not widely realized that, even in the past, there was a lesbian community in Japan. Lesbians chose to live their lives beyond the control of men, pioneering the way for women's employment, cutting through the net of patriarchy to build a new value system. Contemporary lesbianism exists within this flow of history, and it is in this stream that we can build our future. We are hopeful that the Japanese edition of *Our Bodies, Ourselves* will play a useful role in the development of resources and materials for all women who love women as well as in the individual growth of each of us.

MIDWIVES IN JAPAN (p. 307)

Midwifery existed in Japan as a recognized profession from the Edo* Period. The Meiji* Period saw the introduction of a law pertaining to midwifery, which specified that those who passed a standard test could practice as midwives.

Today, midwives have a status similar to that of nurses and can practice in either a hospital or clinic after studying for six months to a year in a school of midwifery and passing a national exam.

Information on regional midwifery services can been obtained through local midwives associations or government health offices.

Any woman in childbirth can be cared for by a midwife in a birthing/obstetrics clinic unless there is evidence of deterioration of the placenta, toxemia, posterior and breech presentations, or a known history of birth complications. Healthy patients can in most cases deliver without the intervention of a doctor; but the progress of any pregnancy is unpredictable, and it must be remembered that there is always a 0.5 percent risk of complication.

THE FUJIMI OBSTETRICS CLINICAL SCANDAL AND HYSTERECTOMIES (p. 470)

The 1980 discovery of rampant malpractice and misdiagnosis at the Fujimi Obstetrics and Gynecological Hospital in Saitama Prefecture had a tremendous impact on many Japanese women who had previously placed their bodies uncritically in the hands of doctors and hospitals.

The following is a description of the nature of the scandal. Women who visited the hospital for regular preventive cancer checks, lower abdominal pain, or light bleeding were made to undergo ultrasound testing. Many were then advised by the director of the hospital, who was not qualified as a doctor, to undergo a complete hysterectomy and ovarian section. In addition, these patients were warned that the surgery was needed urgently and, in some cases, that failure to operate would lead to cancer. More than one thousand women underwent unnecessary surgery in this manner.

A later survey found that most of these women had undergone a complete hysterectomy and the removal of both ovaries. The fact that women who had no sign of cancer were frightened into surgery by the improper methods of this hospital is one root of this scandal. These occurrences, however, were related to the lack of information received by the patients about their supposed medical condition and their consequent belief that they, in fact, had no alternative to radical surgery.

The incident created the impetus for a movement to reconsider the procedures at each stage of a hysterectomy from the perspective of the female patient. Even doctors have started to question the practice of removing both the uterus and the ovaries merely on the basis that they are considered to be primarily reproductive organs and to have no "function" once a woman is past child-bearing age.

After this scandal women made a more concerted effort to be informed and access accurate information. The Association for the Reconsideration of Women's Bodies and Medical Practice published the book *The Trouble With Hysterectomies* (Origin Publications Center). We recommend this book for your careful reading.

ABORTION: THE JAPANESE CASE (p. 282)

Although dilation and evacuation is in use as a method of birth control in Japan, curettage is by far the most common procedure. During the first twelve weeks of pregnancy the combination of dilation and curettage is used, and during the second trimester, from twelve to twenty-four weeks, induced miscarriage is frequent. After the eighth month abortion is only allowed in accordance with those exceptions named in the Eugenics Protection Law. It is also worth noting that in the Japanese case up to 90 percent of abortions are performed under total anesthesia administered by intravenous injection.

Although Japan has the reputation for being "abortion heaven," in fact, in contrast to England, France, and Sweden, where abortions are performed under public health care, in Japan abortion is not covered by health insurance and must be paid entirely by the individual. (In the case of natural or induced miscarriage after the first trimester, it is possible, with the appropriate paperwork, to receive coverage for the portion of treatment that can be described as delivery.) A consent form is required prior to abortion in Japan, and this must include the signature and seal of the husband, lover, or parent (in the case of a minor).

The cost of abortion in Japan, including the procedure and medication without hospitalization, is ¥70,000–100,000. In case of a second-trimester abortion, hospitalization is compulsory, and therefore the cost is generally no less than — and possibly even more than — that for a birth (approximately ¥100,000–120,000).

THE EUGENICS PROTECTION LAW (p. 282)

In the climate of general despair and confusion of the immediate postwar years, backyard abortions flourished. In order to control this confusion and avoid population growth, the government introduced the Eugenics Protection Law in 1948. In the next year the Economic Reasons Clause was added, thus technically legalizing and freeing access to abortion. Introduced as a means of population control, this law had an almost magical impact, reducing Japan's birthrate by over half in a period of fifteen years.

However, the element of guilt associated with abortion since the earliest Meiji law remained embedded in the new legislation. "If you get pregnant, give birth. If not, you are guilty of the crime of abortion." This attitude remains at the core of the current law despite the fact that it came into being specifically as a vehicle for legalized abortion under certain designated conditions. The vast majority of abortions are performed under the Economic Reasons Clause, and therefore, should this clause ever be withdrawn, legal abortion would, for all intents and purposes, become inaccessible. This would amount to the total criminalization of the procedure. The right of Japanese women to choose whether to carry a pregnancy to term continues to stand on shaky ground in the context of a national population policy based on the contradictory legal approaches of criminalized abortion and the pro-choice aspects of the Eugenics Protection Law. In a country like Japan, where there are few religious restrictions, safe accessible abortions are in fact a reality. However, Japanese women must not forget that the circumstances under which abortion rights were

220 » Nakanishi Toyoko

attained in Japan are very different from those in Europe and America, where the fight for legalized abortion as a right was achieved through the women's liberation movement. It could also be argued that low-cost abortions contributed to the failure to gain popular support for the legalization of the pill. In the absence of such effective and accessible contraception it remains vital for abortion to continue to be recognized as legal in order to protect women from the dangers of backyard abortions.

WHAT IS THE MOTHER AND CHILD HEALTH PROTECTION LAW? (p. 327)

The current Mother and Child Health Protection Law boasts that it "guarantees and promotes the welfare of mothers and children . . . and aims to contribute to the advancement of the health of the people of the nation." However, if one reinterprets this to reflect historical fact, it could be restated that "the objective is to reinforce the concepts of motherhood and childbirth, and to nurture a population that is wholesome and superior in both body and mind." In other words, this is a population policy, the equivalent of a human resource development strategy. Instated in 1965, when Japan stood at the threshold of rapid economic growth, this law was designed to identify as quickly as possible children with handicaps, screening treatable cases into clinics and those who would never contribute to the workforce into asylums and other institutions. In the late 1970s, from about the time Japan entered a period of reduced economic growth, there was a new concentration on the prevention of handicapped births. The 1972–74 debate over reform to the Eugenics Protection Law (an attempt to include birth defects as grounds for legal abortion) coincided with the introduction of mass screening for hereditary abnormalities and genetic counseling. Procedures were standardized nationwide and included lists of items to be checked in order to achieve a maximum level of developmental monitoring. As a further part of the detailed system of early screening for handicaps that was introduced at this time, a budget allocation for the examination of babies at eighteen months was added to the existing compulsory (1978) checkup of three-year-olds.

THE MOVEMENT TO REFORM THE MOTHER AND CHILD HEALTH PROTECTION LAW (p. 327)

Having learned from the defeat of the campaign to reform the Eugenics Protection Law (by removing the Economic Reasons Clause from the approved conditions for legal abortion), the government introduced a proposal to amend the Mother and Child Health Protection Law under the rubric of "a policy to prevent unwanted pregnancies" (Study of the LDP Eugenics Protection Reform Investigation Committee). The following three items were pillars of the proposed new policy.

1. The compulsory medical examination of pregnant women and the introduction of mother-child health record books;

2. The introduction of a monitoring system for hereditary defects in newborns;

3. The transfer of mother-child welfare from the prefectural to the city, town, or village level and the legal requirement of a checkup for all children at eighteen months.

However, the amendment did not pass, because of the strong resistance of the handicapped and women. The proposal for maternal medical examinations and records threatened to consolidate the social status of women in the realm of "the maternal" and to control and monitor women's bodies and lives from beginning to end. Many women reacted to this with an explosion of anger.

Since April 1987, even after this defeat, there has been a steady move toward the introduction of a system of medical examination and records for mothers and children (including an expanded list of examination items), together with psychological assessment and detailed physical examination for children at eighteen months.

WHO BENEFITS FROM CHILDREN'S HEALTH EXAMINATIONS? (p. 327)

In addition to the compulsory examination of all three-year-olds, comparative development examinations and medical checkups for infants take place today with considerable differences between government agencies across the country and at varying intervals around three–four months, six months, nine months, and eighteen months. The slightest deviation from the norm leads to an entry such as "close observation recommended" on the record card, which is then sent on to other medical institutions and welfare offices.

Who actually benefits from these examinations? It goes without saying that every child follows his or her own individual pattern of growth and development. Even if a child does have a handicap, it shouldn't be interpreted as a potential handicap to the nation and become the basis for determining the entire future of that child. Supervision and selection are not essential to mother-child welfare. The real function of such a system should be to accept each child on his or her own merits, regardless of whether he or she is handicapped, and to broaden, as much as possible, the horizons available to each child. However, at a time when demands on the national budget are being drastically cut, there is no point in hoping for such services. From another perspective, there is a real concern that the increase in the number of independent facilities developing detailed regional or national computerized data bases as a result of recent government policies of rationalization and decentralization will lead to a continued expansion of the potential to develop and implement eugenic-style controls and selection functions.

FROM THE "EXPECTANT AND NURSING MOTHERS POLICY," WHICH NURTURED THE MOTHERS OF A MILITARIST JAPAN, TO THE "MOTHER AND CHILD HEALTH PROTECTION LAW" OF TODAY (p. 327)

The predecessor of the current policy, with its system of mother-child records was the Expectant and Nursing Mothers Policy instigated in

1942. This was important for carrying out the "Plan for the Establishment of a Population Policy," which had been released the preceding year. The plan called for a concrete policy of population growth in order to "plan for the vigorous and lasting development of the Greater East Asia Co-Prosperity Sphere." It asserted that the job of the women on the home front was to bear at least five children. After the war the name was changed to the Mother-Child Hygiene Policy, but the focus on maternal health and the birth and nurturing of wholesome children continued the old policy's recognition of motherhood as the sole role of women. Indeed the same policy base is still reflected in the current Mother and Child Health Protection Law.

The records of the "guardians" of this policy are becoming increasingly detailed as once again there is an attempt to treat the careful examination of the development of our children in the same light as issues of country and government. We want to state most emphatically that this leads to the supervision and control of the nurturing ability and nurturing style of mothers.

THE MONITORING OF HEREDITARY DISABILITIES (p. 327)

Introduced in 1985 as the central issue of a policy reform movement, the hereditary disabilities monitoring system was explained as "an observation of the introduction of abnormal substances into the environment based on indicators of increases in the levels of hereditary disabilities." Stated in more extreme terms, it amounted to a plan to eliminate "imperfections" by checking the handicapped or nonhandicapped status of every child and then enumerating and controlling this information by computer. There is not a single example overseas of the detection of the substances responsible for disabilities through such a system of monitoring births. Even if a specific cause could be identified, it is hard to imagine that this government, which is so implicated in chemical and other environmental pollution, would take action to introduce systems of control or elimination. It is far more likely that the focus will be increasingly on the hereditary and prenatal environment (the smoking, drinking, and other habits of the mother) with consequent increases in maternal education programs aimed at the birth of healthy children, and on various forms of pediatric and genetic counseling. Without exception, all disabled children will be monitored.

THE NATIONAL POLICY OF GENETIC CONTROL AND MASS SCREENING FOR HEREDITARY DISABILITIES (p. 327)

Currently, two or three days after birth a small quantity of blood is taken from an infant's heel. It is collected on filter paper and used for a series of tests for hereditary defects. In the past, taking a blood sample and testing would have occurred only at the request of the parents, but today most institutions practice this procedure without seeking the direct approval of the parents or offering them any information. The rate of testing is now consistently close to 100 percent of all newborns. However, it is questionable whether this testing is really necessary. For example, more than half of the "abnormal" tests recorded relate to one specific blood test routinely carried out in Japan but excluded from mass screening procedures in North America and Europe. There is no evidence that a negative result in this particular test is any indicator of potential problems in later development of the child. Despite such examples of excess, research calling for the inclusion of still more screening tests for newly discovered hereditary conditions continues to make headway. The filter-paper blood samples mentioned above are frequently used to further this research in what amounts to a clear breach of the privacy of the male and female infants tested.

More frightening is the fact that as long as we remain so unconcerned and continue to permit all newborns to undergo this process of mass screening, interested institutions will collect the results on computers and develop improved systems of control and monitoring. If the data from medical records and the monitoring of hereditary disabilities are combined in such a system, and if the present analytical technology takes a further leap forward, it is conceivable that a simple drop of a baby's blood on filter paper could be used to analyze and record DNA. Imagine the eugenics system that might then be devised to control the genetic and physical makeup of the people of this country. I would still like to believe that it remains possible to put a stop to any such scenario.

OCHIAI KEIKO
Author; Owner-Manager, Crayon House, Tokyo

» » » » » » » » » » » »

OCHIAI KEIKO IS THE MANAGER-OWNER of Crayon House, a complex in downtown Tokyo designed as a commercially based educational and recreational center for children and parents. It incorporates a wide range of activities and resources including an auditorium for performances and movie screenings, a children's bookstore, a toy store, a playground, an exhibition area, a women's bookstore and resource center, a weekly market selling organic produce, and a health food family restaurant. Ochiai began her career as a radio personality but eventually left to become a writer. She has published several best-selling novels, and the earnings from her books helped her to realize the Crayon House project. The structure of Crayon House closely reflects Ochiai's own commitment to the need to reinvent the family in Japan if there is to ever be any substantial change in the status of women. As she explains in her interview, the hidden agenda of the children's book- and toy stores is to create an alternative space in downtown Tokyo for women, and for mothers in particular. The annual women's film festival, the feminist bookstore on the third floor, and regular lectures and other offerings focused on women's issues are at the heart of Ochiai's project.

Ochiai's novels consistently deal with controversial issues such as abortion, rape, and extramarital sex. Her first novel to receive wide attention was entitled *The Rape*. The public controversy created by this book constituted a major step toward breaking the silence surrounding the topic of sexual violence against women. The excerpt translated for this volume appears at the beginning of the book and describes the actual attack and the victim's first reactions. The book goes on to explore the humiliation and psychological violence she experiences at the hands of the police and judicial system once she decides to break the silence and report the crime. Both this book and other novels by Ochiai that deal in equally explicit ways with questions of women's sexual identity have received mixed reviews from some feminists. She has been criticized for writing about such serious issues in a style that is clearly aimed at a wide, popular readership. Some have questioned whether the treatment of rape, sexual violence, extramarital sex, lesbianism, and other sensitive issues in such a popular format isn't received by the readership as little more than soft porn. Ochiai and her defenders, of whom there are many, argue that even if some readers who buy her works only for the "dirty bits," this readership is far outweighed by the importance of the ground that is broken by these forays into the previously unspeakable.

Although Ochiai was infuriated by the film version of *The Rape* and finally refused to be associated with the production, as Miya describes in her essay on the subject, she had a far better experience with her book on sexual harassment. This project was written into a highly successful movie script that appeared on prime-time television. In a country where the concept of sexual harassment was still barely recognized outside a narrow circle of feminists, Ochiai's ability to convince a major network to air this television movie was no small achievement. Once again, there was some criticism of the project from feminists concerned that the strong focus on the beauty and striking figure of the female star who played the lead role contradicted the stated goals of the movie and that the results trivialized a chronic problem in the workplace. But even though perhaps the project popularized or trivialized sexual harassment in the eyes of people who were already aware of the extent and nature of the problem, it did much to open up the issue to a far wider section of the general public than could have been achieved by any other means in such a brief period of time. Ochiai insisted that the movie be firmly grounded in the reality of the politics of harassment by the addition of a series of short interviews with feminists on the topic of antiharassment legislation. These were incorporated into the final stage of the movie.

In her management of Crayon House, the writing of her books, and her dealings with the publishers and the media, Ochiai is always concerned with the politics of power and gender. Until recently there were no men employed at Crayon House, but in response to group decisions within the organization, the first men have now been recruited. Ochiai makes no secret of her frustration with the constant discrimination against women in the media industry. She has won some major battles and lost others in her fight to use the mainstream media as a vehicle for opening up debate on key issues relating to female sexuality and violence in Japanese society. Her preferred strategy is to take advantage of the mainstream media while doing all possible to minimize the compromises necessary to win cooperation. Ochiai has described herself as a realist, in that she recognizes that she cannot do away with the present market system or the monopoly of the media industry on information flow, but that she can develop strategies that enable her to work these systems in ways that support a feminist agenda. There is no doubt that Ochiai's own writing will continue to attract controversy, and there is equally no doubt that she will confront each controversy head on and then move on to the next.

Interview (with Uchida Junko)

SB: Crayon House is a book- and toy store for children?

OK: Yes, but it's also much more than that. There is a lot of space for the children to play safely outside, a restaurant, a theater complex, and an exhibition area. In my own mind this space is as much for parents as it is for children. When I first wanted to put this complex together, I was most concerned with creating a space for women, but the simple truth is that no one was interested in financing such a venture. I could, however, muster enthusiasm for this project. It's ironic, but maybe not surpising, that people place the priority on children's needs rather than those of women, and among women it is mothers' needs that come first. In any case, I have done my best when designing and developing the complex to ensure that areas such as the theater and exhibition area are multi-functional. For example, the theater has been used for puppet shows for children and a festival of women's film. At the moment the exhibition area is being used for a display of art by a well-known illustrator of children's books, and it is also the site of the Japanese Women's Book Fair.

SB: *In addition to running Crayon House, you also write novels, keep a busy lecture schedule, and help coordinate various other projects such as the publication of the magazines* Kodomo *(Children) and* Ongaku Hiroba *(Music Plaza).*

OK: My friends are always teasing me that I am constantly running and never have time to slow down. Maybe that's why I can eat so much and never get fat! It's no coincidence that I built a restaurant into the complex.

Seriously, I do a lot of what I do to try and keep financially afloat. Every month there's an economic crisis. The store's sales alone are just not enough to support a project of this size. I put everything I have into keeping Crayon House going. It is not easy for a woman to find external funding and loans in Japan, especially for an enterprise of this sort.

SB: *How many employees do you have?*

OK: About fifty altogether, and that amounts to a lot of responsibility. Only two of the staff are men. Initially there was a conscious policy of hiring women, but now we are trying to employ some more men when positions come up. It's difficult finding a balance between the desire to create women's jobs and the desire to encourage men to become more involved in areas traditionally designated as "women's work."

SB: *Are you comfortable with your role as manager?*

OK: As the number of employees has grown, I've become more conscious of my role. I try and avoid handing down policy decisions. When decisions are made, everyone is encouraged to participate in the process. Through these group decisions a policy is emerging that is very flexible and yet surprisingly cohesive. I suppose it's not an accident that, as we've hired, we've gathered together a group of people who share a lot of the same values and attitudes.

SB: *Is there any specific policy or set of guidelines relating to the types of books and toys you stock?*

OK: I'm personally not in favor of censorship and feel uncomfortable with the idea of a bookstore or toy shop that screens out whole lines. Different children and different parents have the right to choose for themselves what they will and won't buy. Having said that, however, I think that if you look around Crayon House you won't find a lot of material that could be considered prejudiced or discriminatory, so I suppose that even without any guidelines the staff preferences are reflected in the ordering. We bring out a monthly announcement of what will be purchased, but only after everyone who wants to has had input. More often than not, the staff members know more about a given issue than I possibly can because it is their specialization or they have the hands-on experience with the customers or suppliers. I know that feminists are concerned about women developing alternative structures of leadership, but for me personally the very concept of "leading" is an impossible one. I try to avoid taking on or being put into the "boss" role as much as I can. I see all the people at Crayon House as people I work with rather than people who work for me. The one time this isn't the case of course is when it comes to payday. Then the responsibility is mine to make sure there are enough funds for salaries, and I feel that responsibility very deeply.

SB: *Who are your customers at Crayon House?*

OK: Primarily middle and junior high school girls and mothers shopping with children, but the last couple of years has seen a growing number of fathers coming in, either alone with their children or as a family. I hope this trend continues as it represents some long overdue changes within the Japanese family. We try to create an environment that is just as open to fathers as it is to mothers.

SB: *What motivated you to take on a project of this size?*

OK: Once the planning began, it was clear that a bookstore alone was not enough. What was needed was a space that would allow children to come into contact with stimuli ranging from words to images and sound. The intention from the outset was a multimedia space. Children today are profoundly influenced by the commercial media. Crayon House aims to create an alternative environment where children can experiment with and explore both their own imaginations and the various media themselves. The idea is not to provide either an educational or an entertainment package for the children but to give them the freedom to create for themselves. Wherever possible, we try to make this an experience that can be shared with the rest of the family as well.

SB: *I believe you've written books for children in addition to your novels.*

OK: Yes, I've written two books for children and translated one work from English.

SB: *And then there are the two magazines* Kodomo *and* Ongaku Hiroba.

OK: These are both written for parents but include material of interest to children as well. We try to publish a lot of ideas and materials to help parents explore ways of playing with their children and alternative approaches to educational play. We also include articles on issues related to parenting.

SB: *Your own novels are extremely popular. You seem to be constantly breaking new ground and defying traditional taboos about what is appropriate content for the mass market, for example, your treatment of sexual violence in* The Rape *or female sexuality in* Single Girls.

OK: I think the women who read my novels recognize how difficult some of these things are to write about for a woman and are exploring for themselves in the act of reading as much as I am in the act of writing. On the whole, however, I think men approach my novels very differently. Either they consider them books that only women who hate men would read, or they buy them and read them at a totally different level. I have no control over this. I know that some criticize my novels as sensationalist. All I can answer is that I know my own intent as the author. I cannot prevent people from buying my novel and placing the emphasis where they prefer.

Even dealing with publishers can be difficult. Most of the people in the industry are men, and they are interested in publishing my work only if they think it will sell. They do everything they can in the way they package and market my novels to guarantee sales. A good example is *The Rape*. I had initially written it with the title *Gōkan*, the Japanese word for rape, but they rejected this. I had deliberately chosen not to use the Japananized version of the English, *rēpu*. This word often comes up in romance fiction and television dramas, but the girl usually falls in love with the rapist, discovers her sexual desire through the experience, or some other equally outrageous thing. I wanted to use the Japanese word *gōkan* because it carries all the weight of the reality of rape. I finally gave in and let them use the softer word *rēpu*.

I'd seen various books dealing with rape in the West, both fiction and academic, but there was nothing in Japan. From a very young age I had been aware that within this culture there is a constant denial of the freedom and self-determination of women. I realize this is not a situation unique to Japan, but I do believe that there is much in the nature of gender relations in this country that creates a far more pervasive level of oppression. The forms of this oppression are so diffused across the entire fabric of daily life that they are rendered almost invisible, and this invisibility makes them that much more difficult to articulate and overcome. Rape is the most extreme expression of what women experience in their daily lives. I think it is a good place to begin to try to articulate this condition.

SB: Has there been any change in attitudes toward rape in Japan? The fact that a book focusing on rape could sell so well suggests that something has shifted in the last ten years or so.

OK: I think most women still think that rape won't happen to them and the majority of men think that only certain kinds of women get raped. Rape, however, is a crime against all women; it doesn't have to be experienced to be a personal issue. I think sexual harassment is another issue of which there is a very low public awareness in Japan.

Part of the problem is that once you extend the concept of sexual harassment beyond overt physical harassment to include psychological harassment on the basis of gender, and even innuendo, then you are dealing with the very fabric of Japanese society. We are talking about redefining what is considered "normal" behavior as harassment. You're working on the pornographic comicbooks so you must have a sense of the level of public tolerance. These comicbooks are so much a part of our environment that it's not even a question of tolerance. The "oddball" is the person who is offended by these images on a train or bus, not the person reading the comicbook.

SB: In the late 1970s and early 1980s, there was a problem with the chikan *(perverts) on crowded subways.*

OK: Yes that's another good example. Women tolerated being pinched and manhandled on crowded trains for years. It's also a good example of how opinion can be altered. Once a campaign was started, things changed quickly. The issue is awareness. That's why I was prepared to change the title of my book to *Rēpu* in order to get it published and strike some sort of blow at the taboo against any public mention of rape. Attitudes are shifting slowly. Now we have the Rape Crisis Center in Tokyo. Recently, a group of feminists arranged the showing of a Canadian film dealing with sexual violence, and this drew a lot of attention to the issue. We were very happy with the response to the film. Rape, incest, abortion, there are still too many taboos in place. Women are just beginning to learn to speak their own experience without fear of the consequences. The wheels are in motion, but we are nowhere near achieving the major changes that are needed. The more books and films dealing with these issues, the quicker the resistance will break down.

SB: You are also involved in filmmaking, aren't you?

OK: Yes. I mentioned earlier that we ran a festival of women's films here at Crayon House. I work very closely with Uchida Junko, of the Women's Film and Resource Center. Our long-term goal is to promote women film and video makers in Japan, but we are also trying to provide a forum for viewing foreign women's films. Uchida-*san* keeps us informed of what films are available and worth showing, and we try to run them as often as possible in our theater. We can only seat a hundred people, so the viewings are small; but the enthusiasm for these films is amazing. As for filmmaking, the biggest problem is funding. The Japanese government does not support women filmmakers in the way that, say, the Canadian government does. We arranged for Gail Singer to come to Japan from Canada and tour with her film *Abortion North and South*, and while she was here we talked a lot about the Canadian situation. We were astounded at the level of support the government gives to women in film and video. I still don't think there is a wide enough awareness of feminism in Japan. It's true that the United Nations Decade of the Woman got a lot of attention in this country and led to some public discussion of key issues, but much of this seems to have been mere lip service. The new Equal Employment Opportunity Law is a case in point. A law with no teeth. I also think that the government doesn't have a good enough sense of what is going on in the arts outside Japan. It continues to support the traditional arts but ignores the contemporary art world.

SB: You went to an international festival of women's video in Quebec a couple of years ago . . .

Uchida Junko: I came back both excited and frustrated. Excited at the wealth of video material I had seen, and frustrated at the lack of funds to support similar projects in Japan. I think one option for us is to pursue joint projects with foreign video and filmmakers here in Japan. We're looking at every possible alternative. Whenever an overseas feminist comes to talk or visit at Crayon House, we try to record parts of the visit on video with the dual aims of compiling an information resource and of eventually editing the material down into a video for public showing. The Women's Film and Resource Center is experimenting with video within the limits of its resources. The small number of independent video makers in Japan also tend to be independently wealthy. I think we all are concerned about the content and quality of some of the work that has been taken up in international festivals to represent Japanese women in film or video, but until we can get alternative projects off the ground there's not much we can say or do.

SB: *The Resource Center is also producing quite a lot of printed materials.*

UJ: Yes. We've begun printing a feminist calendar each year and have also produced feminist diaries, posters, and postcards. On the film front we are publishing *Women's Media*. This is a magazine aimed at introducing and critiquing foreign films available in Japan that are either by or about women. It's a valuable resource for anyone interested in women and film. We're also working to create a video library for women. Then, as you saw when you visited, we keep a range of women's books for sale. We aren't well enough staffed at this point to be able to publish a catalogue, but women know that we have a good stock of up-to-date publications and will often come to us rather than go through the inconvenience of trying to track down feminist materials in major bookstores. We would like to expand our book stock; but at the moment the biggest constraint is space, so we will have to be satisfied for now with maintaining this as just one of a range of services.

SB: *Coming back to film for a moment . . . While there certainly isn't an equal representation of women and men in mainstream cinema in Europe and America, there are some women who have successfully established their reputations — Margarethe Von Trotta, for example. Why are women so noticeably absent in Japan's film industry?*

UJ: One reason is the master-disciple system of patronage operating within the industry. There's no room within such a system for young women. You have to understand that the young up-and-coming directors are no better than servants and have to provide for their pater's every need. The system involves a total devotion of time and energy that many women are simply not in a position to make. Often the only reason the men can make this commitment is because they have a woman — wife or mother — playing the servant role in relation to them. The whole thing is insidious, and women are probably better out of it.

Many young directors start out their careers making pornographic films for the subsidiaries of the big movie houses. This again is not an area that a young female director is going to gain easy access to, or find attractive. The few independents have all but disappeared in the wake of the big name movie houses. We have internationally renowned filmmakers, there's no question about that. There are Imamura, Ōshima, and Kurosawa. Whether one would call their films art is another matter. Even if I was to agree that they are art, I would have to add the qualification that they are male art.

SB: Ōshima's In the Realm of the Senses *has received a great deal of critical acclaim in the West even among feminists. How do you react to this foreign reception of a film many Japanese feminists rejected outright.*

UJ: Perhaps it's a problem of context. Could it be that the very "Japaneseness" of the movie is a factor here. It's my sense that a lot of poor-quality Japanese cinema is treated as art outside Japan because of its "exoticism." Kurosawa's latest movies would seem a good example.

Ōshima is a misogynist. I don't understand how anyone can see *In the Realm of the Senses* and not be convinced of it. The radical portrayal of male and female bodies and sex doesn't make for a feminist film. This is the same as the old confusion of sexual liberation and women's liberation. Like all Japanese cinema, Ōshima's movies are about cinematic representations of male desire and fantasy. The fantasy may extend to a strong and desiring female or even castration, but the point of origin of the desire and fears played out on the screen remains masculine. Ōshima's movies are disturbing but not disruptive. Disruption is something quite different, something that we have not even begun to come close to yet in Japanese cinema. It's no secret that Ōshima made pornographic films in the early days of his career, and even until quite recently he was actively involved in late-night pornographic talk shows.

SB: Ochiai-san, has there been any talk of making another of your novels into a film?

OK: I'd be very wary of any such project. Having worked extensively in the media, I'm all too aware of what can happen to a book or play when it's handed over to male directors and producers. I think you're translating a piece by Miya Yoshiko for this book that is her critique of the film version of *The Rape*.

SB: Yes, that's right.
    Could you talk about your radio work? Did you encounter similar gender issues in that environment?

OK: I first became known through my work as a radio compere in the 1970s, but I quit more than ten years ago to explore other options, in particular my writing. Just two years ago, however, I started up a radio program again. This time the program focuses exclusively on women's issues. It's a weekly two-and-a-half hour slot on Mondays. It's called *Hold On, Monday* (*Chotto matte Mandai*). It's a pun on the English and Japanese pronunciations of *Monday* and *Mondai* (problem) — Hold On, Man. We talk about anything we want, no matter how controversial. My policy is to say what we can while we can and not to worry about losing the program until a crisis actually occurs. We combine music and talk. Most of the music is by female performers, and whenever possible we try to chose songs that deal with women's issues. We end up playing a lot of 1960s and 1970s American female vocalists. It's not that we don't want to play more recent music, but we have trouble finding newer material that has any serious political dimension. I just received a CD of Tracy Chap-

man from one supplier, and I have to say she's a breath of fresh air.
The songs are well written, not easy listening, but they amount to
more than bubble and fluff. There's a lot of resistance to our content
from within the station, but that's all the more reason to go on with
it. I think the most difficult thing for me is dealing with male colleagues in the studio. What comes across so strongly is how totally
different our perception of the world we live in can be, and how different our priorities are. We're left with a huge communication gap
that keeps threatening to undermine the program. I started out with
a support staff of five women, but now with a series of changes I'm
down to two men. It's not easy, but I keep trying. I'd hoped that if we
could keep the program going this long, it would have a flow-on effect, and we'd get more women's programming or even a women's
station; but that hasn't happened.

*SB: Are you working on another novel in the midst of all the rest of
your commitments?*

OK: I have a novel I have been piecing together in my mind for some
years, but now I am determined to write it up. It will be difficult,
however, as it's closely tied to my own working through of my identity as a woman and a feminist. It's very personal in that sense and
therefore that much more difficult to articulate. Feminism is a personal thing to me. It's a term I apply to my own experience and goals
as much as to any cohesive group of politically motivated individuals. The book is about the tension between feminism as theory and
feminism as a part of the person I am. I try to live my life in ways that
allow me to stay close to the feminist movement, but there are times
when I am drawn away from this position to follow directions that
are no less my own. I believe that it is these sudden departures in un-
predicted directions which take me onto new, fertile ground where I
grow in ways I couldn't otherwise. I think of them as points of departure. The feminist I was five years ago, am today, and will be five
years from now are all different. My feminism is evolving with each
new departure. The novel will be an attempt to describe all of this. It
is not strictly autobiographical, but traces of me are there in both the

male and female characters. As I write, I am increasingly aware that there is an imperceptible and yet constant erasure of the distance between the male and female characters. I'm not sure where this novel is taking me, but it's very different from anything else I've written.

I think that what I imagine when I imagine change is not a great upheaval but rather a gradual shifting, the opening up of fine cracks, the opening up of new possibilities, new ways of being, new ways of seeing.

The Rape (Chapter 1)

Yahagi Michiko remembered that terrible pain in her left hand. The cigarette she now held had burned down almost all the way to the filter tip and was searing the skin at the first joint of her index and middle fingers. Just as she realized what was happening, the long ash fell. It hit her knee and dissolved into powder. Michiko crushed the cigarette into the ashtray. Even after the butt was out, she continued to stub relentlessly.

"I can't stand it," the words slipped from her lips. "I can't stand it, I can't stand it." Michiko bit down on her back teeth and looked up at the ceiling, as if by doing this she could erase the image she so wanted to be rid of. The louder the sound she made, the harder she bit down.

"I'm looking at a bizarre dream," she thought to herself. A man with a twisted expression stood astride her, staring down at her body. For an instant it seemed that behind the black lenses of the sunglasses, the man's eyes laughed. He put his hands on his belt. He leaves them there a long time, perhaps because he's holding himself back or perhaps because he's shaking. Finally, after a lot of noisy fumbling with the buckle, he takes the belt off and pulls his trousers down to his knees. Then he straddled Michiko's body.

It was at this moment that Michiko grasped what was happening. It wasn't a dream. The man from the car that followed Michiko home

Translated with the permission of the author by Sandra Buckley.

now stood almost naked over her. He attacked her. He was trying to penetrate her.

"Please don't," she screamed, but no sound came. Her voice was trapped in her throat, and she could make no noise. Michiko knocked away the hand stretching toward her face. The hand she struck out with hit the face of the man, and his glasses flew off. A bloodshot light ran across the man's narrow eyes. He struck her on both cheeks with a terrible force.

"I'll be killed . . . If I resist him, I'll be killed." The terror ran through her body, and for an instant she faltered. He grabbed at the opportunity with staggering power and agility. He bound Michiko's wrists with his belt and pulled her arms up over her head. And then he pulled off his underpants. Her glance was arrested by his penis, now a weapon.

"Don't, don't, please don't," she cried out, but no sound came.

Michiko brought her bound hands down hard upon the man's head again and again and flailed her legs. As she hit and kicked at him, he forced his way into her. She felt a sharp cramplike pain. He penetrated her, then laughed silently. He went into a frenzied action on top of her. It was her own body, and yet somehow she felt nothing. She knew what was being done to her body, but she just stared out into the empty space beyond the man's head.

In that space Michiko could see a field of tall grass. She imagined her own body lying there in the field, dead and naked from the waist down. The person here is not me. It's someone else. This can't be me . . . She made a futile effort to convince herself. Let this be a dream, she begged, but the sharp sensation of nausea that rose within her was the harsh proof that she was awake and all this was real.

The man breathed violently as he relentlessly thrust his weapon into her body. How many times did she hear that male voice repeat the same word over and over, "Shit." How long did it last. It felt like five minutes. It felt like an hour. At last the man let out a strange groan and collapsed on top of her. Still lying where she'd been thrown to the ground, Michiko vomited up a sharp-tasting fluid from the pit of her stomach.

"I'm done." It was the first time she'd heard the man say anything else. He sounded a little hoarse, but there was a trace of childishness lingering there in his voice. Having lost its energy, the man's weapon hung wet and shining. He looked down at her as he dressed. "Was it good?" he said. Michiko's whole body was overcome with a violent trembling. His words became another terrible weapon and tore into her. Once again a foul fluid welled up in her mouth. It ran down her chin and around the nape of her neck. The man picked his glasses up from the grass, put them on, undid the belt that had bound Michiko's wrists, and left.

After some time Michiko lifted herself up. The underpants and skirt that had been torn from her lay scattered, vividly white, at her feet. In the midst of her confusion, she recognized that this was the vacant lot near the high-rise apartments. The grass in the place where she had been knocked down by the man was crushed mercilessly. A stray dog that strolled aimlessly out of the grass took fright at Michiko and ran away.

The dull pain of the attack lingered in the pit of her stomach. Things she didn't want to remember kept coming back to her like an endlessly repeating tape, overwhelming her. She thought she'd go mad each time she recalled his question, "Was it good?"

"Don't. Don't."

The memories always had a dreamlike quality in the beginning but quickly became real, pushing Michiko over into the abyss. It was too dreadful to be a nightmare and too cruel to be real.

Michiko lit another cigarette and stared at the back of her left wrist. The veins ran in faint blue lines. A deep cut with a knife would be all it would take to put everything to rest. She could put an end to this broken body, these broken senses. Instead of a knife, it was the cigarette that Michiko stabbed into her wrist. The soft skin smarted under the heat. Heat turned quickly to pain and penetrated her entire body. Not until a dark red blister started to swell did she lift off the cigarette from the skin. The blackened skin embodied Michiko's pain.

Michiko realized that the shaking and nausea were passing. She sat perfectly straight in the middle of the room and looked slowly around her. This is her room. This is her own room, the room that had afforded her the freedom of living alone, the room that had allowed a twenty-eight-year-old woman just the right amount of solitary space and time. Nothing in the room has changed. It is just the same as it was when she left for work yesterday morning. The disruption is within Michiko herself. "I was raped!"

The word *rape* burned into her being. Like ocean waves rushing to the shoreline, humiliation rose and flowed from somewhere deep within her, washing over her consciousness. It swallowed her up and threw her into confusion. Michiko felt the twenty-eight years of her life crushed and scattered in the wake of this wave of humiliation.

She listened to the voices within her. Each of them spoke for one more part of her.

"Just put it down to bad luck and forget about it."

"Be glad that you weren't killed."

"You should be able to forget."

"Some day you will forget."

"You should be able to pretend you've forgotten."

Michiko leaned her throbbing temples against her knees where she sat and glanced in the direction the voices seemed to come from. Even if she couldn't forget, she might be able to pretend that she had. "Was it good?" That vicious voice returned, mercilessly tearing apart her thoughts. With her hands pressed to her ears to block the sound of the man's voice, Michiko felt compelled to examine again her own emotions.

There was no shadow of strangeness or sadness over her heart. And her fear was dissipating. Only hatred and humiliation remained. Presently, Michiko began to notice yet another emotion raising its head beyond the humiliation so deeply imprinted in her being. It was hazy and still had not taken on any recognizable form. Michiko bit down with her front teeth on her bottom lip and sat motionless, staring into the haze. The haze pushed aside the humiliation that had taken possession of her heart and began to mass into a single form. Anger. It was anger.

The severe heat of humiliation had called up the harsh coldness of anger. And that anger set a cold flame to Michiko's heart. In a moment it had consumed her whole body. Spurred on by the flame, she tore off all her clothing. The linen jacket: unnaturally wrinkled and stained with dirt and summer grass. The skirt, the zipper at the waist broken. The blouse, two buttons torn off. The brassiere, one strap ripped away. Stockings, flesh showing through the tear at the knee. Underpants, shredded into a pitiful shape. Now naked, she trampled them all.

Michiko picked up the scissors. She crouched in the middle of the room and cut to shreds the clothing she had worn till no trace remained of their original form. As she cut, she watched her own madness. "If you're going to go mad, go really mad." She kept cutting as she told herself how much easier it would be if she went completely mad. Countless shreds of cloth lay scattered on the floor. For a while Michiko just sat and stared at them.

And then she went to the bathroom and poured buckets of cold water over herself, one after the other. Michiko filled the bucket as many times again and washed and washed her body. No matter how much she washed, the shame didn't fade. Michiko kept washing. Only when she wrapped a fresh towel around her numb flesh did the sobbing vent itself.

Not out of sadness but out of anger, she granted herself the soothing flow of these tears.

Selected Works

Anata no niwa de wa asobanai (I Don't Wanna Play in Your Garden). Kodansha, 1992.

Babara ga utatte iru (Barbara is Singing). Asahi Shinbunsha, 1990.

Gūzen no kazoku (Coincidental Family). Chūō Kōronsha, 1991.

Kekkon ijō (More than Marriage). Chūō Kōronsha, 1985.

Kureyon Hausu monogatari (The Story of Crayon House). Tokuma Shobō, 1992.

Kūru byutei ni yoroshiku (Remember Me to the Cool Beauty). Chūō Kōronsha, 1992.

Natsukusa no onna-tachi (Women of the Summer Grasses). Kodansha, 1987.

Onna to otoko (Women and Men). Mainichi Shinbunsha, 1991.
Rabāzu . . . koibito-tachi (Lovers). Magazine House, 1993.
Sekando kamingu (Second Coming). Shinchōsha, 1992.
Supaisu no yukue (Where Has Spice Gone?). Yomiuri Shinbunsha, 1992.
Supaisu no yuwaku (The Seduction of Spice). Yomiuri Shinbunsha, 1992.
Taikutsu na heddo (Boring Head). Bungei Shunjūsha, 1992.
Watashi o ikiru (Living as I Am). Kairyūsha, 1993.
Za rēpu (The Rape). Kodansha, 1985.

SAITŌ CHIYO
Founding Editor, Agora

» » » » » · » » » » » » »

SAITŌ CHIYO IS BEST KNOWN as the founding editor of the Japanese feminist journal *Agora*. Although she has now stepped down from her editorial position, she remains a central figure in the *Agora* cooperative, which keeps alive the longest running feminist journal in postwar Japan. *Agora* was one of several major feminist journals to appear in the 1970s, but the others, including *Feminisuto* and *Onna Erosu* (Women Eros), have since folded. Saitō sees *Agora* as distinct from the *minikomi* network and very different in its goals. In her opinion, the intensely personal voices and issues that characterize the *minikomi* are both its strength and its weakness. The standard publication format for *Agora* is the special focus issue developed around a specific theme.

Whether the focus is Japan's Equal Employment Opportunity Law, illegal Filipino women workers, the Gulf War, or female sexuality, every effort is made to develop the theme in ways that foreground both the local and global dimensions of the issues and the connections between the two. A major objective of the journal is to publish information that its readers may otherwise not have access to. This flow of alternative information is rare in Japan, as Aoki Yayoi points out in her discussion of the media. *Agora* has also always represented the whole spectrum of feminist voices in Japan. An unknown grass-roots activist may be published side by side with a well-known feminist theorist, and the journal is dedicated to promoting this diversity in the editorial process. Although *Agora* has faced difficult financial times over the last several years, it has managed so far to survive with occasional appeals for additional support from subscribers. The *Agora* offices in Shinjuku also function as a resource and meeting space for women. A small curtain divides off a space at the rear of the large one-room office, and women can come to this space for therapeutic massages, individual counseling, a social chat, or a private English class. Foreign-language courses at affordable rates are held regularly in the offices. There is never a shortage of hospitality or tea for anyone who drops in.

In the 1960s Saitō founded the Bank of Creativity. This was a resource organization that assisted women who had left the workforce to raise children, to retrain themselves and identify prospective jobs. Earlier Saitō had joined forces with other housewives in her neighborhood of Tokyo to form a childcare network. She was frustrated by both ventures and finally decided that these community-based initiatives could only create short-term remedies to specific local problems and could not effect significant structural change. It was on this basis that she decided to found *Agora*, in the hope that a journal devoted to feminist publishing might offer a forum for the expansion of a feminist platform in Japan. Some critics of *Agora* suggest that its editorial policies and priorities are grounded in the politics of the 1960s and 1970s and that there is a need to rethink the viability of the radical strategies of that period of the women's movement in the climate of the 1990s. Saitō for her part rejects suggestions that the strong focus on such issues as war, peace, disarmament, nuclear energy are "dated" or no longer relevant. She sees the recent public furor over the proposal to mobilize Japanese Self-Defense Forces as part of U.N. overseas peace-keeping missions as proof of the ongoing need to sustain a feminist critique of the defense debates in Japan. From this perspective *Agora* plays a key role in maintaining awareness among feminists of the continuous threat of conservative reform in the areas of defense and national security. It is this trend toward a gradual accumulation of conservative legal reforms that also concerns Kanazumi Fumiko in her work as a lawyer and feminist activist.

The pages of *Agora* are open to the voices of the distressed mother of a young man about to be sent to Cambodia on peace-keeping duty; an academic feminist developing an economic argument around the budgetary implications of any increase in the role of Japan's Self-Defense Forces; or a lawyer arguing the fine points of the Peace Article of the Japanese Constitution. This nonhierarchical layering of diverse voices constructs a cohesive site of opposition. The level of attention and pressure the journal has experienced from various government agencies and the police certainly suggests that its activities are seen as potentially disruptive. Saitō is bothered by this pressure but also takes it as a sign that the group is achieving its objective of posing a serious feminist challenge to the dominant structures of power in Japan. With the continued commitment and efforts of the cooperative and its supporters, there is no sign that *Agora* will cease to be a significant landmark on the map of contemporary Japanese feminism in the foreseeable future. The journal's continuing role in the constant redefinition of feminism in Japan is testimony to the political and emotional strength and vitality of its founder, Saitō Chiyo.

Interview

SB: When did Agora *first begin publication?*

SC: In February 1972.

SB: The other two major feminist journals were Feministo *and* Onna Erosu, *but both of these have folded. How is it that* Agora *has managed to survive where the others could not?*

SC: I think we had more people directly involved in the journal from day one. There were a lot of people encouraging us to stick with it. It was also significant that both *Erosu* and *Feministo* had a quite specific focus whereas *Agora* has always aimed at offering a voice to the whole spectrum of women as well as gathering and publishing relevant materials. If *Agora* should ever fold, I think it would be a sign that feminism had run its course here in Japan. The day when Japanese women will no longer have the need of a feminist movement is still far away; there is still a lot of ground to cover.

And so we struggle to stay afloat. We almost had to shut down recently despite the fact that we were all contributing from our own pockets to keep things going. When the word got out, our readers and supporters raised ¥1,000,000 in funds for the journal. We decided to go on as best we could. We're still publishing every month but in a slightly reduced format.

SB: You've been involved in the women's movement for many years. What changes have you noticed?

SC: I first became involved in women's issues when I joined the AMPO movement in 1960, so that's some thirty years now. I think that feminism reached a new peak of activity in the mid-1980s, especially when contrasted with the early 1960s. My concern is whether it has passed its peak and gone into decline. Japanese women seem to be very content these days.

SB: Does this contentedness contribute to the recent neo-conservatism among women?

SC: Indeed. It's a major factor in the repeated electoral successes of the conservatives. They're actually getting stronger, not weaker. The problem lies with the new-found prosperity of the middle class. There is a considerable group of women now who have no desire to work outside the home, who can live comfortably on their husband's salary, and who, once their children have reached school age, have extensive leisure time. Why should they want to work and give up this way of life? Some people go so far as to argue that their husbands have the worst of it. There is no doubt that this prosperous "leisured" class of women is contributing to a new conservative political wave in Japan.

SB: *And where does Japanese feminism stand in the wake of this new conservative wave?*

SC: It comes back to the question of whether Japanese feminism has passed its peak. I don't know where we go from here. I only hope that the movement can muster enough energy to counter the recent trends. I think the movement as a whole is under tremendous pressure to come up with some effective response. We can expect an increasing number of challenges to the Constitution as conservative political interests in Japan continue to expand their influence. The conservative legal reform campaigns we anticipate will have far-reaching implications for Japanese women. We are sure to face another attempt to withdraw the right to legal abortions, for example. And then there is the issue of the military and defense spending, not to mention issues of nationality, illegal immigrant workers, and so on.

Then there is the infamous National Security Act. For the first time since the 1960 AMPO crisis, the political climate has shifted far enough to the right that the government can contemplate reintroducing reforms it was previously forced to abandon. It's not that long ago that the police finally stopped visiting us here at our offices. We were always very cooperative and offered them the latest edition to read. There's every reason to believe now that things will slide backward again. Those of us who lived through AMPO and continued with our political work know that we are blacklisted, that we are photographed occasionally. It is not that many years since the Second World War, when the government launched its campaign against Communist Party members. As long as Japan continues to show signs of moving in the direction of remilitarization, I will do my best to voice my opposition. However, if laws such as the National Security Act should ever be passed, I recognize that I, and others like me, will be at risk.

Of course this situation — the conservative resurgence — is not unique to Japan. A recent visitor from Germany was describing a very similar situation there. However, the continued presence of the Green Party in Europe leaves more room for hope. It's very distressing to read statistics that show women voters outnumbering men in the elections and returning the conservatives. I guess that the possibility of a Socialist Party government or even a left-wing coalition seems too much of a threat to the way of life of those women I talked of before. We describe our middle-class Japanese youngsters as selfish these days, but I suspect they came by it honestly.

SB: There seem to be a lot of stories in the press about the Japan Socialist Party's apparent move toward the center. There does seem to have been a marked shift.

SC: Yes, and I guess there are good and bad aspects to it. One of Nakasone's main objectives during his term in office was to undermine the Japanese labor unions. One of the strongest affiliated unions of the day drew much of its membership from the public sector, in particular from the Japan National Railways; this was also the union that had the closest links with the Socialist Party. When the move to denationalize came, the Socialist Party split in two over the issue. The overall result was that union members felt the JSP had not stood by them when they needed support. This was really the first time the party was accused of moving toward a center position.

I think the basic problem is that the JSP has never had a clear enough definition of its own ideological position. This lack of clarity can lead to sudden fluctuations and shifts of platform. As a feminist, my own experience with the left during AMPO left me suspicious of any move to forge too close a link between the JSP and the women's movement. Feminism is more concerned with a respect for all human rights, while the Japanese socialists seem most concerned with converting people to their Marxist position. I think a concern for the human condition, a sense of humanity, is common to many of the popular protest movements in Japan, not just feminism, and it's this that seems to have been lacking in the JSP.

SB: Let's come back to the question of women's publications in Japan. While Agora *is the main feminist journal today, there are many other less substantial publications in circulation within the minikomi system. Could you tell me something of the history of the* minikomi *in Japan?*

SC: Let me start with my own experience. At the time of AMPO the thing that motivated me to join the movement against the treaty was my memory of the war years. I was only a child, but I still remember clearly the burnt corpses in the streets of Tokyo. We'll never know exactly how many people perished in the incendiary bombings. The people who joined the AMPO protest were sending a message to the government that they didn't want military treaties with any nation; they wanted no self-defense forces. If Japan should be invaded, then fine; better that than remilitarization. The crowds outside the Diet building were phenomenal. I've never seen the like before or after. The most well-represented groups were the unions. The sky was red with union flags. Yet even in the face of this level of public resistance, the treaty went through.

It was this that brought me to an understanding of how Japan entered the Second World War. It's too late to mount a resistance, however large, once the event is already under way. Until that time I had not thought of myself as very political, but in the wake of AMPO I decided to act, not when a crisis arose, but on an ongoing basis, always in anticipation. The first thing I did was to open a kindergarten. There was no childcare facility in the area where we lived, and we all resorted to young teenage girls for help when we needed someone to come in, but this was not good enough. Apart from anything else, our apartments were too small.

There were some 670 houses in the district. We went to each household to solicit support for the kindergarten. The responses were mixed. There were quite a few who felt that this was a very radical, left-wing idea for the times, while others saw it as a threat to the traditional family structure. Still others agreed but just thought it was impossible. I wasn't sure myself that it was really possible, but then the only way to know was to try.

Once the kindergarten was in operation, it became clear that most of the women who were directly involved in the project were not full-time workers seeking daycare but women who'd already given up their jobs because of the lack of support facilities and were now keen to try and reenter the workforce. Unfortunately, in the 1960s it was not that easy to find a job again once you'd left a position to have children. It is much more common, even the norm, these days. And so from the kindergarten project we moved on to develop what we called the BOC — Bank of Creativity. This was in 1964. I put a lot of time and energy into the BOC project, working to bring in job opportunities, but at some point I began to question whether all the running around I was doing was achieving enough for the energy involved. I also felt less than satisfied myself.

And so in 1972 I decided that the energy would be better spent on a project that would build a network of women, a network within which women could reassess both their individual objectives and those of the feminist project itself. That was when I first decided to try and publish a journal. The women who came together to work on *Agora* never intended it to be a *minikomi* project. We saw *Agora* as somewhere between mass communications and *minikomi* — a *midikomi*. We opted for a printed publication in a bound format. We had two main objectives in the materials we collected. First, to feature articles on particular feminist issues (each month had a specific focus) from as wide a range of women's voices as possible. We decided that we would address topics aimed at moving beyond the boundaries of traditional "women's issues." Second, we wanted to bring together and reproduce as diverse as possible a collection of resources on each topic. There is no space in the mass media for the kinds of communication or news we wanted to promote. After all, 99.7 percent of the media employees were male. The mass media is male media. We saw the necessity of an alternative feminist media outlet.

SB: And what of the minikomi?

SC: I wouldn't want to begin to count the number of publications circulating within the *minikomi* network. They are essentially different from our project at *Agora*. Most of the *minikomi* works are short, often hand-written or mimeographed. They tend to feature questions

of a much more personal or individual nature. There are a lot of letters and personal accounts of hardship or self-discovery. The *minikomi* is an important outlet for many women who would otherwise
be isolated from contact with the movement and with one another.
The level of alienation among Japanese urban women is staggering.
The *minikomi* also provides an important vehicle for news related to
local political issues. On the whole, though, the focus of the *minikomi* is closer to traditional "women's issues." Nevertheless, I would
have to say that it has also become an important vehicle for lesbians
to explore and share the experience of "coming out." There are quite
a lot of lesbian *minikomi* publications in circulation these days, re-
flecting a recent move in the direction of a more open gay women's
identity. It's a slow process, though, and these publications play an
important role in opening up opportunities for networking and developing a community.

SB: You do pick up some material from the minikomi *and reproduce
it in* Agora, *I've noticed.*

SC: Oh yes. We read the *minikomi* actively and select items that we
feel are of general interest. One criticism I have of the *minikomi* is
its tendency to focus on individual experiences or individual points
of view. This comes back to the question of selfishness or self-
orientation. Better to open up opportunities for women to come out
of themselves, out of this self-fixation, and network with other
women. There has been so little chance to do this in the past. It may
be an extension of the same issue, but I also find in reading the *minikomi* that the individuals represented tend to take a very strong
stand and push their own point of view onto the reader. This is
something we try hard to avoid in *Agora*. We want, whenever possible, to offer a forum for sharing and exchanging different positions
rather than to push any one point of view. Sometimes *Agora* is criticized for being too disorganized or inconsistent, but that's fine; we
don't mind. The aim is to present as many perspectives as possible
on a given issue. Our readers can then make their own decisions on
where they stand.

SB: You mentioned before in relation to the mass media that 99.7 percent of the media industry was male. Is there no sign that this has changed?

SC: There's the occasional gesture — a female news reader or current affairs reporter — but on the whole I don't see a great deal of change. The *Asahi* newspaper — our major daily — recruited twelve women out of a total intake of thirty-six in 1986, for example, but I'm less concerned with demonstrative gestures of this kind than I am with where the twelve women will be in comparison to their twenty-four male colleagues in five years. I think someone like Matsui Yayori has had a considerable impact on attitudes at the *Asahi*, but at the same time she has had to deal with much aggressive criticism of her work and activities. The harder she's worked, the harsher the criticism has been.

SB: Matsui's name always comes up in discussions of women and the mass media. She seems to have managed to work successfully within the industry without succumbing to it.

SC: Yes. Once you're inside a system like that, it's easy to lose sight of your political objectives. That's one reason why we have been careful to maintain our independence from the mainstream publishing industry. Our choice of smaller printing houses is not only a financial decision.

SB: Agora *is involved in various activities other than the journal itself, I believe.*

SC: We try and offer a range of functions that are all in some way related to the concept of networking and broadening the kinds of options available to women. We have had English classes, for instance, and then there is the acupuncture clinic that also operates from the *Agora* office. We've offered sessions in assertiveness training as well.

SB: Does the assertiveness training relate to the communication skills and language issues we were talking about before the interview?

SC: Yes. Traditionally Japanese women have been taught the art of silence rather than communication. A young girl learns how to speak politely or in a feminine style rather than how to express herself freely. Various studies I've seen have documented the high percentage of emotive and childlike words used by women. All these layers of politeness and femininity act to blur any sense of what a woman is actually thinking. The aim of the assertiveness training was to help women develop the ability to express themselves clearly and directly without having to resort to an aggressive style of expression. We need to find a more effective way of communicating with others as feminists.

At another level we need to have our demands heard in the Diet. We've yet to achieve a political voice that can carry our message convincingly into the public, political arena. There has been talk of establishing a women's party, but our attention is always so fragmented by the endless onslaught of conservative attacks on women's rights these days that there is neither time nor energy for such a major undertaking. And finally, perhaps it wouldn't be a wise strategy for us, as women, to try to subsume all our diverse and often conflicting goals under a single party platform.

SB: *Reading through the materials your contributors submit to* Agora, *do you get a sense that they are struggling with questions of language as they write articles that express their own feminist position within the diversity of feminisms you describe?*

SC: The issue is a very complex one. On the whole, our contributors seem to opt for a voice that is difficult to label as either male or female. I suppose, however, that its tone is less academic than that found in most journals, but that is not to say that the quality is any less serious or well informed. In the *minikomi* you find a lot of women's language. It reads as if it was the written record of an oral narration. The women speak and write in a very natural and feminine style. I think we try and avoid women's language in *Agora*, but we don't dictate any conditions, for that would go against the grain of the whole project.

I don't believe there is any need to do away with women's language. I think the problem lies not so much in the words themselves as in the value attached to them. The general stereotype is that women's language is softer and more emotive, better suited to expressing feelings than facts. On the other hand, men's language is considered more official or authoritative but has the disadvantage of being stiff and dry. The problem for women arises from the negative value attached to the label "emotional." There is nothing intrinsically wrong with emotive language. Men should have more freedom to express themselves emotionally, to voice their feelings, just as women should have the freedom to be straightforward and firm when they choose to do so. It would be preferable if both forms, masculine and feminine, could be value-free and accessible to men and women.

I think my own approach has been a kind of bilingualism. On any given day I find myself in countless different situations and will choose to use whatever style of language is appropriate. For me personally, it comes down to this freedom to choose.

SB: What do you see as the future course of the women's movement in Japan?

SC: I have to admit to being a pessimist. I fear that the number of affluent, leisured women will continue to grow. From a capitalist point of view, I suppose you could argue that if women constitute a major market force, then they have considerable influence, but I don't know that this contented class of women is likely to take up any radical position that might threaten their security. It's true that women are gradually finding their way into more and more senior positions of influence in the public and private sectors; however, I'm not sure that these career women will necessarily work for the same political goals as the women's movement. It's the problem of working from within the system that we touched on before. I don't have a very clear picture of where the women's movement will go in the next few years, but I am sure that it will continue to push ahead. It remains the one serious alternative political force in Japan.

What Is Japanese Feminism?

I first began thinking in terms of a "Japanese-style feminism" as a consequence of the number of times foreign, especially American, feminists asked me whether *Agora* had come into being as the result of the influence of the women's liberation movement in the West. Almost every Western feminist asks me this same question. The BOC (Bank of Creativity) movement, which was the forerunner of *Agora*, dates back to 1960. In the 1960s a multitude of antiwar and citizen's movements originated among nameless, faceless housewives. *Agora* and the women around it constituted one of these movements. Therefore, I always tell these foreign feminists that there was no external influence. What is most interesting to me is the way these women consider feminism to be an exportable commodity. I have an English friend who has been asked the same question repeatedly by American feminists regarding British feminism. I have a suspicion that the French feminists might consider France to be the "motherland" of feminism.

Information is a transferable commodity. Information about feminism can, of course, be both exported and imported, and this trade may influence the various local feminisms. However, it is not so simple for a foreign feminism to take root as the basic ideology of a movement in another country. I think we have reached a stage where we need to look more closely at the various origins and currents of feminism.

How do we translate the term *feminism* into "Japanese"? We are all used to the sound of the Japanized version of the English word *feminizumu*, and yet every time I use the expression it seems increasingly vague. I asked my colleagues at the *Agora* office to look up the dictionary definition of the word. In *Kōjien* (3d ed.; Tokyo: Iwanami Shoten, 1983), Japan's most representative dictionary, the entry for *feminizumu* reads:

Translated with the permission of the author by Sandra Buckley.

A theory calling for the extension of women's rights within society, politics, and the law. Women's liberation. Women's rights. Gender equity. Respect for women. (Feminist: [i] a women's liberationist, women's rights activist, equal opportunities supporter. [ii] A man with a weakness for women, a worshiper of women).

This is quite an old fashioned definition.

The entry in the well-known *Japanese World Encyclopedia* (Tokyo: Heibonsha, 1967) reads:

"Women's rights" and "equal opportunity" are common translations. From the Latin *femina* (woman). There can be no clear theoretical structure attributed to feminism, for it changes across historical periods. The ideology of feminism and the movement by the same name also differ dramatically from country to country. Therefore, feminism is usually subsumed and developed under the umbrella of other theoretical and worldviews — for example, Marxist feminism. There are many different forms of feminism. Within contemporary feminism there are two main streams. One is a theory and/or movement calling for the construction of a society based on the principles of feminism or the equality of the sexes. The other is a feminism based on the primary objective of the defense of motherhood. These two streams of feminism often intersect and have developed in close interrelationship to each other. Which of the two is dominant varies considerably from country to country and across historical periods. The Women's Rights Movement, influenced by the French Revolution, became popular in both America and Britain. The most representative group within this movement was the Suffragists. This stream of feminism called for the abolition of all forms of gender-based inequality, all forms of gender-based exploitation in the workplace. The movement aimed at establishing sexual equality as a fundamental principle of both the law and social custom.

The stream of feminism based on the defense of motherhood developed in Germany and Scandinavia. It came slightly later than the Women's Rights Movement. The main characteristic of this movement, rather than sexual equality, was to leave intact the difference in status between male and female but to demand women's freedom in the areas of childbirth, maternal rights, sexual relations, and marriage. The defense of motherhood has remained a dominant feature of Scandinavian and German feminism. These two streams were united around Marxist feminism. The goals of both were met by Marxist feminism's Women's Rights Movement. This movement was not restricted to demanding the liberation of women but was characterized by its assertion that women's liberation was only meaningful as one step toward the liberation of an exploited and oppressed proletariat. This is a significant departure from the earlier feminisms, which had developed into movements for women's liberation around the issues of the inequality or differences between the sexes.

This definition introduces the two classic forms of feminism, women's liberation and the defense of motherhood, and claims that these two are united under the umbrella of Marxist feminism. In the 1985 edition the definition is revised as follows:

> The word feminism refers to the movement and theory associated with the women's rights movement founded on the principles of sexual equality that spread across Europe and America after first emerging in France in the 1830s. The word "feminist" has come to designate women or men who value women's rights. However, in the context of the women's rights movement dating from the late 1960s the meaning of "feminism" has broadened to refer to the overthrow of all sexual discrimination.

In France, the country where feminism originated, the following definition appears in *Grand Larousse de la langue française* (1973):

> (1) A doctrine or movement calling for the expansion of the rights of women within society. (2) The status of a male who exhibits marked feminine characteristics.

And in *Dictionnaire du français contemporain* (1983):

> A theory or practice focused on the extension to women of equal rights with men.

The representative French encyclopedia *Grand dictionnaire encyclopédique Larousse* writes simply:

> (1) An active movement for the reform and extension of the rights and roles of women within society. (2) A point of view or individual hold-

ing a point of view supporting the reform and extension of rights and roles of women in society.

In the standard English dictionary *Concise Oxford Dictionary* (1982) we find:

Advocacy of women's rights on the ground of the equality of the sexes.

And in the American dictionary *Concise Columbia Encyclopedia* (1983):

A movement for the political, social, and educational equality of women.

Merriam Webster's Dictionary (1974) states:

The theory of the political, economic, and social sexual equality of the sexes. (2) Organized activity on behalf of women's rights and interests.

In *Encyclopedia Brittanica*, used in both Britain and America, there is no specific definition for feminism, only references to the entries under "political rights" and "women's liberation movement." There is also no separate entry in the Japanese edition, *Brittanica International Encyclopedia*. And last, in the *Encyclopedia Americana* we found a somewhat more satisfying description. Starting with Adam and Eve this description covers several pages and covers in detail the circumstances of specific countries. In summary it states:

Feminism is a world-wide cultural movement which, in relation to all human rights — moral, religious, social, political, educational, legal, and economic — aims for the guarantee to women of the exact same rights as men.

Even this definition, however, may not satisfy everyone.

During the past two or three years, feminist discourse has gained a good deal of attention. The debate between Aoki Yayoi and Ueno Chizuko that was carried in the journal *Gendai shisō* and the related feminist conferences in Kyoto in 1985 and 1986 are still fresh in our minds. At the November 1985 conference in Kyoto, entitled "The Spearhead of Feminism," Ueno Chizuko prefaced her speech by saying that she would certainly pay her money to come to a conference with such a prodigious title. She continued:

> On November 3, just the other day, there was a large gathering in Tokyo under the auspices of the Socialist Forum. There was also a Women's Branch meeting. The meeting ran nonstop from 9:00 A.M. to 9:00 P.M., undisturbed even by a power failure. The main session of the meeting was titled "Diverse Feminisms." In other words, the title underlined the fact that feminism is no longer singular. There are various feminisms today. If one group is saying one thing, another is convinced of the opposite, and each of these groups calls itself feminist. We are moving into a period where it is not clear what feminism really refers to.
>
> Let us consider briefly why this situation has come about. The first reason is that feminism has matured to a state of consciousness where such a diversification is inevitable. Because the formations of feminism have become so rich, various new forms have emerged from within it. This situation is one that should be welcomed. And yet I have some doubts about the argument. In this age of theory, the world is approaching its end, and no one seems to know how to achieve any movement. If we can't do anything to change the world, then all we can do is change the way we see the world; this is what has created the demand for theory and the diversification of theories. Seen within this scenario, another interpretation would be that what we are looking at is the proof that feminism has reached the outer limits of its potential. There is the ancient Confucian saying, "When the great moral principles become obsolete, we still have basic humanity and justice," but somehow the idea that "when the movement becomes obsolete, we still have theory" doesn't seem as convincing. As a theorist, I can hardly refuse to take some of the blame, but I do think it is possible that this is the reality of the situation we face. To put it more definitively, feminists don't know what move to make next.
>
> It is not only a question of diversification. Totally opposing groups have emerged around the question of the appropriate strategies for achieving women's liberation. One strategy argues for the steady entry of women into the workplace as the means of achieving liberation. This approach has continued over a long period of time. Recently, however, those who go by the name of ecological feminists have argued the exact opposite of this. Their approach is not "liberation by

access to the workplace" but rather "liberation by rejection of the workplace" as the only course to take. Thus, there are women who call for a complete withdrawal from the workplace. The more time one spends in the workplace, the greater one's complicity and oppression under the capitalist system. This argument has left many women totally confounded by the dilemma of whether to attempt to go out into the workplace. It's difficult for them to know what they should do. The ominous subtitle of the Women's Branch meeting at the Socialist Forum was "Damned If You Go and Damned If You Stay." There is strong support for each of these two quite opposing positions.

Yet another example of the different approaches to feminism relates to female sexuality. When we invited Aoki Yayoi to a symposium in Kyoto last May, she argued that only by placing an extremely strong emphasis on "the feminine principle" can women achieve liberation. I and others responded with the opposite view, that this could only lead to endless trouble. Both camps called themselves feminists. This is the present situation. I think we are at a juncture where it is increasingly difficult to understand which approach is the right one or even what we should do as individuals today.

Ueno went on to say that this situation is not unique to Japan. There are certainly a number of divergent feminist positions in the world today. Some people say that we have entered the third wave of feminism. Even though we speak simply of feminism, we also have translated into Japanese such terms as radical feminism, Marxist feminism, and ecological feminism. There is even an unfortunate trend toward thinking that anyone who is not familiar with the "language" of feminism is out of touch with current thought. Because this "language" is clearly defined in the writings of Aoki Yayoi, Ehara Yumiko, Ueno Chizuko, and others, I won't go into it in detail here.

It is certainly true that during the 1960s, 1970s, and 1980s, feminism changed steadily and new ways of thinking came in quick succession. The issue is not that "there can be no clear theoretical structure attributed to feminism," as claimed in *The Japanese World Encyclopedia*, but that we are in the midst of a major struggle aimed at a coherent theorization of feminism. It comes down to the fact that it is extremely difficult to define feminism. I usually don't like definitions, but if I was asked for my own definition of feminism *today*, I might say the following, emphasizing that it refers only to the current situation:

> An international cultural and human rights movement to "cleanse" experience and knowledge, a movement that adopts a female perspective rather than the traditional male value system. Opposition to the privileging of production and efficiency models. The privileging of human life and sexuality. The elimination of all discrimination based on gender, economic status, race, culture, education, etc.

This would be my definition for the present, but it might well change in the future. It is a definition that is informed by all my own priorities, and so I would invite others to disagree. I believe that the first wave of feminism developed philosophically out of a humanist tradition. If we begin to consider the relationship between humanism and feminism, there is material for a book and still some. I don't feel I am familiar enough with this problem to touch on it here in detail, but as a passing observation I would say that the origins of this relationship go back a long way.

There are various theories as to when the word "feminism" first came into use. The widely told official version is that the term was coined by Alexandre Dumas, the French dramatist, in his work *L'Homme-femme* in 1872, where he used it to name the contemporary movement for women's rights. Other explanations trace the first use back to the eighteenth century, but in all cases the country of origin remains France. In that respect it is interesting to note that despite the fact that there is ample record of the numbers of women at Versailles in 1789, the expression "Freedom, Equality, and Brotherhood" (*fraternité*) excludes sisterhood (*sororité*). The expression *sororité* is still rarely used officially in France today outside limited feminist circles.

The Renaissance is known as the period of the discovery of mankind, the restoration of mankind, and yet, be it the Renaissance or the French Revolution, women are excluded from the category of mankind. Perhaps some will consider it an exaggeration to say that feminism has played a major role in the movement to restore the excluded group—women—but that is my impression. In its earliest forms feminism called for sexual equality in political, economic, educational, and social rights, and these focuses led to the popularization of such terms as "Women's Liberation" and "Women's Rights Movement." However, the radical feminism and second wave of the feminist movement that grew out of the anti-Vietnam and civil rights movements of the 1960s brought major qualitative changes. As early as the nineteenth century some people had questioned whether the Women's Rights Movement went far enough, wanting also to assert the value of woman as reproductive subject. This movement focused on the maternal female. Radical feminism went another step further, calling not only for the glorification of female life and sexuality but also for the feminization of all fixed value systems and future social principles. Perhaps it is because the women of this movement repeatedly brought such massive numbers of demonstrators onto the streets in support of their demands that today American feminists credit their country with the birth of the movement. The Women's Liberation Movement spread quickly across the world under the abbreviated title of "Lib." In contrast to the emphasis on certain aspects of female identity and the fight for equal rights that characterized the classic feminism, the new radical feminism was remarkable in its resolute demand for a realization of the total identity of all women as living subjects. Ueno-*san* has said that we have seen such diversification because feminism has matured and reached its outer limits. From the perspective of feminism's long history, one could say that it has reached a period of maturity, but it is on this solid foundation that radical feminism has come into being. One could call this a step toward the limits of feminism or a step in the development of feminism. For this very reason we can call up the old saying of "a hundred houses, a hundred different voices," but it would be just as true to say "a hundred different blossoms scattered far and wide." While the first wave of feminism worked to expand women's place in the world, the second wave—radical feminism—is attempting to eliminate the logic of male-dominated society. This is not a task that will be achieved in a mere twenty or thirty years.

I believe it is important not to lose sight of the fact that feminism is related to an actual movement. I think that here is another possible explanation for the diversification of feminism. The philosophy of feminism is not just an impractical doctrine; it constitutes the tactics and strategy for action. It will reflect the social conditions of the country, region, and historical period that forms the backdrop of the movement and thus be in a constant process of change. Some argue that the radical feminism of the 1960s grew out of women's rejection of the clearly defined male and female role distinctions within the anti-Vietnam movement. I believe this was not the cause but an opportunity. When people asked questions about sending troops all the way to Vietnam to fight, the links between the structures of discrimination and war were exposed. When people began to ask "Why?" in the 1950s and 1960s — Why are there no seats on the buses for blacks? Why must blacks go to separate schools? — it became clear that there were no places for women either and that this was contrary to the proclamation of "justice" in the U.S. Constitution. These links led to the emergence of Women's Liberation, developed as a mass movement in tandem with the civil rights movement and the anti-Vietnam movement, and from their momentum the move to eradicate the "male principle" that lies dormant in the hearts of men gained its strength.

While one dimension of any movement is an emphasis on basic principles, a movement will also usually confront the reality of its time. Those associated with feminism have consistently called for reforms in the context of all the realities whose paths they have tread, and each of these calls for reform has developed a theoretical base of its own. In response to Ueno-*san*'s claim that the abundance of theoretical positions represents the demise of feminism, I would argue that the richer the movement, the richer the range of theories. I predict that the more women who join the ranks of feminism, the more vigorous feminist discourse will become. I should add, however, that at one level I do agree with Ueno-*san*, when she says that in some sense the proliferation of theory is an attempt to change the way we see the world in the face of the apparent impossibility of changing the reality of the world. When I hear people labeling one another — "Oh, she's a radical feminist." "She's an ecological feminist." — I get the feeling that if theory is ever reduced to just this, a collection of intellectual labels to wear, then the movement will indeed be dead.

If feminist theory and the movement are two sides of the same coin, surely what links them is the fact that both originate from the same basic emotions. This, too, could be seen as another source of the recent proliferation of feminisms. Some people came to feminism from their experience of discrimination in the workplace, others due to hardship caused by the restrictions of the family system or the difficulty for women with young children to return to the workforce. The range of experiences is not unlike that suffered in a state of war. Some suffered psychological injuries, and some the pain of discrimination due to race, culture, class, or other "identifications." For others the starting point was their concern over nuclear weapons or the contamination of food supplies. Still others came to feminism out of a religious love. There are so many paths that bring people to feminism. When I was in New York in 1982 for a peace rally, I tried to meet with as many of the feminist groups there as possible. There were mothers who had become involved over the contamination of milk by radioactive rain, black activists, supporters of cooperation with the third world, minority groups, lesbians, and many others from different interest groups. It is not surprising then that so many different tactical approaches have emerged, ranging from antipatriarchy, the elimination of class, sexual liberation, new ecology, rethinking the body, a rejection of the male principle, and cooperation with the third world to talking from the heart and relaxation.

At yet another level, this diversification is fundamental to understanding the movement itself. The most basic foundation of feminism is each woman's own emotions and perceptions. Feminism is opposed to standardization and regulation. The entrenchment of the standardized concept of "women in the home, men in the workplace" should be questioned. Another example of such questioning is the criticism from lesbians of heterosexual dominance and their call for equal rights for homosexuals. The other unavoidable question is whether the fight for the expansion of rights can be limited to women. The territory has been shifting to include race, culture, birthrights, the handicapped, and others. Even the very category of humanity is coming under question. Ecological feminism, with its call for alternative ways of life that reject high-production society and its questioning of the conditions of human life, will have a major impact.

With this level of diversification it is inevitable that at different times different approaches will generate a barrage of sparks as they come in contact with one another, but as long as no one group attempts to adopt a dominant position, the stimulation of these fiery encounters can become the ground for new ideas and action. It is here that we can identify the boundless potential of feminism. I believe that this diversity will continue to breed still further differentiation.

Let's return to the idea of a Japanese feminism. If we accept the concept of diversity as a characteristic of feminism, then there is no reason why there should not be a multitude of feminisms in direct relation to geographic, historical, and contextual variables. Within this system the possibility that we would nurture a Japanese feminism in Japan is perfectly acceptable, and indeed, I believe it to be the reality. I may not have met even a hundred foreign feminists in my time, but even so they have come from as far afield as Asia, Africa, the Middle East, Central America, North America, Australia, northern Europe, southern Europe, and the Eastern Bloc. I have felt very subtle variations among the feminisms of each of these countries. It is only natural that, given the differences in social conditions in each place, the tone and hue of the feminisms should also differ.

It is often said that northern European feminism is mature while American feminism is radical, and yet surely there are many feminisms in America. It is the social contexts and the sensitivities of the individuals involved that generate its various formations. Isn't it problematic to speak in terms of "American feminism" or "European feminism"? In this sense it is equally strange to speak of "Japanese feminism." There are so many forms of feminism in Japan, and I would argue that the more variations and the greater the number of theoretical positions, the better.

For quite different reasons I have lately come to consider it very important to adhere to the concept of a "Japanese feminism." Although the first wave of feminism is often traced back to Europe and America, the question of whether Japan has a feminism of its own continues to concern me. If feminism is defined narrowly as the expansion of women's rights, then it can be identified only recently in Japan and can certainly be said to have been influenced by European and American feminist theory. The zen saying "Not seeking wealth and honor, making no distinction between rich and poor, watching one's footsteps, accepting self and others" seems to me to be in direct accord with any feminism. And beyond Japan, in regions that still receive little attention, there are other local, distinct feminisms. There is a need for far greater research into the diversity of feminisms worldwide.

The diversity of contemporary feminisms is at one level a reflection of the diversity of value systems in the world today. I have argued that another reason for this diversity is the fact that minority groups, which have previously had no public voice, are now speaking out; their voices are finally penetrating to the surface. Moreover, the individual has come to have a greater voice in relation to the group. We are also in a period when individual positions that diverge from the mass concept of "justice" are less frequently brushed aside under the rubric of "dissident," thus allowing a diversification of voices that constitute a force for increasing social change. There may be much to be gained for feminism if, in the future, those regions that have traditionally been "receivers of information" should instead become active "generators of information" — for example, Asia, Africa, the Middle East, and Central America. I think that information from countries where the "maternal" principle has a strong hold would have a particularly significant impact.

Another important variable is the religious or philosophical differences between countries and regions. When I meet and talk with American and European feminists, I am always aware that there are many fundamental differences. To Western feminists "liberation" always refers to "free from . . . ," and the word that follows can usually be reduced to "patriarchy." It is a mistake to think of patriarchy in terms of the Japanese dictionary definition of the word (father-centered household system). Is it better to think of it as male logic, the father-centered principle, or something as far-sweeping as all dominant ideology to this day? Frankly speaking, I have sometimes sensed traces of the humanist call for liberation from the intolerance of God (the Father) in the use of the term feminism. To what extent can we, as Japanese, hope to understand a call for liberation that is grounded in the historical monologue of those Christians who seek a way to free themselves from the restrictions that are the price of their love for their God.

A simple example is the "abortion problem." I can't help thinking that it is impossible for Japanese women to comprehend the path taken by feminists in Christian, and in particular Catholic, countries in their fight for abortion rights. It is of the same order as an army of ants attacking a concrete structure of the magnitude of our own Diet building and toppling it to put their own doctrine in place. It is truly overwhelming. By contrast, people say that there is no religion in Japan. It is certainly true that there are few people as committed to a religion as Christians are to their faith, and there is no religion that actually regulates the morality of our daily lives. Even so, as long as we are Japanese living in Japan, it can't be denied that we are influenced to some degree by Japanese deities and Buddhism. In contrast to the Christian claim that all humanity is equal in the eyes of God, the Buddhist concept of equality states that man, woman, insects, fish, birds, and all living forms can achieve Buddhahood. Implicit in the belief that "all human beings are equal in the eyes of God" is the relationship of a god who is praised and those who kneel to praise. It was the affliction of this relationship that generated the depth of the Western concepts of equality and freedom. In addition to being words basic to daily thought and life in the West, the gender markers — he and she — are clearly designated linguistically. The singular and plural forms are also marked. The distinction between subjective, predicative, and objective cases is fundamental to sentence structure. Whether it is appropriate to describe our Japanese style of stringing things together in any order (whatever the shape, the substance is the same) as falling into the realm of the "maternal principle," I would not like to say, but I would propose that the Japanese feminisms that have been nurtured under these specific conditions — together with the feminisms of Africa, Asia, the Middle East, and Central America — all open up very different territories from that of American feminism(s). I also have a lingering doubt about how far a Japanese feminism can spread the seeds of discontent in a country that has not experienced the intensity of patriarchy (in the Western sense). The power and authority of Christianity, having penetrated to the level of daily morals, is easier to isolate and identify, and this overtness can help generate the energy for a movement of resistance. It's possible that in the Japanese case, where regulation takes the "soft" form of social custom, the control mechanisms are less easily identified for they are more "mediated." With each level of mediation that is washed away, both the past and future of Japanese feminism will be revealed. In this process we may achieve the power necessary for real reforms. I hold a hope that women, excluded from the doors of traditional scholarship as they have been, will, with the freshness of their vision, throw a new light on our lives.

Selected Works

Josei jinzairon (Talented Women). Yūhikaku, 1980.
Mienai tatakai (The Hidden War). BOC, 1991.

SELECTED TITLES FROM *AGORA*

Danjo byōdō to bosei hoshō (Equality between Men and Women and the Protection of Motherhood). *Agora*, no. 22 (June 1980).
Kinto byōdō hogo (Equal Opportunity, Equality, Protection). *Agora*, no. 89 (August 1984).
Onna no jikoshuchō, kono 10 nen (The Last 10 Years of Women's Self-Assertion). *Agora*, no. 201 (November 1994).

Onna to senso (Women and War). *Agora*, no. 24 (May 1981).

Pekin kaigi e mukete VI (Towards the Beijing Conference). *Agora*, no. 210 (August 1995).

Sekushuaru harasumento: koko made susundeiru Amerika no taisaku (Sexual Harassment: Progress in the American Approaches). *Agora*, no 152 (May 1990).

Other titles available on request from *Agora*, Shinjuku 1-9-4-303, Shinjuku-ku, Tokyo 160.

UENO CHIZUKO

Professor, University of Tokyo; Sociologist

» » » » » » » » » » » »

UENO CHIZUKO, A SOCIOLOGIST who has worked exten-
sively in the area of feminist research, is probably the most internationally well known of Japan's feminists. In addition to her graduate
studies at Kyoto University, she has undertaken research at North-
western University and the University of Chicago. After several years
of teaching at Heian Women's College and Seika University in Kyoto,
she was recently appointed to the faculty of the prestigious Tokyo
University, a move unprecedented for a woman academic of her comparatively young age. Ueno has published prolifically. Her books sell
extremely well for academic publications, a fact that is often attributed to a combination of the high quality of her research, her choice
of controversial research topics, her ability to write in an accessible
prose style, and her frequent use of provocative images that appeal to
a nonspecialist readership. Her work and career have received con-
tinual media attention, and she is frequently called upon as a spokesperson for Japanese "women" and "feminists" both within Japan and
internationally. Ueno is sensitive to criticisms that she has appropriated the voice of "the Japanese Woman" and has attempted in various
publications to acknowledge the diversity of Japanese feminisms. She

has even suggested that this diversity has reached a state of fragmentation that could potentially be the undoing of the familiar forms of feminism. This is a point Saitō Chiyo argues against in her article in this volume.

Ueno has been both praised and criticized for her role in popularizing feminism in Japan. In addition to her scholarly writing, she publishes extensively in newspapers, journals, and magazines. She is a popular guest on interview and talk shows. Her newspaper and magazine articles were recently collected in a volume entitled *Women's Play*, a volume that generated considerable controversy because she chose reproductions of Judy Chicago's "Dinner Party" series for the illustrations. These abstract representations of vaginas outraged some feminists and delighted others, resulting in an extended public debate over the distinction between the erotic and the pornographic. This is an excellent example of how the strategy of popularizing—selecting images sure to attract maximum attention—can create a public space for debating issues otherwise marginalized or ignored by the mainstream media. The issue of pornography and censorship has been a major focus of much feminist research and activity over the last decade. Ueno's book extended the awareness of the debate to a far broader spectrum of Japanese. The use of vaginal imagery was particularly significant in Japan, where until recently the censorship laws prohibited any public representation of the penis or pubic hair (and by reason of anatomical proximity, the vagina).

As I noted in my introduction to Aoki Yayoi, Ueno criticized Aoki in a highly publicized debate focused on the concept of eco-feminism. Ueno has also become well known for her theory of *mazākon* (mother complex). This term, which she developed to describe the intensely intimate and prolonged physical and emotional interdependency of the male child and his mother in Japan has found its way into the popular vocabulary and gained wide currency among both intellectuals and the general public. Critics of the concept claim that it places excessive responsibility on mothers for the male condition while ignoring the larger social context within which women and children are positioned. Once again, it has to be said that even though this concept should be interrogated thoroughly, its popular circulation has raised the general awareness of the need to examine the nature of the mother-child relationship in the contemporary Japanese family.

Most recently, Ueno has been active in establishing a new feminist book series with the appropriate title of "New Feminisms." She and her co-editors are committed to publishing new theoretical feminist research focused on issues of the body, technology, and sexuality. The first three issues demonstrated Ueno's penchant for the outrageous or provocative. The issue on pornography carried numerous full-frontal nude shots of men in a clear challenge to the censorship laws. The decision to also include in the series a substantial number of translations of recent writings of some Western feminists is consistent with Ueno's contention that the dynamic future of Japanese feminism rests, at least in part, on its ability to network internationally in the new age of global communication and information flow.

While it is clear that Ueno will remain a highly influential figure in Japanese feminism, some people predict that the move to a large, national university will lead her to pull back from some of her more provocative strategies and her role as media feminist. Others see her new-found status as a license to continue stretching the limits of Japanese discourse on gender and sexuality. Only time will tell.

Interview

SB: In a recent commemorative issue of Agora, *Saitō Chiyo raised some questions regarding statements you made about the present state of Japanese feminism. In particular she was responding to your suggestion that feminism has reached the limits of its possibilities in Japan and that this is the reason for its recent fragmentation into different camps or factions.*

UC: I would rather use the word diversification than fragmentation. It has less of a negative connotation to it. While I am suggesting that there is a certain limited span to the life of a Japanese feminism and that we may be reaching the outer limit of that span, I don't see this as necessarily a negative or undesirable stage. I do believe that feminism has already peaked as a movement in Japan. It is clear from recent election campaigns that feminism has become far more widespread, or popularized, in recent years. I think it should be said, however, that the women who constitute what is being described by the media as the "women's vote" are not necessarily voting as feminists. In fact, the women who make up the majority of this "women's vote" may pose the greatest dilemma for Japanese feminism. It is these women who in some way have defined or set the limitations of a Japanese feminism over the past decade.

SB: Who are the women who make up this group you're describing?

UC: In a recent book I wrote on women's networking in Japan, I coined the term "*enjo*-ists." It's a wordplay combining English (*enjoy*) and the Japanese word for women's networking, *joen*. I inverted the syllables to make a new word to describe women who enjoy all the benefits of the networking but don't necessarily participate in the efforts to achieve those benefits. At the time I was writing that book, I started thinking in more detail about the relationship between the *enjo*-ists and feminists. These women have made conscious decisions to marry and to stay married. For them divorce would be the last and worst possible choice that they could make. These women are generally middle class and are often very active in such groups as the consumer protection organizations. These groups are definitely concerned with women's issues, but whether they can be described as feminist is a quite different issue. They are concerned largely with questions related to the traditionally defined roles of women in Japanese society. Over the years these groups have excelled at organization and lobbying. Many of the women involved in these organizations share a set of particular characteristics: they are well educated, their economic status is relatively high (this status is often attained through marriage), and they live in urban settings. The divorce rate among these women is lower than the average. There is too much at stake for these women. Any feminist looking at the inequalities operating within these marriages might think that divorce was an obvious

and desirable option. However, for these women it is the last option
and one they would almost never consider.

*SB: You would see the group you've just described as the one that led
the vote against the LDP in recent elections?*

UC: Yes. I would have to disagree with any attempt to declare this
trend a victory for feminism, even though it is clearly a victory for
women. I would view the major success of women candidates in the
1989 Upper House election in the same way. I simply don't think that
the political and economic agenda of the *enjo*-ists is the same as a
feminist agenda. These women have made very practical and realistic
choices in the context of contemporary Japanese society. They take
advantage of their status even though they are clearly a disadvantaged group.

SB: Could you explain this?

UC: There is no question their husbands and society take advantage
of these middle-class, educated, urban women, as full-time housewives who must care not only for children but also the elderly and
handicapped. Even so, these women are not inclined to want to for-
feit the security of their position. What they *can* do is take advantage
of the resources of time and money that their status offers them. At
some level they can be said to enjoy (*enjo*) a good deal of freedom. Of
course, they are not really free to do want they want with their lives,
but they are free to do what they want with the time and money at
their disposal within the parameters set by their status as wife and
mother.

*SB: It's a freedom of lifestyle rather than a political or economic
freedom?*

UC: Yes, *raifusutāiru* (lifestyle) is a very real concept to these women,
but it is a commodity that is purchased rather than a freedom that is
fought for. I may sound as if I am criticizing them, but I should add
that they are only doing what is perfectly reasonable given the limited number of options available to them. They have learned to take

advantage of the situation they find themselves in and to make their lives as comfortable as possible. For a very long time there was nothing in the lives of Japanese women that they could even turn to their own advantage in this way. It is the fact that their situation is so materially comfortable that makes them so unlikely to leave it or take any other action that would unsettle their *raifusutāiru*.

SB: How representative is this group that you're describing? There are obviously many Japanese women who are not middle or upper class and don't have these resources of money or time.

UC: Are you asking about lower-class women?

SB: I'm wondering what percentage of Japanese women these conditions would be true for.

UC: Recent statistics show that less than 40 percent of married women in their forties are full-time housewives. This means that 60 percent of households are double-income families. I think this figure would be true for both working-class and middle-class families. There are very few women who could be classified as full-time activist housewives. They certainly form a privileged minority in that they can devote all their energies to activist work. The resources the *enjo-ists* have to draw on will often include some additional income from their own part-time labor. They make careful choices to establish a balance between the necessary household income and their desired leisure time. I'm really not sure that it makes sense to try to maintain the distinction between lower and middle class in Japan today when talking about the status of women. It is very difficult to draw the boundaries clearly.

SB: One of the comments made by various feminists I have interviewed is that they are tired of Western feminists always asking them to comment on the influence of Western feminism on Japanese feminism. They argue, justifiably, that this type of question ignores the specific conditions of the development of a Japanese feminism. I am interested, however, in what you would identify as the important differences between the two.

UC: The first thing that I would have to say is that North American feminism developed under very unique circumstances. You have to look at it in the context of world history. It is not so much that North American feminism is unique but that the context in which it developed is unique — North American society. That society developed in an almost artificial way. It is a recent society, which made strong and deliberate choices on such issues as individual rights and freedom. It developed in a very planned or conscious way, and the feminist movement developed within the context of a freedom closely associated with the autonomy of the individual. Japanese feminism has far more in common with the feminisms of the other countries of East Asia.

I'd also argue that there are similarities between Japanese feminism and the movements in some European countries. I think there are serious problems when one tries to make any simplistic cross-cultural comparison on the basis of statistics. A good example would be the recent U.N. ranking of the status of women in member countries. The criteria focused on labor-force participation, women elected to government, and other measures of women's access to male domains. Japan was ranked 34th, I think, in that study. I believe statistics often misrepresent the status and influence of women in gender-segregated societies if they use criteria that are developed in accord with the objectives of non-gender-segregated societies.

In any East Asian culture you will find that women have a very tangible power within the household. This is often rejected by non-Asian feminists who argue that it is not real power, but I would disagree. Asian women do have significant power, although it is not a form of power recognized by non-Asian feminists. I think that we need a far greater sensitivity to cultural differences. It is possible for Asian women to develop a feminism that is the product of their own cultural context and meaningful to them. To impose the goals of other feminisms onto those women or use foreign goals as a measure of the quality of the lives of Asian women is problematic. Japanese women may not be as visible in the public sphere as their American counterparts, and this may lead observers to the conclusion that women are less liberated in Japan. On the other hand, Japanese women look at the low status attributed to the domestic labor of housewives in North America and feel that this amounts to a denigration of a fundamental social role — whether it is performed by a man or a woman. The domestic role is highly valued, some would even say overvalued, in Japanese society. This is something Japanese women do not want to give up.

SB: *In the 1989 election a Kyoto woman was elected to the Upper House as a Japan Socialist Party candidate. On the night of the election she was asked by an interviewer if she agreed that the finance minister in Japan should be a woman, given that women had always run the economy from the home. The JSP candidate responded quite angrily that she thought this was a ridiculous comment. She went on to say that while women do have a great deal of say in domestic budgets, they don't have equal earning capacity in the workplace and remain economically dependent on men. Her position seems quite different from your own.*

UC: When this kind of argument is used by men, it becomes a tricky and elusive ideology for trapping women within the household. I would still argue that women who choose domestic labor over entry into the workplace should be respected for that choice, and their labor should not be devalued. It is very easy, however, for this approach to be turned around into a form of entrapment as Sasano Teiko — I believe that was the name of the JSP candidate — points out.

Just to go back to the question of North American feminism for a moment, I think that this is another important area of difference. American feminists have devoted themselves to the issue of freedom of speech for women. Many feminist campaigns have focused on catching up with men in the public sphere through equal access. The women of NOW are radical individualists at the same time that they are feminists. A good example is the ambiguous position taken by some feminists in relation to the recent maternal leave case in the California courts. The question of maternal care is a low priority for many American feminists. There has been a devaluing of the maternal or nurturing role. The situation in Japan is quite different. The controversy that surrounded the reform of the Equal Employment Opportunity Law exemplifies the differences. Most Japanese women were opposed to the concept of equality and sameness. Equality with protection is an acceptable feminist position here. At that time we found ourselves in the ironic position of having the Japanese government confront us with the American example. It argued that if Japanese women really wanted to be equal, they also would have to accept an equal employment opportunity law without protection clauses. We responded that such a policy may fit the reality of the lives of American women, but it did not reflect the conditions of Japanese women's lives in the 1980s. The reforms went through despite the resistance. We are now living with the consequences of that legal reality, but this doesn't change the fact that in Japan the mothering, nurturing function is a key concern of feminists and seen as something that must be protected. Our primary goal is not to be like men but to value what it means to be a woman. This aspect of Japanese feminism is deeply rooted in the history of the women's movement in Japan as well as the individual experience of women. It's a double-edged sword, I admit, but it is also fundamental to the identity of Japanese feminism. The emphasis on mothering over the individualism of American feminism is a characteristic shared by East Asian and some European women. There are many similarities.

SB: Even within East Asia the status of women varies considerably despite some common factors such as the influence of Confucianism. In what ways do you see the situations being similar?

UC: You've already mentioned Confucianism, and that is an important common thread between the cultures of East Asia and how they regard women. Another factor is the shared experience of living within households traditionally based on an agrarian social structure. The status of women in agricultural communities will always be higher than it is in nomadic cultures. The religions of East Asia also tend to place a high value on women and the qualities associated with the feminine identity. Some might argue that this is just a form of compensation, but I feel that it has been significant in the formation and continued dominance of gender-segregated social structures in Asia. If you look at European society, you find that it was also gender-segregated until quite recently. It has only been with the process of modernization that the system has collapsed. Japan, on the other hand, has gone through a process of modernization, as distinct from Westernization, and kept its traditional gender segregation. It is worrying when this is used as evidence that Japan is not "successfully" modernized. It simply means that Japan has modernized differently. I often speak of Japan as being a mixture of the pre-modern and the hyper-modern. This is a unique characteristic of Japanese society.

SB: *How does what you're describing now relate to the debate between yourself and Aoki Yayoi? One of your major criticisms of Aoki seems to be that the link she draws between ecology and feminism is basically essentialist. Isn't what you are saying now about the maternal function quite similar in some respects?*

UC: It's true that in the debate with Aoki in the 1980s, I took what was closer to an individualist feminist position in opposition to Aoki's so-called ecological feminism. I did this because I felt that the association between the maternal function and "ecological feminism" was a particularly risky one and that someone had to take a strong counter-position. That does not mean, however, that I am opposed to the maternal function per se. What I am opposed to is any movement proposing that the maternal function is the only acceptable or worthwhile function for all women. This is very dangerous politically. For example, I am concerned that the antinuclear movement in Japan is demonstrating just this tendency. There has been considerable controversy among the women participating in the antinuclear movement over the terms of address used by speakers at their rallies. Often most of the people attending a rally are women. The speakers consistently refer to their audience as mothers. There are many women who are opposed to nuclear arms and power who are not mothers and may have even made a deliberate choice not to be. In focusing their campaign on mothers, they devalue all the other women in the community who are concerned with the same issues. The effect of the controversy has been to lead some feminists to regard the antinuclear movement with some suspicion. While it may be antinuclear, it is not clear that it is antipatriarchal. I'm not sure how it can be the former and not the latter.

SB: You've also commented at various times on the concept of the feminization of the male, a concept you've associated with Ivan Illich's work.

UC: This is a very interesting and difficult area to talk about with a Western feminist. I have given you a copy of my paper on reverse Orientalism. In that paper I look at this question in the context of Orientalism and the reactive reverse Orientalism that occurs at certain times in Japan. Within Orientalism the West is equated with the masculine and the East is equated with the feminine. What is peculiar is that Japanese men are then characterized as feminine by their identity as East Asians. Japanese men are quick to respond to a feminist strategy for the feminization of the male. They argue that because they are already so much more feminine than their Western counterparts, they should not have to give any more than they already have. Some of the cleverer Japanese male intellectuals have developed quite elaborate antifeminization arguments around the difference between Western and Eastern men.

SB: You did argue quite strongly for this strategy yourself in your paper at the Japanese Studies Conference in Melbourne in 1984.

UC: Yes, that's true, but since then I have realized the risks in pursuing this direction too far.

SB: What other alternative strategies do you now envisage for dealing with gender issues in Japan, or elsewhere for that matter?

UC: I suppose that a simple answer is a combination of the feminization of the male and the masculinization of the female. It is the polarization of the two that needs to be overcome. While Japanese male intellectuals may argue that they are already feminized in relation to the masculine West, I would argue as a Japanese woman that there is still a lot that could be done to get men to participate more in the domestic and nurturing roles. Unless women can teach men how to move into these areas, I don't think things will change.

SB: So when you speak of feminization, you are talking about men's taking up the social functions that have been traditionally defined as feminine.

UC: I agree with the early radical feminist position that the condition of the "feminine" is nurtured and not natural. We learn what it is to be feminine, and it must be possible for men also to learn. I realize that there are some feminist theoreticians who still argue for a feminine nature or essence that we are born with as women, but I feel very uncomfortable with this idea. I believe that the French feminists who take this stand are generally considered out of touch with the activist feminists in France today. The gap between the theoreticians and the activists seems to be immense there.

SB: What is the situation in Japan? Among the postwar feminists you would be one most known for bringing theoretical content into her writing.

UC: It's true that I am given a lot of labels — theoretical feminist, institutional feminist, academic feminist, leading feminist. What do all these labels mean? In Japan the movement has never been guided by theory. I believe that the activists are ahead of the theoreticians in Japan. Academic feminists are trying to catch up with the activists. In my work I see myself following the direction taken by the women in the movement and finding the words and ideological framework to capture, or express, what they are doing.

SB: Are you concerned, as feminist theory gains more currency in Japan both among intellectuals and in the mass media, that the gap between feminists working with theory and grass-roots feminists will widen?

UC: One thing that will limit the growth of the gap you're describing is the limited access women have to the academic institutions. There are still very few women academics, not to mention feminist academics. I think that it is the institutionalization of feminism that poses the greatest threat to communication between theoretical feminists and the movement. Another factor in Japan is the prominence of the fringe intellectual community. These intellectuals may or may not have a university affiliation. They build their careers around their relationship to the mass media and a large popular audience. I think that I have been able to take advantage of this system by using it to spread feminist ideas to a large number of people, especially young people.

SB: *You would see yourself filling a gap then . . .*

UC: Well, I hope so. I think the biggest gap we face as feminists in Japan is the generation gap. There are very few young people, males or females, who know the history of feminism in Japan even over the last twenty years or so. Young people often seem shocked by the most basic facts I publish in my books. The task is twofold in the sense that we have to find a voice for ourselves in the academic institutions and also find a voice for ourselves among the young. These are the two gaps I am keen to fill in my own work.

SB: *Another criticism I know you are sensitive to concerns the effect of popularization. Some women have expressed concern that this can lead to the dilution or weakening of feminism at the level of both theory and the political movement.*

UC: I am aware that I have my critics among feminists, but I feel no need to apologize for popularizing feminism in Japan. Most of my critics feel that there is some pure form of radical feminism that must be protected, but I personally find this romantic or even elitist. It's at least as important to me to share my ideas with the women of the *Hanakozoku* as with radical feminists. These young women are the readers of *Hanako* magazine, a consumer magazine with almost no content other than advertisements for expensive designer goods. The young women model themselves and their *raifustāiru* on the images they find in *Hanako*. The pictures come complete with prices and store locations. The message is that you can have anything you want if you have the money to buy it. The *Hanakozoku* believe in being open to their desires, being true to themselves, and doing whatever they want. These young women are usually perfectly happy, however, to be full-time wives. They enjoy the privileges of a good marriage and don't want to change anything. I've talked about this before. It is quite a challenge to find a way of getting a feminist message through to these women.

SB: When you talk about desire are you referring to sexual desire or only the desire for consumer goods?

UC: As you know, Japanese couples get married for the institution and not out of romantic love. The *Hanakozoku* go into marriage with very low expectations of romantic or sexual satisfaction. They choose the institution of marriage because of the material advantages it offers them. They secure their lives financially and socially with a good match. That is not to say that they give up their sexual desire. There is no question of this. They simply don't pursue that desire within marriage.

SB: The idea of a Japanese wife having an extramarital affair is so far outside the dominant stereotype . . .

UC: There is still very little public discussion about the extramarital relations of Japanese wives, but there is no question that there have been drastic changes in this area in recent years.

SB: In the comicbooks for adult female readers there has been, in the last several years, a dramatic increase in the number of stories of wives taking lovers.

UC: Oh yes, and this is not just fantasy. I know that not all women have the time or money to take up this option, but it is certainly a growing reality among Japanese married women.

SB: Let me ask you a question in a slightly different but related area. You introduced the term mazākon *(mother complex) several years ago. Today, it is used extensively by other people and yet is still often referred to as "Ueno's concept of mazākon." It has become a very popular and widely used term. Could you describe something of the background to the concept in your own work?*

UC: *Mazākon* is a direct product of the gender-segregated system in Japan. Women — and society — define the roles of wife and mother as primary. However, given that the husband is absent so much of the time, the wife tends to devote all her attention and energy to the male child. That it is the male child, and not the female, also reflects the traditional value system, the Confucian influence we touched on before. It's also a fact that sons and not daughters will be most likely to succeed in Japanese society today. The mother's success and fulfillment is achieved indirectly by identifying with her son's achievements. A daughter is still seen as someone who will eventually marry out of the household and leave. Japanese girls grow up aware that if there is a son, he will take priority over them. It is a life lived in the shadow of abandonment, if not in childhood, then at marriage, when she is sent out into another household. These things haven't changed. One might think that young boys would try to escape from the hold of their mothers, but unfortunately the system in Japan is so harsh and competitive that boys understand from a very young age that they can only succeed if they work closely in an alliance with their mother. Surveys taken among male high school students taking university entrance examinations show a very strong sense of obligation toward the mother. It almost seems that the strongest motivation is to please the mother rather than individual success.

SB: *In your writings on the theme of* mazākon *you describe a mother-son bonding that is far stronger than any identification with an absent father. And as in the case of the high school students, this bonding extends even beyond puberty. This situation doesn't seem to fit the standard Freudian construction of male subjectivity, and, at the same time, it seems to raise many interesting possibilities for a Freudian analysis of the mother-son relationship in Japan.*

UC: There is certainly something very different happening in the Japanese family in terms of any psychoanalytic reading. The major difference is the absence of the father from the family unit. His influence is minimized by the high demands placed on him to devote his energy to the workplace. The mother's energies, on the other hand, are exclusively channeled into the family and, in particular, the son. There is no social expectation of breaking or cutting the bond between mother and son at any age, even during adulthood. It is not unusual for the strongest influence in a man's life to remain his mother even after marriage. This is not an easy scenario for the young Japanese wife, and yet we see wives replicating the same system in the relationships they develop with their own sons. I fear that this kind of relationship is intensifying in contemporary Japanese society. Two important factors are the exorbitant costs of education and the lack of any viable welfare system for the elderly. Children cannot hope to get into the elite educational stream unless they have the full support of their mother. Mothers (who are far more likely to be the surviving parent in old age in Japan) cannot depend on the state for a decent pension or welfare later in life. The result is a bond of mutual dependency and obligation that lasts a lifetime. When I look at the children in Japan today, I feel they are being treated more and more as a commodity or an investment. Within the present system they become one more source of status and security for women who have no other options. Children, for their part, take full advantage of the resources their parents offer. The *mazākon* bond is oppressive and advantageous to both mother and son.

SB: There has been an increased interest in the media recently in the relationship between teenage male violence and television, videos, and comicbooks. It is generally argued that the intense levels of overt violence in the media are directly related to recent violent crimes. How do you feel about the link that is being drawn between representation and violence?

UC: I am suspicious of the suggestion of a direct conjunction between the media and real violence. You may know of the recent case of boys who raped a young girl and killed her. It is true that the media have been giving detailed coverage of these cases lately, but the level of violence among Japanese youths, especially sexual violence, is still extremely low. You can't even begin to compare the Japanese and American situations. One explanation is that we live in a less violent society, but you could also say that we live in a much more controlled society. Given the popularity of pornographic images in Japanese culture, if there was a direct link between the media and real violence, I think this society would be uninhabitable.

SB: It seems that one effect of the recent emphasis on the influence of the media has been to deflect attention away from the family as a source of violence.

UC: The conjunction of media representation and real violence is always assumed but can never be proven. The possible link between violence and the family structure in Japan — *mazākon*, for example — is something that is easier to understand and can be researched, but as you say little has been done in this area yet. There has been an attempt to set up a Japanese version of the American "Take Back the Night" project, but I can't help feeling that we are importing, or superimposing, something that doesn't grow out of the circumstances of women in Japan.

SB: This comes back to the question of the family. Japanese statistics for rape by strangers are very low. The vast majority of victims of sexual violence identify their attacker as an acquaintance or family member.

UC: Yes. The truth of the matter is that while the media has chosen to emphasize a small number of cases of sexual violence where the perpetrator is a stranger, it really is comparatively safe for women to walk the streets in Japan. This is not New York or Chicago. The source of danger is closer to home. We need to develop campaigns that fit our lives and not just follow trends in America that are quite specific to the conditions of that society.

SB: *There is a tremendous silence in Japan when it comes to the sex industry. It is a huge industry in Japan that touches the lives of most Japanese women. There are all the Japanese women employed in the* mizushōbai, *and then there is the relationship between the sex trade and marriage.*

UC: It's a lot easier to deal with the question of prostitution at a distance. The *mizushōbai* problem comes very close to home for many women, including feminists. The case of the sex scandal surrounding former prime minister Uno Sōsuke's relationship with an under-age geisha has surprised many people. Usually such cases don't become major media stories in Japan, but for some reason this particular story has unleashed a tremendous level of anger among Japanese women, especially married women. This is a clear case of prostitution, but we shouldn't confuse bar-women and prostitutes. There are many women working in the *mizushōbai* who are not prostitutes. I think that we have to be careful of slipping into moralistic judgments of women in the sex trade. Feminists in France have fought for the rights of prostitutes; in Japan, however, the rhetoric often remains one of antiprostitution. This approach effectively denies the right of women to exploit every economic path available to them in a world filled with inequity. We cannot judge women who make the choice to be entertainers or prostitutes.

SB: *Society goes to great lengths to disguise the continuity between the institutions of marriage and prostitution.*

UC: Of course, and feminist campaigns against prostitution often buy into this deception. If we argued that men shouldn't take jobs in any industry that puts the environment at risk, we would be shutting off the majority of job opportunities for men. There is almost no job that isn't in some way implicated in aspects of our society that we might consider ideologically questionable. Why do we take such a strong stand against women in prostitution, but not all these other jobs? What about a woman who works for a large corporation that is destroying the environment? On what basis do we make such arbitrary distinctions?

SB: If we could just go back to the question of the family . . . We saw a wave of publications on the "family in crisis" during the early 1980s, and more recently there has been a number of books on "singles culture." What changes do you predict in the Japanese family structure in the next decade?

UC: The Japanese family is not in crisis. Look at who wrote those books — men and some of the more conservative feminists. The conditions of postmodernization in Japan today are reinforcing the structure of the family unit. It's ironic but true. The government's decision to continue to pursue what they call "Japanese-style welfare" means that the responsibility for children, the sick, the elderly, and the handicapped will continue to fall on the shoulders of the family. Structures such as *mazākon* also work to reinforce the family from within. Unfortunately I see things continuing in this conservative direction.

SB: In Japan married women, even Hanakozoku, *have been prepared to take a very strong stand against conservative attempts to restrict access to abortion. Recent Supreme Court decisions in the States have been seen as a blow to women's rights in that country. Do you think that there will be any flow-on effect in Japan given the previous levels of cooperation between the Moral Majority in the United States and anti-abortion campaigners in Japan?*

UC: I don't believe so. I think that the crisis around the abortion issue in the States is the product of Christianity. The anti-abortion movement is always linked to religious questions. In Japan it is far more difficult to construct an anti-abortion campaign that can carry the same emotional weight. We don't have a religion of sin or guilt here. Women are reluctant to have abortions if they can avoid it. They regret the need to terminate a pregnancy and may be emotionally distressed by an abortion, but these are all personal reactions and not grounded in any religious ideology. In the absence of religion the decision to have an abortion or carry a fetus to term rests with the woman, who may or may not consult with the father. Japanese women will continue to fight to protect that right.

SB: *What about the recent increase in the occurrence of* mizuko jizō? *Some Buddhist temples are making a lot of money from selling these statues to women and charging large amounts for prayer services for the aborted fetus. All of this is marketed by the temples as tradition, and yet it seems closer to a Christian concept of guilt than any Buddhist practice.*

UC: I think that profit had a lot to do with the motivation of the temples. There is no doubt that the practice of *mizuko jizō* has a long history, at least back into the Edo Period, but it was not something that grew out of guilt or shame. It had an almost magical quality to it then. Women didn't keep the *mizuko jizō* as an act of appeasement but more as an act of compensation for a personal loss. The motivation was grief rather than guilt. Recent conservative anti-abortion campaigns have tried to distort this natural sense of loss into a form of guilt through the images and emotive language they use.

SB: *This is another example of a North American strategy being superimposed onto the Japanese situation, but this time by the conservatives.*

UC: Yes, it is not a movement that reflects the reality here. I should add, however, that if there is to be a single major influence in the lives of Japanese women in the future, it will be the new religions. These groups, like their counterparts in the United States, are extremely good at motivating people who are in need of social support networks, people in crisis. They are masters of human management. This worries me, for women seem to be very vulnerable to these new religions at the moment. The isolation of the urban lives they lead makes them prime targets. This is something feminists should watch out for.

SB: *Let me ask you one last question about your own position. Watching the shelves in Tokyo bookstores, there is a constant flow of books and journals on recent theoretical developments in the West and Japan, but there is really no other woman who is as central to current theoretical debates in Japan as you are. Do you see this changing in the near future? Do you think that other women will find their way into the ranks of the so-called new academicians?*

UC: Yes, I think this is already starting to happen. There are excellent young women working in feminist theory now, and they are becoming increasingly well known. It used to be at lot more lonely. Now I am aware of having a circle of colleagues to work with. I should say that these women are not just following the directions I take but are branching out into new areas of their own original research. These women are very powerful and controversial. An interviewer once asked me who would be the post-Ueno feminists. The feminists of my own generation were much more fortunate than those of the pioneer generation. We didn't have to fight all the same fundamental battles that they did. The way was paved for us by our predecessors. I think the young feminists coming up today in Japan are sometimes not aware of how much easier things are now than in the prewar or early postwar years. I have never felt completely alone in my work. Networking among feminists today has made our lives and our work much less isolated. With the recent diversification of feminism, there is now a proliferation of feminist theoretical approaches. The next few years should be very exciting in that way. Radical feminism is no longer the dominant feminism in Japan.

SB: You used to refer to yourself as a Marxist feminist. Is that still how you would describe yourself?

UC: I think I would still consider Marxist feminism an important aspect of my own work, but I am concerned that there has been a move away from Marxist analysis at the very time it is most needed in Japan. We call ourselves a middle-class society, and women enjoy all the benefits of a middle-class status. However, the high level of *raifustāiru* we enjoy is supported by a growing distance between Japanese who are members of the middle class and Japanese and non-Japanese who fall outside it. I am talking in particular of the immigrant workers who are becoming a crucial presence in our domestic workforce and also of workers in the countries to which Japan has exported so much of her manufacturing industry. These people exist within a class relationship to the Japanese middle class, but we erase them from our sense of reality. The disappearance of clearly defined class differences in Japan has made it that much more difficult to identify and address gender issues. The complexity of women's relations to the women — and men — of other countries becomes invisible in the absence of class analysis.

If there is one thing that makes me less than optimistic about Japan's future it is this willingness to erase difference. If there is to be any significant change in Japanese society, it will only come through the rediscovery of difference, and here feminism has much to contribute.

Are the Japanese Feminine? Some Problems of Japanese Feminism in its Cultural Context

A remarkable intellectual event in Japanese feminist theory has taken place. It is the publication of a book about Takamure Itsue, a critical biography of one of the greatest Japanese feminist philosophers and historians of the prewar period. The book, written by a young feminist scholar, Etsuko Yamashita, is an attempt to reevaluate Takamure's achievements in the light of developments in recent French postmodernist philosophy.

This attempt is itself rooted in two wider intellectual contexts: first, the rediscovery and reevaluation of pre-modern thought as postmodernist; second, the reconstruction of a critical history of feminist thought that also problematizes the active participation of Japanese feminists in the Second World War. The former reflects the current revisionist tendency to reevaluate what was once considered to be backward. The latter demonstrates a feminist "reflectiveness" in relation to women's history. The latent messages are, in the first case,

Translated with the permission of the author by Sandra Buckley.

that the Japanese are not always wrong, and in the second case, that women are not always victims. As a cultural product, contemporary Japanese feminism is located within the same cultural context. Feminism is under considerable pressure to respond to these two trends. The purpose of this paper is to see Japanese feminism as a constructed cultural ideology and place it within a wider political context. To this end I will use a "sociology of knowledge" approach. In a sense, this is an attempt at a meta-anthropology of gender.

In the concept of Orientalism proposed by Edward Said, the East is to the West as woman is to man. Taking an Orientalist approach to national identity, Japanese intellectuals have described Japan as an oppressed woman. Some have gone even farther, to equate Japan with a poor woman raped by the West, particularly when describing the period after the Second World War. After the Western concept of Orientalism was imposed on the East, the intellectuals of this region took up the same framework as a basis for their own expression of self-identity. The use of gender metaphors to refer to the East and the West has become common. However, on reflection, this is somewhat tautological, given that gender difference is shaped by a romantic worldview that sees men and women as existing only within such binary relations as positive/negative, active/passive, rational/irrational, dominant/subordinate, and ultimately, superior/inferior. However, the "East-as-woman" is inhabited by both men and women. By implication, within this framework Oriental men can, to some extent, be assigned such feminine "traits" as passivity and irrational thinking. Some research has shown that if an individualist orientation is used as the criterion of gender difference, then Japanese men are more feminine than French women. However, this finding does not mean that a Japanese man adopts a woman's role more than a French woman does. He is after all a man. There will always be gender politics regardless of the ethnic context.

With the rise of new nationalism since the 1970s, in the wake of the so-called Japanese economic miracle, there has been a tendency for Japanese indigenous thought of the prewar years to be reevaluated as postmodernist, as ideas that had the potential to overcome the constraints of Western-influenced models of modernization. The reevaluation itself has only taken place in the light of the most recent wave of European philosophy. Japanese intellectuals repeatedly take advantage of the cycles of self-criticism within European thought. This could be described as the product of *reverse Orientalism*—a process of devaluation followed by a process of reevaluation, in which an Orientalist perspective is taken up to define a positive national identity. This approach both fits the existing dominant paradigm for the East and is appealing for its ability to express a fundamental weakness of Orientalism, namely, Western ambiguity toward the non-Western world.

It is in this context that the reevaluation of an indigenous feminist thinker, Takamure, can be understood as an example of reverse Orientalism. Takamure shaped her thought in the face of the modern world, more specifically in reaction to the disintegration of the traditional community structures that had been based on such oppositions as rural/urban, nature/culture, and human/technological.

Takamure's own counter-modernism is obviously a modern product, something that would not have existed without modernism. It is a reactionary response to modernism. Takamure stood for the past, for tradition, for things that were rapidly disappearing. She was particularly worried about what she considered the loss of traditional gender roles or identity. The recovery of national identity and gender identity were the same thing for her. She attempted to achieve both goals by tracing women's history all the way back to ancient times. With no professional training as a historian, she strove to prove the existence of matrilineality in ancient Japan by tracing the genealogical documents of the ancient clans. Though she mistook matrilineality for matriarchy, she did offer a challenge to a dominant historical view that had never admitted to the possibility of women's power.

In her search for women's power, Takamure also turned to the Japanese creation myths. According to those cosmological myths, Japan's first great ancestral goddess was Amaterasu, from whom all creations derived. Takamure proposed the idea of "maternal self" as a Japanese cultural ideal, identifying herself and all Japanese women with the first, great goddess. For her, this solution went beyond the Western individualism to which she attributed the destruction of Japan's traditional community structures. Within her concept of a "maternal self," woman is at the center of everything. There is no conflict between community and individual in this ideal culture, and it is only women who can lead.

Her argument was an exercise in counter-modernism and problematized the questions related to the debate surrounding the overcoming of modernity. The counter-modernists generally sought a process of modernization that was not bound to Westernization or Western models. Among these counter-modernists, Nishida Kitarō was an outstanding philosopher who wrote extensively on these issues. He questioned the Western modernism that appealed so much to young Japanese intellectuals of the prewar period. The same young men later had to fight the United States in the Second World War. When the time came, Nishida encouraged them to participate in the war. The anti-Westernization of counter-modernism lent itself to nationalist goals.

Takamure offered a feminist counterpart of counter-modernism. Her counter-modernism also led her to participate actively in the war. In the late 1930s, she wrote: "The maternal self sees humankind as one family. As our sacred war is a challenge to what interferes with this familyhood, the war is ours, for women." She also described what she saw as the close relationship of women and fascism: "Fascism, which encourages women to have more children, values womanhood and therefore is liberating for women."

Takamure was committed to forming a maternalist feminism, as opposed to an individualist feminism. From her point of view, individualist feminists, with their focus on such issues as the woman's vote, were effectively destroying feminine virtues and cultural tradition in their attempts to overcome male standards. This was not the first debate between individualist and maternalist feminists in Japan. The most famous precedent occurred as early as the 1910s.

The two main figures in that debate were Hiratsuka Raichō and Yosano Akiko. Raichō was the founder of the first feminist journal in Japan and a strong maternalist. She argued for the specificity of womanhood and demanded maternal welfare from the state and the community. From the beginning, Japan's indigenous feminism defined itself as distinct from Western individualism. Takamure considered herself a legitimate heir to this first maternalist feminist and received her enthusiastic approval. Takamure's emphasis on motherhood and femininity functioned as an attempt to overcome Western individualism. She was by no means a right-wing woman or a conservative, but a strong feminist from the start. However, once locked into a framework of reverse Orientalism (the rejection of the Western model in the search for a Japan-specific one), she became increasingly implicated in fascism.

Not only Takamure, but also leading feminists in the struggle for the women's vote, participated actively in the war effort. In order to earn their share of political rights, women felt obliged to demonstrate a positive contribution to the state in the time of national crisis. A problem shared by most Asian feminists is that of locating a female identity and a feminist movement in relation to questions of national and cultural identity. Since feminism is frequently criticized at the local level as a Western import, feminists are under continuous pressure to distinguish themselves from Western feminists and must always define themselves negatively or oppositionally in order to establish a distinctly indigenous feminist identity.

This is confusing in a country such as Japan, where the national identity is already, at least to some extent, constructed as a somewhat feminine identity. If the Japanese as a cultural group are considered to have "feminine" traits, and to have internalized the understanding of their own culture as "feminine" (in contrast to other cultures, such as that of North America, which might be characterized as "masculine" within this framework), then feminists are faced with a dilemma: on the one hand, if feminists ask for equal rights, they are accused of being anti-Japanese; on the other hand, if they stress feminine virtues, men think it over and say, "Look, in contrast to Western men we are already feminine enough. Why do we have to become more feminine?"

This dilemma was reproduced in the 1980s, a half century after the first feminine/feminist controversy. The feminist debate in the 1980s was between "maximalist" and "minimalist" feminists. Maximalist feminism was a new wave of feminism that followed radical feminism. It was also referred to as "ecological feminism" and drew support from a counter-cultural movement for alternative technologies. Its critique of Japanese industrial society paralleled the logic of the earlier counter-modernist movement. It began to resemble a new nationalism when it proclaimed the virtues of such concepts as nature, motherhood, and "vernacular" values (after Ivan Illich).

An oppositional or reactive cycle of Orientalism and reverse Orientalism has been reproduced again and again throughout Japanese history. During the Edo Period Motoori Norinaga*, a philosopher, proposed a counter-Orientalism of the Japanese mind, in opposition to Chinese universalism (*karagokoro*, or Chinese mind). The Chinese model of the Orient and its relation to the rest of the world was the dominant model of identity in the East. Japan was as much the "other" to China as it was later to the West. Before contact with the West, everything—writing, law, technology, philosophy, and art—derived from China. Norinaga was a student of the classical literature of the Heian Period. He was particularly known for his study of the *Tale of Genji*, a work written by a woman of the court and renowned as the world's oldest novel. In the Heian Period Japanese official documents were always written in Chinese, but women were not allowed to use the Chinese language. It was during the same period that the Japanese writing system, *kana*, was developed. This invention took place among the court women. Gradually a system emerged within which women and men had clearly distinguishable written and spoken languages. Paradoxically, women could express themselves more easily than men in the vernacular of women's speech and the indigenous *kana* syllabary. The Heian Period is considered to have seen the birth of Japanese culture as opposed to Chinese universalism.

Norinaga developed his own theories of the *Tale* and of a Japanese aesthetic, theories which were based on the premise that the Japanese mind could be characterized as feminine while, by contrast, Chinese universalism could be characterized as masculine. Ironically, the creation of a "Japanese" culture led to the ghettoization of Japanese traits. The particularism of this conscious production of cultural identity is still evident in many contemporary theories of Japanese culture and society. In its attempts to define the feminine positively, maximalist feminism shares much with Japanese cultural particularism. We could point out the following similarities: first, this particularism falls within the same frame of binary oppositions as that imposed by Orientalism — nature/technology, soft/hard, positive/negative, masculine/feminine. It is actually a reversed expression of universalism, Western or Chinese, in that it strives to redefine or reallocate the positive and negative qualities of the existing, traditional oppositions. Second, this particularism is achieved only by ghettoizing the same qualities it claims to valorize. The dominant paradigm is ultimately left intact.

The nature of the relation of feminism to nationalism starts to become ambiguous when feminism and cultural particularism approach one another. In more recent times, a right-wing woman, Hasegawa Michiko, has criticized feminism as being responsible for the destruction of cultural traditions. As a philosopher and, not coincidentally, a student of the works of Norinaga, she has referred to feminism as *karagokoro*, or "Chinese mind." Hasegawa is a Japanese equivalent of Jean Bethke Elshtain, the American political scientist who, rather confusingly, claims to be a feminist. Fortunately, our "Japanese Elshtain" distinguishes herself clearly from feminism, so we can comfortably and fairly position her as antagonistic.

Hasegawa made a speech at the sixtieth anniversary of the Shōwa emperor's reign, in which she referred to the emperor as the "mother of the nation." Strangely enough, her statement did not cause any anger on the right. Though the Japanese imperial system is patrilineal, the emperor is no longer a powerful patriarch but an embracing mother; conservatives also agree with this view of the Japanese empire. There has been a transmogrification of the image of the emperor from a fatherlike to a motherlike figure. The current imperial system has gone through changes parallel to the transformation of capitalism — from hard to soft, visible to invisible, industrial to information- and service-oriented, centered to decentered. Accordingly, the entire discourse surrounding imperialism has changed. The new discourse of a soft, invisible empire was first posited by the French philosopher Roland Barthes in 1970 in his book *L'Empire des signes*, or *Empire of Signs*. In this book, he describes the emperor as an empty center: the center is there, but it is an empty, passive one. Japanese postmodernists were quick to take up his vocabulary. It is now common to refer to the emperor as the zero sign of Japanese culture: everything derives from this empty center, and everything collapses into one at this center. It functions like a black hole. This model has served as a strategy for enabling the imperial system to survive the transformation of Japanese capitalism. The transformation of the emperor into an empty center can be seen as equivalent to the emergence of the "soft capitalism" of the 1980s, a process often described as a feminization.

To sum up, we find ourselves trapped in a vicious circle that oscillates between Orientalism and reverse Orientalism. Feminism as a cultural product can not escape from this closed framework. It is especially difficult when gender is fundamental to many of the oppositional metaphors mobilized in the production of cultural identity. When a feminism chooses to stress the feminine, as in the case of maternalist and maximalist feminists, any alignment with either position will be achieved only by the effective ghettoization of "Japaneseness" and "womanhood." How can we avoid getting trapped by these frustrating alternatives?

In conclusion, it should be said that although I have limited this discussion to the Japanese case, these problems are in no way unique to Japan but are common to all nations. These issues are particularly evident in developing societies where mechanisms of reverse Orientalism have prevailed in the attempt to define local identities. Developed societies in which the formation of a national identity is at issue will also be faced with the same potential problems. Any feminist backlash that effectively ghettoizes the feminine — for example, the emergence of women's religions — also raises these same questions. In considering the issues I have raised here in relation to Orientalism and reverse Orientalism, feminist and cultural particularism, and nationalism — all of which are specific (not mutually exclusive) strategies for the construction of identity — it would be naïve to forget the political specificity of difference.

Selected Works

Joen ga yo no naka o kaeru (Women's Networks Changing the World). Nihon Keizai Shinbunsha, 1988.
Kafuchōsei to shihonshugi (Patriarchy and Capitalism). Iwanami Shoten, 1990.
Kindai kazoku no seiritsu to shuen (The Rise and Fall of the Japanese Modern Family). Iwanami Shoten, 1994.
Kōzōshugi no bōken (Explorations in Structuralism). Keishō Shobō, 1985.
Nihon no Feminizumu (Feminism in Japan). Vols. 1–8. Iwanami Shoten, 1994–95.
Onna asobi (Women's Play). Gakuyō Shobō, 1988.
Onna wa sekai o sukueru ka (Can Women Save the World?). Keishō Shobō, 1986.
Shihonsei to kaji rōdō (Capitalism and Domestic Labor). Kaimeisha, 1985.
Shufu ronsō o yomu zenkiroku (Reading the Japanese Domestic Labor Debate, 1 and 2). Keishō Shobō, 1982.
Sukāto no shita no gekijo (Theater Under the Skirt). Kawade Shobō, 1989.
Watashi sagashi geimu: Yokubo shimin shakairon (Looking for My Self: Collected Essays on the Consumer Society in the 1980s). Chikuma Shobō, 1987.

CHRONOLOGY OF SIGNIFICANT EVENTS
IN THE RECENT HISTORY OF JAPANESE
WOMEN (1868–1991)

» » » »

Compiled by Sandra Buckley with Sakai Minako

Introduction

This timeline has been compiled from a wide range of sources including Japanese-language histories of women and feminism, government
publications and white papers, feminist journals and reference works,
and assorted *minikomi* publications. The historical period covered by
the timeline runs from the first year of the Meiji Period (Meiji 1,
or 1868), the point generally (if somewhat arbitrarily) identified as
marking Japan's entry into a process of modernization, to 1991, the
last year for which reasonably complete data were available at the
time that the project was concluded. When references are made to individuals, events, or historical periods that fall prior to 1868, they are
taken up in the Glossary. We decided to extend the timeline back to
1868, rather than commencing at 1945 with the end of World War II,
as a means of creating some historical context for the conditions of
emergence of postwar feminism in Japan. It was felt by all involved in
the project that it would be important to emphasize the historical

roots of the "second wave" of feminism in the postwar period in the strong and clearly articulated political movement of the "first wave" of feminists. As can be seen in the timeline, women's protest and activism over the Meiji, Taishō and early Shōwa Periods posed a challenge to the state agenda that was disruptive enough to require an ongoing process of state response.

In the Preface I addressed the reasoning behind the decision to produce a timeline rather than an historical overview in the form of an introductory essay. I hope that the reader will find the layout accessible both for "spot checking" the historical context of specific events, individuals, or movements and for a fuller reading. As we compiled it, we were struck by an unexpected advantage of this format. The linear and minimalist quality of a timeline foregrounds certain long-term patterns of repetition in a compressed space as well as patterns of continuity or linkages across events over shorter periods of rapid change. An example that demonstrates both patterns is the "motherhood debate" (*bosei ronsō*). This debate surfaced in the late 1910s between Hiratsuka Raichō and Yosano Akiko, again in the eugenics and labor policies of the war years, in relation to the drafting of the Constitution under the Allied Occupation, in the 1950s "housewife debate," and most recently in the 1990s resurgence of policy issues relating to women's paid and unpaid work. The timeline offers an overview of the historical tenaciousness of this fundamental debate over the reproductive (unpaid) and productive (underpaid) labor of women while allowing a close-up view of the strategic intersections of the discursive practices (legal, medical, educational, etc.) that defined the distinctiveness of each of these instances of debates surrounding motherhood and women's identity in Japan over the last century. Other issues such as reproduction and contraception, employment equity, educational access, legal status (in divorce, marriage, inheritance, nationality, etc.) can be similarly read across the span of the timeline.

There is an inevitable imbalance between the level of detail available for the earlier years and the more contemporary period. While this is partly explained by the comparative paucity of accessible historical records of women's affairs in the Meiji and Taishō Periods, it also reflects a conscious decision to provide a more comprehensive listing for the postwar years as a means of offering the reader a reasonably detailed context for the the interviews and translations collected in the volume. It is hoped that this level of detail will facilitate an easier analysis of the emergence of new areas of contestation and negotiation. Clusters of organized activity or government policy reform around a specific issue — for example, nationality law, abortion access, the PKO Bill, or illegal women immigrant workers — help identify the shifting map of feminism in contemporary Japan.

Some Final Comments on Style

There are some peculiarities in the format of Japanese translations that should be explained. At their first appearance the names of all organizations and institutions are offered in Japanese with the English translation in parenthesis. Thereafter, only the Japanese title is used. However, in the case of specific laws and acts of government, the English translation is provided at the first appearance, followed by the Japanese original in parenthesis. We felt that this system would be the most accessible for both specialists and nonspecialists. The proper names of organizations and institutions are seldom known or used in translation in Japan, and it was therefore considered more useful to the reader to become familiar with the original Japanese title. However, in the case of laws and acts it seemed more helpful to all readers if the English title was used throughout. In the case of organizations or institutions whose English title is widely recognized in and out of Japan — for example, Temperance Union or YWCA — Japanese has been replaced by the translation. All Japanese personal names are given with the surname first.

CHRONOLOGY

» » » »

	Opening of the first International Women's Congress in Paris
1880 Meiji 13	Campaign against legal prostitution at Japan International Conference of the Association for Abolition of Prostitution
1881 Meiji 14	Campaign by Kishida Toshiko for democratic rights.
1882 Meiji 15	Speech by Kishida Toshiko at Rikken Seito Enzetsukai (Women's Social Gathering) in Okayama
1883 Meiji 16	Political speech by Kageyama Eiko
	Founding of Joko Gakusha (School for Girls) by Kageyama Eiko
1885 Meiji 18	First female doctor of medicine (Ogino Ginko)
	Founding of Meiji Jogakkō (Meiji Women's School)
	Arrest of Kageyama Eiko and others in relation to Osaka Incident (arrest and trial of liberal politicians who plotted a military expedition to Korea in 1885)
	Founding issue of *Jogaku zasshi* (Magazine of Women's Learning)
1886 Meiji 19	First Japanese strike at Kofu Amamiya Silk Mill
	Founding of Tokyo Women's Christian Temperance Union
	Founding of Joshi Shokugyō Gakkō (Vocational School for Women)
1887 Meiji 20	Open trial of Kageyama Eiko, attended by large numbers of women
1888 Meiji 21	Submission of Temperance Union proposal to Chamber of Elders for revisions to Monogamy Law
1889 Meiji 22	Strike by female workers at Osaka Silk Mill
	Publication of *Onna daigaku* (New Women's Higher Learning) by Fukuzawa Yukichi
1890 Meiji 23	Founding of Zenkoku Haishō Dōmeikai (National Federation for Abolition of Prostitution)
	Ban on political activities and promulgation of political meetings by women
1891 Meiji 24	Abolition of prostitution in Gunma Prefecture
1892 Meiji 25	Presentation of Women's High School Education Bill (*Joshi kyōiku ni kansuru kunrei*)
1893 Meiji 26	Founding of Japan Women's Christian Temperance Union
	Publication by Tamura Naomi of critique of Japanese family system in *Nihon no hanayome* (The Japanese Bride)

1894 Meiji 27 Strike at Osaka Tenma Silk Mill
1895 Meiji 28 Establishment of Edict on Women's High School Education (*Kōtō jogakkō ukitei seitei*)
1896 Meiji 29 Publication of *Joshi kyōiku* (Women's Education) by
Naruse Jinzō
Death of woman author Higuchi Ichiyō
1897 Meiji 30 Submission by Temperance Union of petition for prosecution of male adulterers (House of Representatives and
House of Peers)
Attendance by Inoue Tomoko at conference of Interna-
tional Women's Christian Temperance Union in
Canada
1898 Meiji 31 Strike of female workers at Tomioka Silk Mill
1899 Meiji 32 Publication of *Tōyō no fujo* (Oriental Women) by Ueki
Emori
Enactment of Higher Girls School Order (*Kōtō jogakkōrei
seitei*) — Policy of Good Wives and Wise Mothers
1900 Meiji 33 Founding of Joshi Eigaku Juku (Girls' English School) by
Tsuda Umeko
Founding of Tōkyō Joigakkō (Tokyo Women's Medical
School) by Yoshioka Yayoi
Salvation Army campaign for liberation of Yoshiwara
prostitutes
1901 Meiji 34 Founding of Aikoku Fujinkai (Patriotic Women's Association)
Founding of Nihon Joshi Daigaku (Japan Women's University) by Naruse Jinzō
1902 Meiji 35 "Fujin to shakaishugi" (Women and Socialism) article published in *Yorozu chōhō* by Kōtoku Shūsui
1903 Meiji 36 Founding issue of *Katei zasshi* (Home Magazine) by Sakai
Toshihiko
Employment of first woman as ticket clerk by National
Railroads (*Tetsudōin*)
1904 Meiji 37 Conference of Socialist Women
Publication of *Warawa no hanshogai* (Half of My Life)
and *Warawa no omoide* (My Memories) by Fukuda
(Kageyama) Eiko
1905 Meiji 38 Campaign by Imai Utako and Sakai Tameko for revision of
Article 5 of Public Order and Police Law (*Chian kei-*

satsuhō) banning women's attendance at political meetings)

Presentation of Bill for Abolition of Socialism in Women's Secondary Schools by Ministry of Education

1906 Meiji 39 Submission of petition to House of Representatives by Temperance Union for prosecution of male adulterers

1907 Meiji 40 Founding of magazine *Sekai fujin* (Women of the World) by Fukuda (Kageyama) Eiko

1908 Meiji 41 Founding of magazine *Fujin no tomo* (Woman's Friend) by Hani Motoko

Establishment of *Nara Joshi Kōtō Shihan Gakkō* (Nara Women's Normal College)

1909 Meiji 42 Campaign by Temperance Union for abolition of brothel districts

1910 Meiji 43 Arrest of Kanno Suga (female political activist) in relation to the Taigyaku Incident (alledged socialist plot to assassinate Meiji emperor)

Amendment of Higher Girls' School Order

Founding of Jitsuka Jogakkō (Women's Technical High School)

1911 Meiji 44 Founding of Seitōsha (Bluestocking Society) and founding issue of *Seitō* (Bluestocking Magazine) by Hiratsuka Raichō

Announcement of death sentence for Kanno Suga

1912 Meiji 45 Founding of workers union Yūaikai (Friendship Association) and recruitment of female workers over age of 13 as associate members

Admission of first women by Tohōku University

1913 Taishō 2 Ban of sales of February and April issues of *Seitō*, focusing on question of nontraditional identity of the "new woman" of Meiji Period

First admission of female student to Tokyo Imperial University

1914 Taishō 3 Strike of female workers at Tokyo Muslin

1915 Taishō 4 Itō Noe, well-known political activist and supporter of women's rights, becomes editor of *Seitō* magazine

1916 Taishō 5 Establishment of Women's Branch (first women's union) within Yūaikai

Founding of *Yūai fujin* magazine (Friendship Women)

Founding of *Fujin kōron* magazine (Women's Review); discontinuation of *Seito*

1917 Taishō 6　Founding of *Shufu no tomo* magazine (The Housewife's Friend) by Ichikawa Takeyoshi

Conference of Zenshōgakkō Jokyōin Taikai (Conference of All-Japan Women's Elementary School Teachers)

1918 Taishō 7　Publication of debate on protection of motherhood (*bosei hogo mondai*) among Yosano Akiko, Hiratsuka Raichō, and Yamakawa Kikue published in *Taiyō* (Sun) and *Fujin kōron*, focusing on role of education for women and women's right to work

Rice riots by women in Toyama Prefecture over pricing

1919 Taishō 8　First question-and-answer session on women's suffrage in House of Peers

Tanaka Takako attends the first Women's International Labor Conference

1920 Taishō 9　Founding of Shin Fujin Kyōkai (New Women's Association) by Hiratsuka Raichō and Ichikawa Fusae

Founding of *Josei dōmei* magazine (Women's League) by New Women's Association

1921 Taishō 10　Founding of Sekirankai (Red Wave Society; organization of socialist women) by Yamakawa Kikue, Itō Noe, and Sakai Masae

Founding of Nihon Fujin Sanseiken Kyōgikai (Japan Women's Suffrage Council) by Ochimi Kubushiro

1922 Taishō 11　Revision of Article 5 (Public Order and Police Law) to allow women's participation in, and organization of, political meetings

Dissolution of Shin Fujin Kyōkai

Granting of maternity leave to female teachers by Ministry of Education

1923 Taishō 12　Founding of Fujin Sansei Dōmei (Women's Suffrage League)

First International Women's Day

Founding of Zenkoku Kōshō Haishi Kisei Dōmei (National League for the Abolition of Legal Prostitution)

1924 Taishō 13　Founding of Fujin Sanseiken Kakutoku Kisei Dōmei (Women's Suffrage League; affiliation of previous suffrage groups)

1925 Taishō 14   Renaming of Fujin Sanseiken Kakutoku Kisei Dōmei as
               Fujin Kakutoku Dōmei
               Publication of *Fujin mondai to fujin undō* (Women's Issues
               and Women's Movements) by Yamakawa Kikue
               Publication of *Jokō aishi* (The Sad History of Women
               Workers) by Hosoi Wakizō
               Granting of universal male suffrage

1926 Taishō 15   Submission of petition to ban late-night work for women
    /Shōwa 1   and youths

1927 Shōwa 2   Founding of Kantō Fujin Dōmei (Kanto Women's
              League)
              Founding of Zenkoku Fujin Dōmei (National Women's
              League)
              Strike by Tōyō Muslin women workers for freedom to
              leave factory premises and dormitories

1928 Shōwa 3   Founding of Fujin Shōhi Kumiai Kyōkai (Association of
              Women's Consumer Unions) by Oku Mumeo
              Lobbying of Diet for women's suffrage

1929 Shōwa 4   Ban of late-night work for women and youths
              Founding of Rōdō Onna Juku (Women Workers' School)
              by Tatewaki Sadayo, for female employees of Tokyo
              Muslin Kameido Factory, with focus on sewing skills

1930 Shōwa 5   First Zen-Nihon Fusen Taikai (Conference of Japan
              Women's Suffrage)
               Founding of Fujin Setsurumento (Women's Settlement) by
              Oku Mumeo
              Founding of Dai-Nihon Rengo Fujinkai (All Japan Federa-
              tion of Women's Associations) under Ministry of
              Education

1931 Shōwa 6   Musan Fujin Taikai (Conference of Proletarian Women) on
              suffrage issues
              Granting of first menstruation leave in Japan at Senju
              Shokuryō Kenkyūjo (Senju Food Research Institute)

1932 Shōwa 7   Founding of Dai-Nippon Kokubō Fujinkai (Women's Na-
              tional Defense Association) supported by Ministry of
               the Military

1933 Shōwa 8   Granting of permission to women to take qualifying exam
              for the bar
              Ban of pit work for women under 16 years of age

1934 Shōwa 9   Founding of Bosei Hogohō Seitei Sokushin Fujin Renmei (Women's Federation for Promotion of Motherhood Protection Law) by Yamada Waka; renamed next year as Bosei Hogo Renmei (Motherhood Protection League)

1935 Shōwa 10   Successful strike at Tokyo Muslin for right to unionize
Establishment of Tokyo Municipal Home for Mothers and Children

1936 Shōwa 11   Further tightening of Restrictive Labor Law for Women and Children (*Reigai rōeki kinshirei*)
Total ban on midnight pit work by women
Publication of *Dai-Nihon josei jinmei jisho* (Japan Biographical Dictionary of Women) by Takamura Itsue

1937 Shōwa 12   Promulgation of Mother and Child Protection Law (*Boshi hogohō*)
Founding of Nippon Fujin Dantai Renmei (All-Japan League of Women's Organizations)
Publication of *Nōson fujin mondai* (The Problems of Women in Japanese Farming Villages) by Maruoka Hideko

1938 Shōwa 13   Kokumin Seishin Sōdōin Fujin Dantai Renraku Iinkai (Liaison Committee of Women's Organizations for the National Spiritual Mobilization Movement)
Qualification of first three women lawyers in Japan

1939 Shōwa 14   Easing of ban on women's pit work in mines
Founding of Fujin Jikyoku Kenkyūkai (Research Center for Women's Issues) by Ichikawa Fusae
Ban on permanent wave hairstyles.

1940 Shōwa 15   Founding of Fujin Dantai Toitsu Kyōgikai (United Council of Women's Organizations)
Dissolution of Women's Suffrage League and League for Acquisition of Women's Suffrage
Enactment of National Eugenics Law (*Kokumin yūseihō*), restricting birth control access and promoting genetic screening

1941 Shōwa 16   Enactment of Bill for United Women's Association (*Fujin Dantai Tōgō ni kansuru kengisho*)

1942 Shōwa 17   Founding of Dai-Nihon Fujinkai (Greater Japan Women's Association)

Announcement of plan for national mobilization of women's labor

1943 Shōwa 18 Enactment of Law for Mobilization of Unmarried Female Students (*Joshi gakuto doinrei*)

Commencement of late-night shifts for women and youths

1944 Shōwa 1 Founding of Joshi Teishintai (Women's Volunteer Brigade)

End of publication of *Fujin kōron*

1945 Shōwa 20 Founding of Sengo Taisaku Fujin Iinkai (Women's Committee on Postwar Counter-Measures) by Ichikawa Fusae, Yamataka Shigeru, and Akamatsu Tsuneko in cooperation with Occupation authorities

Founding of Shin Nihon Fujin Dōmei (New Japanese League of Women)

Granting of women's suffrage

1946 Shōwa 21 Ban on legal prostitution

Founding of Fujin Minshū Kurabu (Women's Democratic Club) by Matsuoka Yōko, Miyamoto Yuriko, and others

First general election after World War II — 39 female candidates elected

1947 Shōwa 22 Founding of Minshū Fujin Kyōkai (Democratic Women's Association) by Yamakawa Kikue and Kamichika Ichiko

Establishment of Fujin Shōnen Kyoku (Women and Minors Bureau) at Ministry of Labor; first director, Yamakawa Kikue

Operation of Standard Labor Law for Women and Minors (*Joshi nenshōsha rōdō kijun kisoku*)

1948 Shōwa 23 Founding of Shufu Rengokai (Housewives Association of Japan) by Oku Mumeo

Introduction of new tertiary education system for women's colleges

First International Women's Day since Second World War

Enactment of Eugenics Protection Law (*Yūsei hogohō*), including Economic Reasons Clause for wide abortion access

1949 Shōwa 24 13 women's colleges open under new school system

Establishment of prefectural family court system

Founding of Nōson Fujin Kyōkai (Association of Rural
Women) by Kawasaki Natsu and others

1950 Shōwa 25 Submission of a peace petition by Hiratsuka Raichō and
four other women to John Foster Dulles (U.S. Secre-
tary of State, assigned to Allied Occupation GHQ)

Change of Name from Shin Nihon Fujin Dōmei (New
Japan Women's League) to Nihon Fujin Yūkensha
Dōmei (Japan League of Women Voters)

Founding of Zenkoku Nōgyō Fujin Dantai Renraku
Kyōgikai (National Council of Women's Agricultural
Cooperatives)

1951 Shōwa 26 Submission of a joint statement for peace and demilitariza-
tion of Japan to John Foster Dulles (see 1950) by six
women's organizations

1952 Shōwa 27 Attendance of Moscow World Economic Conference by
Takara Tomi

National Conference of Zenkoku Chiiki Fujin Dantai Renraku Kyōgikai (National Federation of Regional
Women's Councils)

Revision of Eugenics Protection law (Boshi yūsei hogohō)
to reduce medical fees for abortion operations and
simplify procedures

1953 Shōwa 28 Founding of Zen-Nihon Fujin Dantai Rengokai (All-Japan
Coalition of Women's Organizations) by Hiratusuka
Raichō

Opening of first Zenkoku Fujin Kaigi (National Women's
Conference)

Founding of Fujin no koe magazine (Women's Voices) by
Yamakawa Kikue

1954 Shōwa 29 National Women's Conference aimed at total ban of prostitution

Human rights strike at Ōmi Silk Mill

Founding of Gensuibaku Kinshi Suginami Kyōgikai
Shōmei Undō (Women's Ban the Bomb Petition Movement)

1955 Shōwa 30 Attendance of International Council of Democratic
Women by Hani Setsuko and Maruoka Hideko

First session of Nihon Hahaoya Taikai (Japan Mothers'
Congress)

1956 Shōwa 31 Enactment of Maternity Leave Replacement Teachers Law
(*Sankyū hojo kyōin sechihō*)
First annual meeting of Hataraku Fujin no Chūō Shūkai
(First National Conference of Trade Union Women)
Promulgation of Antiprostitution Law (*Baishun kinshihō*)
Attendance of First World Conference of Women Workers
by 12 Japanese women delegates

1957 Shōwa 32 Founding of Nihon Seikatsu Kyōdō Kumiai Rengokai Fu-
jin Katsudō Zenkoku Kyōgikai (National Women's
Action Council of the Federation of Japanese Con-
sumer Cooperatives)
Attendance of Asia-Africa National Conference by
Kuboyama Suzu

1958 Shōwa 33 Founding of Nihon Fujin Kagakusha no Kai (Association
of Japanese Women Scientists)
Change of name from Zen-Nihon Fujin Dantai Rengokai
to Nihon Fujin Dantai Rengokai (Japan Coalition of
Women's Organizations)
Organization by Nihon Hahaoya Taikai (Japan Mother's
Congress) of conference and demonstration against
revision of U.S.-Japan Security Treaty (*Nichibei anzen
hoshō jōyaku*, usually abbreviated as AMPO)

1959 Shōwa 34 Defeat in courts of Tokyo Electric proposal for retirement
of women at time of marriage
Marriage of crown prince to commoner (Shōda Michiko)

1960 Shōwa 35 Call for Abolition of U.S.-Japan Security Treaty and complete disarmament, organized by prewar feminist ac-
tivist Hiratsuka Raichō
Opening of AMPO Hijun Soshi Zenkoku Fujin Taikai (National Women's Congress to Block Ratification of
U.S.-Japan Security Treaty)
Death of female student (Kanba Michiko) in anti-AMPO
demonstration at Diet building
Attendance by 12 Japanese representatives at International
Women's Conference for the 50th anniversary of International Women's Day

1961 Shōwa 36 Attendance of Conference of Asian and African Women by
9 Japanese female representatives
National meeting of mothers opposed to consumer price

rises, educational achievement tests, and Law for Prevention of Political Violence

Attendance by 17 Japanese representatives at World Conference of Women for Disarmament

1962 Shōwa 37 Founding of Nihon Fujin Kaigi (Japan Women's Conference) by Tanaka Sumiko and others

Founding of Shin Nihon Fujin no Kai (New Japan Women's Association), headed by Hiratsuka Raichō

Founding of Fujin Mondai Konwakai (Group for the Informal Discussion of Women's Issues) by Tanaka Sumiko and Yamakawa Kikue

1963 Shōwa 38 Declaration of opposition to atomic submarines from Jinken o Mamoru Fujin Kyōgikai (Women's Association for the Protection of Human Rights)

First national conference of consumers

1964 Shōwa 39 Promulgation of the Motherhood Welfare Law (*Boshi fukushihō*), including provision of allowance and other welfare benefits for single mothers and their children

National Women's Conference on Nursery Schools

Publication of *Kodomo hakusho* (White Paper on Children) by Kodomo o Mamorukai (Association for the Protection of Children)

Meeting of Chūō Fujin Shūkai (Central Women's Conference) to oppose increases in rice prices

1965 Shōwa 40 Campaign by women's groups against ratification of Japan–South Korea Treaty (*Nikkan jōyaku*); part of an attempt by Japan to ratify peace treaties with all nonsocialist countries in Asia

Commemorative Conference of 20th Anniversary of Women's Suffrage

32.9 percent participation in labor force by married women

1966 Shōwa 41 Promulgation of Mother and Child Health Protection Law (*Boshi hōkenhō*). This law includes measures to protect and support pregnant women, mothers, and infants with a particular focus on the provision of information and education on issues related to pregnancy and child-rearing. The legislation proves controversial among feminists, with some lauding the move to support mothers while others contest the intrusive nature of the measures.

Attendance by Yamaguchi Yūko and others at World Conference on Children

Submission by Fujin Shōnen Mondai Shingikai (Council of Women and Youth Affairs) to government of proposal concerning the employment conditions of middle-aged and elderly female workers

1967 Shōwa 42 Ratification of ILO Article 100 on equal employment

National meeting of women to call for early return of the Okinawan Islands

1968 Shōwa 43 Formal introduction of leave system for nursing mothers at the Nihon Telegraph and Telephone Company (first in Japan)

Founding of Shūfu Dōmei (League of Women)

Percentage of male voters in national elections outnumbered by that of women for first time

1969 Shōwa 44 Ratio of female elementary school teachers exceeds 50 percent

Number of female students entering senior high school exceeds that for males for first time

Establishment of Rōdō Kijunhō Kenkyūkai (Research Bureau of Labor Standards Law) at Ministry of Labor

Case brought by Tatenaka Shūko against Tokyo Heavy Metals for discriminatory retirement system

1970 Shōwa 45 Promulgation of Industrial Home Work Law (*Kanai rōdohō*), aimed at improving conditions for women in "cottage industry" workforce

Workforce rationalization strategy of dismissal of married women employees declared legal

Organization by coalition of consumer groups of successful color television boycott over pricing

First women's liberation mass demonstration in Japan

1971 Shōwa 46 Organization by Temperance Union of meeting to protest Yasukuni Shrine State Patronage Bill (*Yasukuni jinjahō*). The bill is seen as a challenge to the constitutional separation of state and religion; it is also opposed by peace activists because it involves the enshrinement of all war dead at Yasukuni.

General demonstration by women's groups against ratification of agreement between Japan and U.S. for return of Okinawan Islands. Women protesters call for complete removal of all military bases.

Presentation of awards to 24 female activists at government ceremony commemorating 25th anniversary of women's suffrage

Introduction of Child Allowance Law (*Jidō teatehō*), with provision of regular allowance to families

Award of Order of Cultural Merit to Nogami Yaeko, woman writer renowned for her commitment to social issues

1972 Shōwa 47 Enactment of Working Women's Welfare Law (*Kinrō fujin fukushihō*), aimed at promoting welfare of working women. This law continued to maintain the separate status of women in the workplace and was therefore seen by some feminists as sustaining discriminatory employment conditions in the name of welfare and protection. Others supported the recognition of the distinct needs of working women.

Granting of maternity leave to female public servants

Establishment of Fujin ni Kansuru Mondai Chōsa Kaigi (Research Bureau of Women's Issues) in office of prime minister

Appointment of Japan's first female chief justice (Niigata Family Court)

1973 Shōwa 48 Submission of proposal to increase wife's legal claim to husband's property from one-third to one-half. Drafted by Zenkoku Fujin Zeirishi Renmei (National Federation of Women's Licensed Tax Accountants)

Establishment of Bosei no Kenkō Kanri ni Kansuru Senmonka Kaigi (Special Conference on Maternal Health Measures)

Successful campaign by women's consumer groups for end to synthetic protein research projects

Organization by Ichikawa Fusae of group to discuss problems of working and single mothers and to protest discriminatory court judgments on women's issues

Protest by 30 women's groups blocking conservative campaign for removal of Economic Reasons Clause from Eugenics Protection Law

1974 Shōwa 49 Founding of group to promote coeducational home economics in schools

Coalition of 15 women's organizations in opposition to Yasukuni Shrine State Patronage Bill

Founding of Zenkoku Mukyoka Hoikujō Renraku Kyōgikai (National Liaison Association of Nonregistered Nursery Schools)

50th anniversary commemorative meeting of Fusen Kakutoku Dōmei (National Union of Acquisition of Women's Suffrage)

Successful court challenge by women workers at Nagoya Broadcasting to policy of compulsory retirement at age 30

Passing of Employment Welfare Law (Koyō Hokenhō)

Establishment of *Chupiren* (The Pink Helmet Brigade), radical feminist group committed to direct action)

1975 Shōwa 50 International Women's Year

Establishment of first public nursery specializing in babies under 1 year

Opening of International Women's Year Conference in Mexico City

Opening of International Women's Year Conference in Tokyo under sponsorship of 41 women's organizations

Successful court action by women clerks at Akita Sōgō Bank against discriminatory wage practices

Passage of Women Teachers and Nurses Childcare Leave Law (*Joshi kyōin kangofu hobo tono ikuji kyūgyōhō*)

Inaugural publication of *Fujin hakusho* (White Paper on Women)

1976 Shōwa 51 Establishment of Fujin Mondai Kikaku Suishin Honbu (Central Office for Planning and Promotion of Women's Issues)

Designation of Ogata Sadako as ambassador to the U.N., marking most senior posting for woman in diplomatic corps

Founding of Josei no Kenri ni Kansuru Tokubetsu Iinkai
(Special Bureau of Women's Rights) at Nihon
Bengoshi Rengōkai (Japan Federation of
Lawyers)

Submission of report on female workers by Shūgyō ni
Okeru Danjo Byōdō Mondai Kenkyūkai (Research
Group on Gender-Based Employment Equity)

Submission of proposal demanding equal employment opportunity and promotion by Fujin Shōnen Mondai
Shingikai (Council of Women's and Youths' Affairs)

Opening of first session of Conference on Women's Issues
in Japan under sponsorship of Ministry of Labor

Japan Television loses case brought against it by female
employee transferred from her position as announcer
because of age-related changes in appearance

Revision of Civil Divorce Code to allow wife to retain
name of ex-husband

1977 Shōwa 52 Announcement of government's Fujin no Jūnen Kokunai
Kōdō Keikaku (Domestic Action Plan for Decade of
the Woman)

Revision of Child Welfare Law (*Jidō fukushihō*) to allow
men to qualify as nurses

Opening of Tokyo Women's Counseling Center Refuge for
Women

Announcement of Ministry of Labor plan to abolish discriminatory retirement systems for women

First International Conference of Women for Autonomous
and Peaceful Unity in Korea

Inauguration of International Women's Studies Association and Japan Women's Studies Association

Ruling by Supreme Court that firing of women on basis of
marital status is not illegal. Decision is seen as major
blow to feminist campaign for reform in judicial
system.

Implementation of vocational-training allowance of
¥67,500 per month for single mothers

1978 Shōwa 53 Submission to U.N. of petition for total ban on nuclear
weapons

Submission of *Danjo kōyō kintō hōan* (Equal Employment

Opportunity Bill) by Nihon Shakaitō (Japan Socialist Party)

Establishment of Tōkyō-to Fujin Mondai Kaigi (Tokyo Metropolitan Government Conference on Women's Issues) headed by Kaji Chizuko

Announcement by Ministry of Education of draft of directive concerning high school education. Four credits in home economic classes are still compulsory for girl students; the classes are also open to boy students on request.

Appointment of first female vice-principal in Tokyo Metropolitan High School system (Kurahashi Toshiko)

Public controversy over statement by Minister of Justice Setoyama that "women should stay in the home" (*onna wa katei ni*)

Appointment of Ogata Sadako (Japanese ambassador to U.N.) as chairperson of UNICEF

Instructions by Ministry of Labor to 14,200 companies to eliminate discriminatory retirement systems

1979 Shōwa 54 International Children's Year

Founding of Watashi-tachi no Danjo Kōyō Byōdōhō o Tsukurukai (Group to Frame Our Own Equal Opportunity Act)

Appointment by Ministry of International Trade and Industry of its first woman department manager, Kawaguchi Junko

Employment of women as officials in 12 areas of national public service

Gaining of women's right to take entrance examinations for University of Air and Maritime Security and University of Meteorology

Loss of discrimination case by Nissan Motors brought to Tokyo Supreme Court by Nakamoto Miyo over discriminatory retirement system

Ten-year commemorative demonstration of support for Tatenaka Shūko's struggle against Tokyo Heavy Metals' policy of compulsory retirement on childbirth

Passage of National Bar Exam by 40 women (highest number yet recorded)

Submission of proposal by Nihon Bengoshi Rengōkai
(Japan Association of Lawyers) to implement *Danjo*
byōdōhō (Equal Employment Opportunity Law) to
Ministry of Labor

1980 Shōwa 55 Naming of Takahashi Nobuko as Japan's first woman ambassador; assigned to Denmark

Election of Tanaka Sumiko as first woman vice-
chairperson of Shakaitō (Japan Socialist Party)

Partial revision of Civil and Family Law (*Minpō*) to allow
increase of legal portion of inheritance of property by
spouses from one-third to one-half (implemented
1981)

Commemorative conference marking midyear of United
Nations Decade of the Woman. During this year national women's and student groups organized large
numbers of activities and demonstrations against discriminatory employment practices.

Approval by Japan Airlines of return to work by female
employees after childbirth, and ending of discriminatory retirement age for women (set at 58 for men and
women)

Demand by Baishun Mondai to Torikumukai (Association
for the Elimination of Prostitution) for reform of
Kōshū yokujōhō (Public Bathing Laws) and active
prosecution of bathhouse customers by Ministry of
Health and Welfare

Victory for Tatenaka Shūko in eleven-year-old lawsuit
against Tokyo Heavy Metals. She is awarded ¥15 million in compensation and reinstated.

70,000 copies sold of first issue of *Torabayu* (*Travaille*)
(magazine of employment listings for women)

1981 Shōwa 56 Survey of employment and management of female workers
showing that 73 percent of companies recruit only
men from among university graduates

1,451 successful candidates in principal senior A class entrance examination for public service, including 44
women, 20 more than previous year

Death of Ichikawa Fusae (leading feminist and member of
Upper House)

Supreme Court ruling against Nissan Motors appeal in
Nakamoto Miyo discrimination case

Conference held by Nihon Fujin Kaigi on theme of Japanese medicine and gynecological abuse

Ruling by Tokyo Supreme Court that *Fukei yūsen kettō shugi* (*jus sanguinis* through father only) is legal

Publication of Ministry of Health and Welfare study entitled *Bēbi hoteru mondai ni taiō suru tame no nyūjiin no katsuyō to ni tsuite* (On the Subject of Childcare Facilities and the Baby Hotel Problem) with request to extend legal hours of operation of registered childcare centers

Complaint brought by Iwate Bank union to Ministry of Labor about women's lack of access to company-based child and family allowances

Proposal submitted by Kokusai Kekkon o Kangaerukai (Association for International Marriages) to Ministry of Justice for revisions to Nationality and Registration Law (*Kokuseki oyobi kosekihō*) to allow Japanese nationality to children of both Japanese fathers and mother, and to modify alien registration procedures

1982 Shōwa 57 Release of interim report by Ministry of Labor advising companies to abolish discriminatory retirement age standards for men and women employees. As of March 1982, 12,300 out of 18,800 companies had abolished discriminatory rules, while 300 companies had regulations for women's retirement at less than 40 years of age or at marriage or childbirth.

Attendance of 600 participants at women's symposium concerning issues on aging

Survey showing that 80 percent of listed companies have no plan to employ women college graduates

Opening of Shōkadō Women's bookstore in Kyoto, specializing in women's books and publications

Release of Ministry of Labor statistics showing a total number of 13,910,000 women workers and an average wage differential of 46.7 percent

1983 Shōwa 58 Founding of Kōreika Shakai o Yokusuru Josei no Kai (Women's Association to Improve Aging Society) by Higuchi Keiko

Married women's rate of employment at 50.8 percent, of
which 26 percent is in part-time jobs.

Founding of Tōkyō Gokan Kyūsai Sentā (Tokyo Rape Crisis Center)

Request by Kokusai Fujinnen Renrakukai (Committee for
the International Year of the Woman) that Minister
for Health and Welfare not present proposed Eugenics
Protection Law reforms to Diet. Women and student
groups actively campaigned and mounted protests
throughout this year to successfully block the proposed restriction of abortion access.

Support by Hōsei shingikai Kokusekihō Bukai (Legal Ad-
visory Committee on the Nationality Law) of reforms
to grant nationality through both maternal and pater-
nal line

Approval by Kobe District Court of first divorce after minimum 18-month absence of husband

Organization by Kokusai Fujinnen Renrakukai of conference on the theme of revisions to the Eugenics Protection Law and Nationality Law

Ministry of Health and Welfare survey showing that 75.9
percent of women favor separate pension fund for
women

Founding of Ajia Joshi Rōdōsha Koryū Sentā (Asian
Women Workers Center) under leadership of
Shiozawa Miyoko

Average age of 43.2 years for women performing contract
labor in own home; average of 5 daily work hours;
average wage of ¥313 per hour

Various opposition parties and Ministry of Labor separately develop policy options for new Part-time Labor
Law (Pāto rōdōhō) to improve working conditions for
part-timers

Attendance by 16,000 of 29th Conference of Nihon
Hahaoya Taikai, on theme of peace

527 "baby hotels" catering to 13,080 infants, of which
only 22 percent meet government standards

Ministry of Labor survey showing that 59.3 percent of
companies have undertaken office automation leading

to reductions in part-time positions for women and female high school graduates

Birth of Japan's first test-tube baby

NHK's broadcast of television serial "Oshin" (popular history of long-suffering Meiji woman), drawing 62.9
percent viewer rating

Release of Economic Planning Agency "White Paper on the
Life of the Nation — Fulfilling Household Budgets and
the New Family Image"

1984 Shōwa 59 Decision by Defense Agency to accept women examinees
for Bōei Ika Daigaku (National Defense Medical College)

Passage in Diet of revised Nationality and Registration
Law recognizing nationality rights of both father and
mother, to become effective Jan. 1, 1985

Release of Ministry of Labor "White Paper on the Female
Workforce," showing that 50.3 percent of 30,420,000
housewives have jobs, surpassing full-time homemakers for the first time

Appointment of Ishimoto Shigeru as cabinet minister (second woman minister since Second World War

Submission by Kokusai Fujinnen Renrakukai of request to
Ministry of Health and Welfare for improvement of
women's status under national pension plan

Average household income of ¥4,444,000. 43.3 percent of
household incomes were subsidized by wife's income
(averaging ¥1,386,000). 54.6 percent of working
wives stated income supplementation as primary reason for employment.

Active campaign by women's groups and peace movement
against nuclear weapons on Japanese soil with specific
focus on mobilizing Tomahawk Missiles on U.S. bases

Intensification of campaign between opponents and supporters of Equal Employment Opportunity Law due
for ratification in 1985

Increase in annual tax exemption for part-time employment income ¥900,000

Publication of first "White Paper on Divorce" by Ministry
of Health and Welfare: 41.2 percent of marriages end

after 10 years, and custody of children is awarded to
women in 70.1 percent of cases

Tōkai Bank survey showing average monthly childcare cost
of ¥13,000 for infant and ¥28,000 for three-year-old.
42.1 percent of survey respondents indicate that they
co-reside with parents

Appointment by Bank of Japan of 3 out of 10 career-track
women recruits to out-of-town rotational posts, an
important step toward management-track promotion

Lifestyle survey of wives of union members showing that
72 percent of husbands do not take annual leave and
only 27 percent of families eat evening meal with
father

1985 Shōwa 60   Admission of 8 women to National Defense Medical
College

Equal enforcement by Ministry of Health and Welfare of
livelihood assistance for men and women.

Passage of Equal Employment Opportunity Law in Diet

Refusal by prestigious golf club (Koganei Country Club) of
right to play to Moriyama Mayumi, female parliamentary vice-minister

Ratification of U.N. Convention on the Elimination of All
Forms of Discrimination against Women

Appointment of Akamatsu Yoshiko as ambassador to Uru-
guay (second appointment of women as ambassador)

Documenting by government of 366,000 noninstitu-
tionalized bedridden elderly patients and a further
110,000 in institutions. 90 percent of caretakers are
women.

Recommendation by Ministry of Health and Welfare that
single mothers should work rather than draw welfare

Publication by Nihon Keizai Chōsa Kyōmukai (Japanese
Institute for Economic Research) of "Education for
the Twenty-first Century," expressing concern that
women are currently seeking satisfaction in outside
employment rather than focusing on primary responsibility for the family. The document recommends that
women reevaluate their relation to the family.

Office automation survey identifying 58.3 percent of respondents experience increased work stress due to new technologies

Campaigns by both government and nongovernment groups to focus attention on need for increased assistance to families caring for bedridden elderly at home

Reform of Child Allowance Law eligibility rules to reduce maximum yearly income of recipient households to ¥3 million

Claim by Miura Shūmon, head of Bureau of Culture, in popular press articles that his comment that "all men should be strong enough to rape a woman . . ." was meant as a joke

Granting of public service leave for marriage and childbirth for both sexes

Ruling by Ministry of Labor that it is not illegal to advertise positions for women only

First government survey on part-time workers, recording 3,280,000 *pāto* employees and an average hourly rate of ¥572

31st conference for Hataraku Fujin (Working Women) on Equal Employment Opportunity Law, attended by 2,000 people

Enactment of Revised Child Allowance Law granting child allowance only beginning with second child and shortening period of allowance

1986 Shōwa 61 First appointment of woman as director of Ministry of International Trade and Industry (Sakamoto Haruno)

Seiyū Supermarket starts employee childcare system under which both men and women workers can shorten working hours while engaged in childcare

Appointment of Doi Takako as chairperson of Japan Socialist Party (first female leader of a major political party in Japan)

Successful lawsuit by Matsushima Chieko in Tokyo Supreme Court against Japan Heavy Metals for discriminatory retirement system

Active campaign by women's organizations against revision of Mother and Child Health Protection Law

Survey by Ministry of Law showing significant increase of

Southeast Asian illegal female sextrade workers.
4,942 illegal workers are identified.

Participation by 130 women in conference against National Security Act

Survey of female high school teachers showing that 2 out
of 3 female teachers suffer from poor health and cannot afford adequate hospital care

Granting of subsidies by Ministry of Labor to employers of
women who return to work after three years of child-
rearing

Establishment by Temperance Union of Josei no Ie: HELP
(House of Women: HELP), counseling and resource
center for Southeast Asian workers in Japan

Ministry of Agriculture, Forestry, and Fisheries survey
showing that 52 percent of farming women work
more than 10 hours per day in peak seasons; 50 percent take maternity leave in weeks leading up to birth
of first child; 99 percent take two weeks leave after
delivery

Survey showing that a drop in the gender wage differential
from ¥7,002 to ¥3,264 since the introduction of the
Equal Employment Opportunity Law

Women at 1.8 percent of academic staff at national
universities

Average life expectancy: 74.8 years for Japanese men and
80.46 for women

Survey by Ministry of Health and Welfare estimating that
by 2015, the number of single elderly who live by
themselves will be 5,554,000, of whom two-thirds
will be women. 50 percent of families would prefer to
live with their extended family members. 60 percent
are currently living in a nuclear family unit.

Attendance by 20,000 at 32d Conference of Hahaoya Taikai, held in Saitama Prefecture

Lobbying of Ministry of Labor by Tōitsu Rōsō Konfujinbu
to block revision of Standard Labor Law that would
remove night shift restrictions for women

Assignment of overnight duty to policewomen by 39 police

stations in Osaka in association with introduction of
Equal Employment Opportunity Law

Numerous campaigns by women's organizations against
National Security Act

Protest by women's and peace groups against Prime Minister Nakasone Yasuhiro's approval of increase in defense budget to more than 1 percent of GNP

Attendance of first International Female Journalists Conference in Washington by Matsui Yayori, Shimomura
Mitsuko, and Miyazaki Midori

Submission by Hōsei Shingikai (Council for Legal Issues)
of a proposal to introduce gender equality in all issues
relating to international marriage and divorce

Successful lawsuit by Maeda Fujiko against discriminatory
retirement pensions in Tottori District Court

Amendment to Geriatric Health Act (*Rōjin hokenhō*) to increase medical fees for elderly

Decision by Ministry of Health and Welfare to increase
level of compulsory health check-ups for infants

1987 Shōwa 62 Appointment of first female chief justice of the Supreme
Court (Noda Aiko)

Organization by Kōdō Suru Onna-tachi no Kai (Women in
Action) of conference on issue of pornographic writing and pictures in sport newspapers and adult
magazines

Election of unprecedented number of female candidates to
local assemblies

Appearance of Agnes Debate in *Bungei Shunjū* between
Hayashi Mariko (female writer) and Agnes Chen
(actress) over Chen's decision to take her baby to
work leads to extensive public controversy in media
over working mothers

Forcible repatriation of illegal foreign workers. 60 percent
are women, of whom more than 90 percent work in
entertainment industry.

Acquittal of woman accused of murder after pushing man
who harassed her from station platform into path of
inbound train

Assumption of office by Nagao Tatsuko, first female director of Ministry of Health and Welfare

Decision by Curriculum Council of Ministry of Education
to make home economics compulsory for both boys
and girls in junior high, and optional in senior high
schools

Death of first Japanese female AIDS patient (Kobe Prefecture)

Presentation of survey by Nihon Yūshoku Fujin Kurabu
Rengōkai (Japan Alliance of Working Women) on
Equal Employment Opportunity Law and discriminatory job advertisements. In October 1985, 38 percent
of advertisements targeted only men; by June 1986,
the figure dropped to 11 percent.

Decision by Sanyō Electric Company to lay off 1,200 part-
timers (mainly housewives) for economic reasons.
One part-timer brings case to court.

Attendance by 10,000 consumers at conference against introducing consumer sales tax

Four female members appointed to committees for
Akutagawa and Naoki literary awards

Japanese suicide rate for elderly women ranks second
among developed countries

Survey on employment showing that less than 30 percent
of women employees take childcare leave

Extensive campaigns to promote compulsory childcare
leave. Four opposition parties submit proposal to Diet
for childcare leave.

19 new "baby hotels" are constructed

Pay scales of 80 percent of new graduates entering employment determined irrespective of gender

Comment by Minister of Education Shiokawa Masajuro
that mothers should stay at home during children's period of compulsory education

Nationwide meetings organized by Kokka Kimitsuhō ni
Hantai Suru Josei no Kai (Association of Women Opposed to the National Security Act) to protest incor-
poration of sweeping police and censorship powers in
proposed act

Increase in number of female local assembly members to 1,420

Organization of meeting by Josei no Ie: HELP on theme of Filipino illegal women workers in Japan

Ruling by Hiroshima High Court that it is illegal for a husband to rape his wife

Announcement by Ministry of Education that level of attendance at culture centers in major cities numbers 1,360,000. 80 percent of attendees are women; these centers offer cultural activities and community and adult education.

Survey by life insurance company showing that 75 percent of housewives working in part-time jobs seek employment for economic reasons

Deportation of 1,036 illegal foreign workers, of whom 90 percent are female prostitutes

1988 Shōwa 63 Survey by Prime Minister's Office indicating 19 percent drop since 1986 in rate of young women rejecting idea that men work outside home while women keep house

7th Hansen Marason Supīchi Kontesuto (7th Antiwar Marathon Speech Contest) held by Sensō o Yurusanai Onna-tachi no Kai (Women Against War) on issue of National Security Act

Survey showing that 46 percent of people caring for bedridden elders are patient's daughter-in-law

Extensive campaigning and conference activity around issue of protecting female part-time employees

Increase from previous year of 66.4 percent in number of illegal foreign workers. 75 percent are Filipino.

Strike by nurses to protest heavy workloads

Reelection of Doi Takako as leader of Japan Socialist Party

Announcement by Supreme Court that more than 70 percent of divorce cases brought to family court in 1987 were initiated by wives

Survey by Ministry of Labor showing that working women number 16,150,000. This is 790,000 more than number of housewives without outside work. 1 out of 3 working women are part-timers.

Meetings held by media watch groups of Kōdō Suru Onna-
tachi no Kai to protest extensive use of swimsuit posters and calendars in bank advertising

Lawsuit brought against state and new university employer
by Sekiguchi Reiko for right to continue using maiden
name at workplace

Midosuji Subway Incident, in which woman who accused
2 men of sexual abuse in subway train is raped by
them

Holding of conference by Nihon Josei Eizu Kikin (Japan
Women's AIDS Foundation) on AIDS and women

Enactment of AIDS Protection Law (*Eizu yobōhō*), requiring reporting of AIDS patients to local government
office

Submission of proposal by Josei no Ie: HELP to protect human rights of illegal Asian female workers

Campaigns focusing on illegal Filipino female workers and
Filipino brides in farming areas. Various organizations, including Firipin Mondai Shiryō Sentā (Center
for Filipino Issues) and Firipin Hanayome o Kangaeru
Kai (Association for Filipino Brides), organize lobbying efforts all over Japan.

Proposal by U.N. that Japanese government introduce legislation to protect Asian illegal workers

Opening of counseling center for illegal Asian workers by
Ministry of Justice

Focus of feminists on government survey indicating that
only 14 percent of commercial companies have introduced childcare leave policies; 43 percent of those eligible actually utilize the system, and salaries are not
guaranteed for those who claim leave

Widespread attention to welfare and working conditions
of part-time workers in feminist publications and
campaigns

Survey by Ministry of Labor showing that number of
housewives who undertake paid work in home is less
than 1,000,000, indicating strengthening of new trend
toward outside part-time employment

Organization by Ministry of Labor of Pāto Taimu Rōdō

Mondai Senmonka Kaigi (Council for Part-time
Workers Issues) to enact Part-time Welfare Law (*Pāto
taimu fukushihō*)
Decision by Minister of Labor to loosen employment security eligibility for part-timers
1988 International Women's Studies Conference in Tokyo
selects theme of women and communication in high-
tech society
Lawsuit by de facto couple in Tokyo to end discriminatory
legal treatment of their children
Organization of national conference by Fūfu Besshi
Hōseika o Jitsugen Surukai (Organization to Legalize
the Use of Maiden Names After Marriage)
Campaign by Nihon Josanpukai (Japan Midwives Association) against accreditation of men as midwives
Survey by Ministry of Health and Welfare showing that
88.5 percent of women and 81.6 percent of men consider that single life is more attractive than married life
Employment by Japan Airlines of first female aviation me-
chanics in world by major international carrier
Permission by Ministry of Labor to assign overnight postal
work to women
Legal guarantee of women's right to accommodation in
company-owned dormitories for unmarried employees
Controversial survey published in major Japanese medical
journal suggesting that rates of miscarriage are higher
among working women
Active campaign by women's groups for review of emperor
system in light of emperor's imminent death
Submission of proposal to prime minister's office by conservative group Shinfujin (New Woman) requesting
that inauguration ritual of new emperor should be
treated as a national rite
Organization of conference by Sensō e no Michi o
Yurusanai Onna-tachi no Kai on theme of emperor,
war, and women
Participation of 12,000 people in public meeting to protest
Recruit Scandal (political bribes) and new consump-
tion tax

1989 Shōwa 64   Report by Tōkyō Bengoshikai (Tokyo Lawyer's Associa-
/Heisei 1   tion) advocating optional use of separate surnames for
        married couples

Election of 22 female candidates to Upper House (largest
    number of successful female candidates since 1946);
    The election focused on two issues: "Uno Scandal" (a
    woman disclosed that she had an affair with Prime
    Minister Uno Sōsuke while she was a geisha and then
    received money from him to keep quiet) and the re-
    cently introduced consumption tax

Rate of women entering universities and junior colleges at
    36.8 percent, exceeding that for men (35.8 percent)
    for first time. Ratio of men is higher in 4-year univer-
    sities while ratio of women is higher in 2-year colleges.

Appointment of Moriyama Mayumi as secretary of Envi-
    ronmental Agency and then as chief cabinet secretary

Appointment of Takasu Sumiko as secretary of Economic
    Planning Agency

Record number (166) of women pass Principal Senior En-
    trance Examination for public service

Survey by cabinet secretariat showing that average
    monthly salary level for married women exceeds
    ¥100,000

Survey by Ministry of Labor announcing that average
    hourly wage for female homeworkers is ¥374

Rate of women between 59 and 69 years of age active in
    workforce reached 41 percent

Extensive protests by women's organizations at introduc-
    tion of consumption tax

Submission to Bureau of Economic Planning of Shufuren
    proposal to abolish consumption tax

Organization by Tōkyō Gōkan Kyūsai Sentā of seminar on
    theme of women's sexual freedom and independence

Organization by Dai-ikkai Zenkoku Rōjin Hōmu Josei
    Shisetsuchō Fōramu (First All Japan Forum for Fe-
    male Directors of Homes for Elderly) of conference on
    future of elderly care

Organization by Osaka Metropolitan Government of first
    Asia-Pacific International Women's Forum

Successful lawsuit by female bus guide in Okinawa charging discriminatory retirement at 35; legal retirement
age extended to 60

Serious shortage of nurses, leading to opening of four
"nurse banks"

Opening (2:00 P.M.–10:00 P.M.) of registered late-hour
nursery school in Takamatsu City

National conference sponsored by Tōkyō no Sankairyō o
Kangaerukai (Group to Examine Tokyo Maternity
Clinics) on recent increase in medical scandals in ma-
ternity hospitals

Meetings on human rights of illegal Asian female workers,
cooperatively organized by women's groups

Submission to Ministry of Education of proposal to revise
gender roles in school textbooks

Submission of proposal to Ministry of Justice by Hiteki
Shūtsushi Sabetsu no Haishi o Motomeru Renrakukai
(Committee for Campaign Against Discriminatory
Treatment of Illegitimate Children) to abolish discrim-
inatory treatment of illegitimate children on grounds
of violation of U.N. Treaty on Rights of the Child

Organization of various conferences and meetings by feminist groups around issues of pornographic videos and
sexual violence against women

Strong reaction to one-day telephone counseling service on
sexual harassment; survey showing 1 out of 4 female
employees quits job over sexual harassment

Draft of report on sexual harassment by Dai-ni Tōkyō
Bengoshikai Ryōsei no Byōdō ni Kansuru Iinkai (Second Congress of Tokyo Lawyers Association on Sexual Equality)

Strong feminist support for sexual harassment court case
in Fukuoka

Protective custody by Osaka Immigration Office for three
Filipinas after they were forced into prostitution

Protest by women's organizations of revision of Eugenics
Protection Law to reduce legal period for abortion
from 24 to 22 weeks. The decision to modify the regulated period of legal access was made by using a legal

loophole that allowed the Ministry of Health and Welfare to act without referral to the Diet for approval.

Protest by 1982 Yūsei Hogohō Kaiku Soshi Renrakukai (Committee against Revision of '82 Eugenics Protection Law) of plan to shorten eligible period for abortion

Request by Shinfujinkai that Ministry of Health and Welfare implement measures to reduce unwanted pregnancies and abortion

Recommendation by Jintsu Sokushinzai ni Yoru Higai o Kangaerukai (Group to Examine Harmful Effects of Oxytocin) that Ministry of Health and Welfare investigate evidence of excessive use of oxytocin in births and the associated risks

Active recruitment of women because of decreasing popularity among men of Defense Forces as choice of career

Announcement by Ministry of Health and Welfare of introduction of 400 local nursery schools for children of part-timer workers

1990 Heisei 2   Release of pamphlet entitled "Good-bye, Boy-First School Rollbook" by Kōdō Suru Onna-tachi no Kai

Release of Ministry of Health and Welfare white paper analyzing reasons for Japan's decreasing birth rate (1.57 births per woman): (1) decrease in number of women of childbearing age; (2) tendency for women to marry later (average age 25.9); (3) economic and mental burden of childraising (e.g., compatibility of jobs and housing conditions)

Appointment of Satō Ginko as first female bureaucrat of ministerial class in Ministry of Labor

Extensive criticism of appointment of Takahashi Sakutarō as first male head of Rōdōshō Fujin Kyokuchō (Bureau of Women's Affairs, Ministry of Labor)

Ruling by Tokyo District Court that gender-based salary increments and promotions are illegal

IPU (Inter-Parliamentary Union) survey of 130 countries showing average rate of women members in national assemblies at 12.7 percent, with Japan ranked 112th in world at 14 percent

Protest by women's groups of Ministry of Health and Wel-

fare decision to shorten period of access to legal abortion from 24 to 22 weeks

Organization of meeting by 1989 Chūzetsu Dekiru Jiki no
Tanshuku ni Hantai Suru Joseitai chi no Kai (Women's
Group to Protest Reduction in Eligibility Period for
Legal Abortion) to prevent revision of Eugenics Pro-
tection Law

Recommendation by Ministry of Health and Welfare that
local governments shorten eligible abortion period
from 24 weeks to 22 weeks

Election of 12 female candidates in general election for
House of Representatives

Organization of conference by Onna no Jinken to Sei Jikko
Iinkai (Committee for Women's Rights and Sexuality)
entitled "The Risky Reproduction Revolution"

Decision by National Defense University to admit female
students after 1992

Organization of meeting by Seibōryoku to Tatakau Onna-
tachi no Nettowāku 1990 (Women's Network Against
Sexual Violence 1990) entitled "Liberty Security
Power"

Proposal by Baishun Mondai to Torikumukai to stop
erotic entertainment bus tours in Japan

Homework Law jurisdiction extended to include part-time
word-processing at home

Coordinated nationwide protests by women's organizations against beauty pageants

Acceptance of female participation in traditional festival in
Shiga Prefecture that had always excluded women

Survey on family planning showing that 26.5 percent of respondents think that low-dosage contraceptive pills
would be harmless; 20.5 percent think they are harmful; 49.2 percent do not have sufficient information.
The full legalization of pill remains controversial.

Ratification by Japan ILO annual meeting of treaty allowing women's late-night work

Conference on sexual harassment sponsored by Fukuoka
City. A related survey showed that 60 percent of
working women had experienced sexual harassment.

Survey by Tokyo Metropolitan government showing that more than 50 percent of popular comics on market include sex scenes

Proposal sent by Fudanren to 28 international women's organizations to cooperate in international opposition to occupation of Iraq

Publication by Tōkyō Gōkan Kyūsai Sentā of *Rape Crisis: Kono mijika na kiki* (Rape Crisis: Danger in Our Lives)

Active protest by various women's groups against PKO bill — part of government strategy to dispatch Self-Defense Forces to Gulf War as peace-keeping troops

Demands by Korean "comfort women" that Japanese prime minister recognize Japan's responsibility for forced prostitution during World War II

Organization by Onna no Jinken to Sei of meeting on decline of birth rate

Survey showing 35 percent of husbands in their thirties plan to attend wife's childbirth, and 61 percent place more priority on their family than on their job

Survey by Ministry of Education showing that employment rate of four-year female university graduates at 81 percent, same rate as that of male students

1991 Heisei 3   Decision by several major employers (Takashimaya Department Stores, Tokyo Motors, Oki Electrics, Nichii Supermarkets) to extend family and childcare leave policies to both male and female employees

Publication of Japanese-language newspaper by Filipinas married to villagers of Higashi Iyayama in Tokushima Prefecture

Survey from prime minister's office showing 30 percent of Japanese favor freedom to choose same or separate surnames after marriage

Establishment by Japanese Lawyers Association of national emergency dial-in service on women's rights

Significant advances for women in joint local government elections: 2,030 out of total 66,444 (31 percent)

Election of Kitamura Harue as mayor of Ashiya (first female mayor in Japan)

Establishment by Japan International Cooperation Association of office for women involved in environmental development projects

Development by prime minister's office of policy to approve family and childcare leave for men in order to enable them to participate more actively in family life

Establishment in Osaka of Hello Work, first job placement office for women only

Appearance of first female baseball announcer, on TBS television network

Meeting of International WID (Women in Development) specialists in Tokyo for discussions focused on role of feminist movements in aid-receiving nations

Senshu University survey on workplace sexual harassment (first university-based harassment survey in Japan), showing 70 percent of respondents had experienced workplace sexual harassment; 50 percent of assaulters were superiors; 22 percent were senior colleagues

Opening of U.S. surrogate mother agency in Tokyo

Institution by government of system for subsidizing nurseries that contract with companies to care for children on nights and holidays

Death on September 14 of Filipina who was working at nightclub in Fukushima Prefecture. The body is sent back to her family, which claims that it has found traces of abuse. The Philippine government stops sending laborers to that prefecture.

Replacement in revised edition of *Kōjien* dictionary of sections considered discriminatory against women

Publication of new edition of *Gakuyō shobō* (Women's Networking) with some 600 listings of women's groups

Announcement by Ministry of Labor that 20 percent of companies have introduced a reemployment system for women after childcare leave

Survey by Asahi Television showing only 23 percent of women approve of unmarried mothers as compared with 35 percent of men

Announcement by Ministry of Labor that one-third of all families were now double income households

Women primary and secondary school principals at 27.5
   percent
Active protest from women's organizations at beginning of
   Gulf War
Demonstrations by 31 women's organizations in Ginza to
   protest Japanese government support of Gulf War
Submission by 42 female parliamentarians of letter to Gen-
   eral Secretariat of U.N. protesting against the Gulf
   War
Sexual harassment seen as major issue for women's groups,
   gaining significant attention in media and political
   forums
Ruling by Tokyo District Court that man who sexually ha-
   rassed woman should pay ¥3 million damages
Campaign by Shin Nihon Fujin no Kai against Dial Q-2,
   telephone sex party line
Protest by Temperance Union against prostitution tour to
   Indonesia organized by Sōgō department stores
Organization by Kita Kyushu City of first Ajia Josei Kaigi
   (Conference of Asian Women)
Proposal by Shintsujin that franchised convenience stores
   regulate pornographic comicbook sales
Submission of childcare leave proposal by Ministry of Labor to Bureau of Women and Youth Affairs. The proposal does not guarantee an equal position after
   childbirth or paid leave, and there are no penalties.
Nurses' strike for better working conditions
Ruling by Tokyo Supreme Court that illegitimate children
   can claim equal share of parental inheritance
Revision of Child Allowance Law, effective from January
   1992. A monthly child allowance of ¥5,000 provided
   to first- and second-born children who were covered
   by the previous policy. The period of the allowance is
   shortened to less than three years. Annual income eligibility is reduced to ¥6,500,000 from ¥7,500,000.
Enactment of Childcare Leave Law (Ikuji kyūgyōhō),
   granting one-year leave for all employees with primary responsibility for infant under 1 year of age
Inauguration of Annual Nurses' Day

Organization by Kōdō Suru Onna-tachi no Kai of conference entitled "Freedom of Expression and Sexual
Discrimination — Protest Against Restrictions on Pornographic Comicbooks." The conference is intended
to counter recent feminist procensorship campaigns.

Organization by Ministry of Agriculture, Forestry, and
Fisheries of Nōsangyoson no Fujin ni Kansuru
Chōchōki Bijon Kondaikai (Council on Future Prob-
lems of Women in Rural and Fishing Communities)

Attendance of 27,000 participants at 37th Hahaoya
Taikais

Protests by Baishun Mondai to Torikumukai against Mie
Police's handing over of Thai prostitutes to *yakuza*
groups

Campaign by 49 women's groups against passage of PKO
bill

Founding of coalition of women's protest groups opposed
to PKO bill, Heiwa o Tsukuru Josei-tachi no Kai (Association of Women Peace Makers)

Survey by Ministry of Labor on impact of Equal Employment Opportunity Law, showing that 40 percent
thought there had been no major change while 30 percent recognized some change in treatment of women

Media attention focused by women's groups and antiprostitution campaigners on issues of prostitution
through range of organized national activities

Intensification of demands for compensation from Japanese government by Korean "comfort women"

Request by Baishun Mondai to Torikumukai to chair of
House of Councillors and female parliamentary members that Japan apologize to comfort women and pay
compensation

Nurses' strike to improve working conditions

Enactment of Childcare Leave Law for Public Servants

Feminist and Related Women's Organizations

» » » »

Kyoto

Shōkadō Bookstore (Shōkadō Shoten)
Address: Nishitōin-iru, Shimodachiuri-dōri, Kamigyō-ku, Kyoto
602. Phone: (075) 441-6905. Fax: (075) 441-6905. Activities: book
sales; mail order; women's books and other publications. Publications: women's books; catalogues of women's books.

Kyoto City Women's Information Center (Kyōto-shi Fujin Jōhō Sentā)
Address: c/o Shakai Kyōiku Sōgō Center, Shichihonmatsu-
nishiiru, Marutamachi, Sakyō-ku, Kyoto 604. Phone: (075)
802-3141. Activities: library service specializing in women's books;
women's studies workshops. Publication: *Sentā Letter* (Center
Letters).

*Organization of Women for the Protection of the Constitution (Kenpō o
Mamoru Fujin no Kai)*
Address: c/o Jugaku, 10-1 Jotoku, Ueno-chō, Muko-shi, Kyoto 617.
Activities: meetings on global peace.

*Women's Group for Improvement in an Aging Society: Kyoto (Kōreika
Shakai o Yokusuru Josei no Kai: Kyoto)*
Address: c/o Satō Tazu, 29 Kinugasashimo-chō, Ryūan-ji, Ukyō-ku,

Kyoto 616. Phone: (075) 463-6315. Activities: seminars; conferences on aging in an affluent society. Publication: newsletter.

Equal Child Care for Both Men and Women: Kansai Branch (Kansai Ikujiren Otoko mo Onna mo Ikujijikan no Renrakukai: Kansai Ikujiren)
> Address: 15-20, Yahata-chō, Nishino, Yamashina-ku, Kyoto 607. Phone: (075) 502-4853. Activities: campaign against gender-role reform. Publication: *Ikujinasu tsūshin* (quarterly).

Osaka

Amnesty International: Osaka Office
> Address: 3-17-5, Nakatsu, Kita-ku, Osaka 531. Phone: (06) 376-1496. Activities: support for human rights. Publication: *Amnesty Newsletter*.

Women Against All Forms of Discrimination (Arayuru Sabetsu o Yurusanai Onna-tachi no Atsumari)
> Address: c/o Kasahara, 2-38, Ichizumi 8-2, Minami hon-chō, Yao-shi, Osaka 581. Activities: movies and lectures on gender, peace, and discrimination.

By the Hearth (Iroribata)
> Address: 2-7-26-1002, Uriwarihigashi, Hirano-ku, Osaka 547. Phone: (06) 794-8640. Activities: research resources; scrapbooks of publications on the aged from newspapers. Publication: *Oi no ryōbun* (Old People's Territory).

Woman's Cinema House (Umanzu Shine Hausu)
> Address: c/o Rakudo, 5-26-28, Izumi-chō, Suita-shi, Osaka 565. Phone: (06) 380-2656. Activities: production and projection of movies produced from women's points of view. Publication: *Women's Cine House News*.

Women's Center Osaka (Women's Sentā Ōsaka)
> Address: 1-3-23, Gamo Joto-ku, Ōaka-shi, Osaka 563. Phone: (06) 933-7001. Fax: (06) 933-7001. Activities: psychology classes; physical and mental counseling. Publication: *Onna no kurinikku nyūsu* (Women's Clinic News); *Women and Health in Japan* (English newsletter).

Osaka Gay Community OGC (Ōsaka Gei Komyūnite)
Address: c/o Hirano, 6-1-26 Amamigado, Matsubara-shi, Osaka
580. Phone: (0723) 30-0870. Activities: meetings on gay life in a heterosexual society. Publications: *Musubikko* (Integrity); *Gei ribu to
feminizumu wa deaeru ka* (Can Gay Liberation and Feminism get
along?).

Osaka City Women's Education Center (Ōsaka Shiritsu Fujin Kaikan)
Address: 5-6-21, Ueshio Tenji-ku, Osaka 543. Phone: (06)
772-0061. Activities: library service; lectures on women; function
rooms.

Osaka Prefecture Women's Center (Ōsaka Furitsu Fujin Kaikan)
Address: A-10, Kami-machi, Chūō-ku, Osaka 540. Phone: (06)
762-2658. Fax: (06) 762-2658. Activities: counseling service; seminars; function rooms. Publication: *Ms. Fōto* (Ms. Fort).

Women's Labor Union: Kansai (Onna Rōdō Kumiai: Kansai)
Address: Excellent Building 303, 5-5-13 Tenjinbashi, Kita-ku,
Osaka. Phone: (06) 354-2270. Activities: Speaking out against gen-
der roles and sexual harassment and for better working conditions.
Publication: *Onna-tachi no genkiryū* (Women's Cheerful Way).

Kansai Mischievous Lesbian Power (Kansai Yancha Rezubian Pawa)
Address: MBE Sentā 335, Ōsaka Ekima Dai-san Biru, B1-61, 1-1-3
Umeda, Kita-ku, Osaka 530. Activities: center for lesbian action and
culture. Publication: *Sekushuaritē tte nandarō* (What Is Sexuality?);
Women's Festival 1990 Report.

*International Women's Year Association in Osaka (Kokusai Fujinnen Ōsaka
no Kai)*
Address: 7-1-39-202, Tamimachi Chūō-ku, Osaka 540. Activities:
promotion of the goals of the International Women's Year; lectures;
meetings. Publications: *Ōsaka kusanone—fujin hakusho* (Ōsaka
Grass-Roots Women's Movement White Paper); *Eporado*
(newsletter).

*Women's Group Against the National Security Act: Naniwa (Kokkai Kimit-
suhō ni Hantai Suru Onna no Kai: Naniwa)*
Address: c/o Matsui, 1-9-20-404, Nishitenma, Kita-ku, Osaka 530.
Phone: (06) 365-5678. Activities: workshops. Publication: *Akanwa!
Kokka kimitsuhō* (No! To the National Secrets Law).

Organization for the Rethinking of Gender Roles in Advertising
(Komāsharu no Naka no Danjo Yakuwari o Toinaosukai)
> Address: 14-11, Amagawa, Chinmachi, Takatsuki, Osaka 569.
> Phone: (0726) 73-3356. Activities: advertisement censorship; com-
> mercial awards. Publication: newsletter.

Association of Permanent Resident Korean Women in Japan: Osaka Head
Office (Zainichi Kankoku Minshū Joseikai: Ōsaka Honbu)
> Address: 1-1-202, Azihara-chō, Tennōji-ku, Osaka 543. Phone: (06)
> 765-3370. Activities: see Tokyo branch.

Association Against Discrimination Toward Illegitimate Children
(Kongaishi Sabetsu to Tatakaukai)
> Address: 14-202, Shimonoikejūtaku, 545-34, Nagasone-chō, Sakai-
> shi, Osaka 591. Activities: fight against the birth registration and
> marriage systems of Japan. Publications: *Konsakai tsūshin* (newslet-
> ter); *Shussei todoke no minigaido* (Handbook of Birth Registration);
> *Konna mono iranai — koseki* (We Don't Need a Family Register).

Sakai City Women's Organization (Sakai-shi Josei Dantai Renraku
Kyōgikai)
> Address: 4-1-27, Shukuin-chō, Higashi Sakai-shi, Osaka 590. Phone:
> (0722) 23-0333. Activities: fight against beauty contests; Provide
> education on environment issues. Publications: newsletter; *Miss*
> *Contest Now.*

Sashisawari
> Address: c/o Soyokaze Planning, 1-21-2-1109, Higashi Nakajima,
> Yodogawa-ku, Osaka 533. Phone: (06) 324-1133. Activities: reading
> group; talks by disabled women on the making of a new society. Pub-
> lication: *Onna to shōgaisha — kara no messeiji* (Message from
> Women and the Disabled — Newsletter).

Osaka Women Against Sexual Assault (Seibōryoku o Yurusanai Onna no Kai)
> Address: P.O. Box 15, Higashiyodogawa, Post Office, Osaka. Phone:
> (06) 322-2313. Activities: telephone counseling; lectures. Publica-
> tions: *Faito bakku* (Fight Back [newsletter]); *Nakineiri shinai onna*
> *no tame no handobukku* (A Handbook for Women Who Do Not
> Give Up)

Labor Unions Against Sexual Harassment: Purple (Sekushuaru Harasu-
mento to Tatakau Rōdō Kumiai: Pāpuru)

Address: 4-8-1-301, Tenjinbashi, Kita-ku, Osaka. Phone: (06) 354
5193. Activities: fight for good working conditions for women. Publication: *Sore yuke onna-tachi* (Let's Go, Women [newsletter]).

*Osaka Organization Against Gender-Based Wage Discrimination (Danjo
Sabetsu Chingin o Nakusu Ōsaka Renrakukai)*
    Address: Kita Building 2-301, 4-6-19, Nishitenmma Kita-ku, Osaka
    530. Phone: (06) 364-0746. Fax: (06) 365-1109. Activities: lectures;
    pamphlet publications on equal rights. Publications: *Futsū no OL no
    tame no jūbai tokusuru kintōhō* (Equal Laws for Female Clerks).

Women's Studies Research Association of Japan (Nihon Joseigaku Kenkyūkai)
    Address: SH Esaka 4B, 5-3, Enoki-chō, Suita-shi, Osaka 564. Phone:
    (06) 386-8837. Fax: (06) 386-8837. Activities: women's studies
    meeting. Publications: *Joseigaku nenpō* (Annual Report of Women's
    Studies); *Voice of Women* (monthly).

*Japan Women's Conference: Osaka Head Office (Nihon Fujin Kaigi: Ōsaka
Honbu)*
    Address: 3-9-27, Tenjinbashi, Kita-ku, Osaka 530. Phone: (06)
    353-3245. Activities: education on children, women, medicine, and
    the environment. Publication: *Fujin shinbun* (The Women's News-
    paper); other publications.

Philippine Grass-Roots Trade Group (Firipin Kusanone Bōeki no Kai)
    Address: c/o Yoshida, 2-17-5, Katsura-chō, Yao-shi, Osaka 581.
    Phone: (0729) 96-8271. Activities: sales of cards made by Filipinas.
    Publication: *Isang Palay*.

*Osaka Liaison Association: Women Against the Revision of the Mother and
Child Health Protection Law (Boshi Hokenhō Kaiaku ni Hantai Suru Onna-
tachi: Ōsaka Renrakukai)*
    Address: c/o Toshimitsu, 7-7-2, Higashitokiwadai, Toyono-chō,
    Toyono-gun, Osaka 563-01. Phone: (0727) 38-0485. Activities: sem-
    inars; negotiation with local governments against systematic man-
    agement of women's bodies.

Ms. Crayon House: Osaka
    Address: 5-3, Enoki-chō, Suita-shi, Osaka 564. Phone: (06)
    330-8071. Fax: (06) 330-8075. Activities: bookstore specializing in
    books for women and children; lectures; workshops. Publication:
    Crayon House tsūshin (Crayon House Letter).

Osaka Organization Against the Revision of Eugenics Protection Law
(Yūsei Hogohō Kaiaku Soshi Ōsaka Renrakukai)
> Address: P.O. Box 182, Ōsaka Nishi Post Office, Osaka. Phone: (06)
> 328-8284. Activities: monitoring Eugenics Protection Law and revi-
> sion movement. Publication: newsletter.

Theatrical Company Taihen Kim Manri (Gekidan Taihen Kim Manri)
> Address: 3-8-51, Awagi Higashi, Yodogawa-ku, Osaka 533. Ac-
> tivities: theatrical company of the disabled; testimony by disabled
> women. Publication: *Watashi wa onna* (I Am a Woman).

Tokyo

International Feminists of Japan (IFJ no Kai)
> Address: c/o Deguchi, 1-1-2-211, Kaita-chō, Higashimurayama-shi,
> Tokyo 189. Phone: (0423) 97-5609. Activities: meetings in English.
> Publication: *IJF Newsletter*.

Association of Asia (Ajia no Kai)
> Address: c/o Shimada, 3-18-46, Iguchi, Mitaka-shi, Tokyo 181.
> Phone: (0422) 32-5325. Activities: meetings for the study of Asia.
> Publication: *Gekkan Ajia* (Asia Monthly).

Asian Women Association (Ajia Onna-tachi no Kai)
> Address: 14-10-211, Sakuragaoka, Shibuya-ku, Tokyo 150. Phone:
> (03) 3508-7070. Activities: action for Asian women, especially for
> working women from Southeast Asia and ODA (Overseas Develop-
> ment Aid). Publications: *Asian Women's Liberation* (English journal,
> twice a year); *Women from Across the Seas* (English booklet).

Support Center Tachiyori
> Address: 14-10-211, Sakuragaoka, Shibuya-ku, Tokyo 150. Phone:
> (03) 3463-9752. Activities: providing Asian women in Japan with
> support and advice. Publication: *Harō harō*.

Asian Women Workers' Center (Ajia Joshi Rōdōsha Kōryū Sentā)
> Address: 2-3-18-34, Nishiwaseda, Shinjuku-ku, Tokyo 169. Phone:
> (03) 3202-4993. Activities: seminars; lectures; newsletter publica-
> tion. Publication: *Resource Materials on Women's Labour in
> Japan/Ajia no nakama* (Asian Friends Company, bimonthly).

Pacific Asian Resource Center: PARC (Ajia Taiheiyō Shiryō Sentā: PARC)
  Address: 1-30-402, Jinbo-chō, Kanda, Chiyoda-ku, Tokyo 101.
  Phone: (03) 3291-5901. Fax: (03) 3232-6775. Activities: rethinking
  Japan's relationship with Asia; PARC Free School. Publication: *Sekai
  kara* (From the World, quarterly) *AMPO* (English book).

*Amnesty Japan Team for Women and Human Rights (Amnesty Nihon Josei
to Jinken Chīmu)*
  Address: 2-3-22, Nishiwaseda, Shinjuku-ku, Tokyo. Phone: (03)
  3203-1050. Fax: (03) 3232-6775. Activities: protecting women's human rights. Publication: *Amnesty Newsletter.*

Alisu
  Address: 3-14-2, 5F, Nishiwaseda, Shinjuku-ku, Tokyo. Phone: (03)
  3208-1165. Fax: (03) 3208-1165. Activities: book and journal publications on women in movies. *Imai Masa zen shigoto* (Complete
  Work of Masa Imai).

Express (Ikusupuresu)
  Address: c/o Ikeda, 3-17-503, Tsuda-chō, Kodaira-shi, Tokyo 187.
  Phone: (0423) 44-3493. Fax: (0423) 44-3493. Activities: book information service. Publication: *Ari no mama no jibun ga ii* (Take Pride
  in Yourself as You Are).

LIP, Lesbian in Pain (Ijimerarekko no Kai: LIP)
  Address: c/o Regumi Studio, Nakazawa Bldg. 3F, 23 Araki-chō,
  Shinjuku-ku, Tokyo 160. Phone: (03) 3226-8314. Activities: support
  for lesbians.

A.L.N. (Asian Lesbian Network), Japan (A.L.N. Nihon)
  Address: c/o Regumi Studio, Nakazawa Bldg. 3F, 23 Araki-chō,
  Shinjuku-ku, Tokyo 160. Activities: networking with Asian lesbians;
  international conferences.

*Women's Group Against the AIDS Protection Law
(Eizu Yobōhō o Haian ni Suru Onna-tachi no Kai)*
  Address: Nakazawa Bldg. 3F, 23 Araki-chō, Shinjuku-ku, Tokyo
  160. Activities: AIDS-related issues; fighting against discrimination.
  Publication: *Onna-tachi no eizu mondai* (Women's AIDS Issues).

L.F. Center (Eru Efu Sentā)
  Address: P.O. Box 84, Nakano Post Office, Nakano-ku, Tokyo. Ac-

tivities: Criticism of heterosexist culture and marriage system; promotion of women's liberation. Publication: *Poruno wa onna e no
bōryoku da* (Pornography Is Violence Against Women; slides).

Open House (Ōpun Hausu)
> Address: Hoken Kaikan Bekkan, 1-2 Sadohara-chō, Ichigaya,
> Shinjuku-ku, Tokyo 162. Phone: (03) 3235-2638. Activities: coun-
> seling on women's health, gender issues, contraception; medical ser-
> vice for women.

*Ochanomizu University Institute of Women's Studies (Ochanomizu Joshi
Daigaku, Josei Bunka Kenkyū Sentā)*
> Address: 2-1-1, Otsuka, Bunkyō-ku, Tokyo 112. Phone: (03)
> 3943-3151. Activities: interdisciplinary research; information service
> for women's culture. Publication: *Josei Bunka Kenkyū Sentā nenpō*
> (Annual Report of the Women's Culture Research Center).

Ochanomizu Library (Ochanomizu Toshokan)
> Address: Ochanomizu Square Bldg. 9F, 1-6, Surugadai, Kanda,
> Chiyoda-ku, Tokyo 101. Phone: (03) 3294-2266. Activities: library
> service exclusively for women (admission ¥100).

*Equal Childcare for Both Men and Women (Ikujiren Otoko mo Onna mo
Ikujijikan o Renrakukai)*
> Address: c/o Masuno, 4-7-14, Ekoda, Nakano-ku, Tokyo 165. Phone:
> (03) 3385-2293. Activities: achievement of nursing time for men in the
> workplace; meetings. Publications: *Ikujiren* (newsletter); *Otoko to
> onna de hanbunko-ni suru* (Equal Share Between Men and Women).

*Committee for the Festival of Women's Film (Onna-tachi no Eigasai Jikkō
Iinkai)*
> Address: Tōto Rejidensu 410, 4-28-5, Yoyogi, Shibuya-ku, Tokyo
> 151. Phone: (03) 3370-6007. Fax: (03) 3370-8440. Activities: film
> loan service; film information; film production by female directors.
> Publication: *Women's Media* (information magazine).

Women's Movie Production Group (Onna-tachi no Eiga Seisaku Iinkai)
> Address: Hatagaya Cōporasu 101, 1-12-11, Hatagaya, Shibuya-ku,
> Tokyo 151. Phone: (03) 3485-2935. Activities: production and loans
> of women's movies. Publications: *Uman nau: Josei ga shakai o kaeru
> toki* (Women Now: When Women Change Society); *Hansen o utau
> onna-tachi* (Women Sing Against War).

*Organization for Women's Bodies and Medication (Onna no Karada to Iryō
o Kangaerukai)*
Address: Nihon Fujin Kaigi, Higashi Puro Bldg., 1-33-3 Hongō,
Bunkyō-ku, Tokyo. Phone: (03) 3816-1862. Fax: (03) 3816-1824.
Activities: research on the female body; lectures. Publication: *Onna
no karada to iryō* (Women's Body and Medicine).

Group for Women's Rights and Sexuality (Gurupu: Onna no Jinken to Sei)
Address: Fujin Kyōdō Hōritsu Jimusho, Mezon Kaneko 202,
1-45-11, Higashi Ikebukuro, Toshima-ku, Tokyo 170. Phone: (03)
3985-3308. Fax: (03) 3971-5565. Activities: demanding a new system and laws for protection of the female body. Publications: *Onna
wa naze kodomo o umanai no ka* (Why Women Decide "No Children"); *Chūzetsu jiki no tanshuku ni kansuru kinkyu hōkoku*
(Urgent Report on Shortened Period for Abortion; pamphlet).

*Women's Association Against Police Sexual Violence (Keisatsu no
Seibōryoku o Yurusanai Onna-tachi no Kai)*
Address: c/o Sakazume, 2-29-2-1215, Takashimadaira, Itabashi-ku,
Tokyo. Activities: abolition of sexual violence by the police against
women; meetings only for women.

*Women's Association to Improve in Aging Society (Kōreika Shakai o
Yokusuru Josei no Kai)*
Address: No. 31 Kyūtei M. 802, 2-9-1 Shinjuku-ku, Tokyo 160.
Phone: (03) 3356-3564. Fax: (03) 3355-6427. Activities: research re-
sources; annual meeting; lectures. Publication: *Koreika Shakai o
Yokusuru Josei no Kai kaihō* (newsletter).

Women in Action (Kōdō Suru Onna-tachi no Kai)
Address: Nakazawa Bldg. 3F, 23 Araki-chō, Shinjuku-ku, Tokyo
160. Phone: (03) 3357-9565. Fax: (03) 3357-9565. Activities: lectures; publications. Publication: *Kōdō Suru Onna* (Active Women,
monthly).

*International Education Resource Information Center: ERIC (Kokusai
Rikai Kyōiku Shiryō Jōhō Sentā)*
Address: Tsuda Bldg. 1F, 1-21-18, Tabata, Kita-ku, Tokyo 114.
Phone: (03) 5685-1177. Fax: (03) 5685-0550. Activities: informa-
tion service on environment, peace, and human rights. Publication:
ERIC Newsletter: Warudo sutadizu (World Studies).

Organization on Women Workers and Computers (Konputā to Josei Rōdōsha o Kangaerukai)
> Address: c/o Nihon Fujin Kaigi, Higashi Puro Bldg., 1-33-3, Hongō, Bunkyō-ku, Tokyo. Phone: (03) 3816-1862. Fax: (03) 3816-1824. Activities: hearing from women in computer work; lectures. Publication: *Onna/komputā* (Women and Computers; bimonthly).

Association of Permanent Resident Korean Women in Japan (Zainichi Kankoku Minshū Joseikai)
> Address: Shinko Bldg. 5F, 3-6-8, Ogawa-chō, Kanda, Chiyoda-ku, Tokyo 101. Phone: (03) 3295-2638. Activities: meetings for Korean women in Japan. Publications: *Minshū josei* (Democratic Women, newsetter); *Kankoku josei mondai shiryōshū 8: Chōsenjin jūgun ianfu* (Reports on Korean Women's Issues, No. 8: Korean Comfort Women).

Sappho (Safo)
> Address: c/o Kido, 2-2-5-909, Ōmori-kita, Ōta-ku, Tokyo 143. Activities: parties for lesbians. Publication: Safo *kawaraban* (Sappho Newspaper).

Socialist Women's Association (Shakaishugi Fujin Kaigi)
> Address: Dai-ichi Shinwa House 202, 2-23-25, Mejiro, Toshima-ku, Tokyo 171. Phone: (03) 3984-5105. Fax: (03) 3984-5210. Activities: thinking about socialism, feminism, and women's liberation. Publication: *Fujin tsūshin* (Women's Communication; monthly).

Joki: The Joint Office for Women's Liberation (Joki: Josei Kaihō Gōdō Jimusho)
> Address: Nakazawa Bldg. 3F, 23 Araki-chō, Shinjuku-ku, Tokyo 160. Activities: studio facilities.

Association of Female Architects (Josei Kenchiku Gijutsusha no Kai)
> Address: c/o Hana Sekkei Kōbō, Dai-ichi Kumano Bldg. 5-C,2-26-1, Yoyogi, Shibuya-ku, Tokyo 151. Phone: (03) 5388-7813. Fax: (03) 5388-7813. Activities: networking for female architects. Publication: *Jōgi* (A Ruler; newsletter).

Research Center for Women and Politics (Josei to Seiji Kenkyū Sentā)
> Address: c/o Mitsui Mariko Jimusho, 2-19-11-101, Asagaya Minami, Suginami-ku, Tokyo. Phone: (03) 3318-5860. Activities: research and information service on female politicians. Publication: *Mitsui Mariko no shiten* (Mitsui Mariko's Viewpoint).

CHOISIR (Showajiru)
> Address: 3-6-29-101, Amanuma, Suginami-ku, Tokyo 167. Phone: (03) 3391-4919. Activities: self-reflection of women's sexuality. Publication: *CHOISIR* (monthly).

Newspaper Data Press (Shinbun Shiryō Shuppan)
> Address: 3-25-13-103, Nishiogi-kita, Suginami-ku, Tokyo 167. Phone: (03) 3399-8592. Prewar article collection from newspapers. Publication: *Shinbun shūsei: Shōwa hennenshi* (Showa Chronicle of Collected Articles).

Women's Network Against Sexual Violence 1990 (Seibōryoku to Tatakau Onna-tachi no Nettowāku 1990)
> Address: c/o Project Tatakau Akazukin, P.O. Box 35, Fussa Post Office, Fussa-shi, Tokyo 197. Activities: campaign against pornography and sexual harrassment. Publication: *STON 1990* (newsletter).

Japan National Women's Journal (Zenkoku Fujin Shinbun)
> Address: Hoko Nishishinjuku Bldg., 3-7-28 Nishishinjuku, Shinjuku-ku, Tokyo 160. Phone: (03) 3343-1846. Fax: (03) 3348-1890. Activities: newspaper publications. Publication: *Zenkoku fujin shinbun* (National Women's Newspaper; journal).

Women Opposed to War (Sensō e no Michi o Yurusanai Onna-tachi no Renrakukai)
> Address: c/o Nihon Fujin Kaigi, 1-33-1, Hongō, Bunkyō-ku, Tokyo 113. Phone: (03) 3816-2057. Activities: meetings for peace on memorial days; workshops on the Peace Constitution. Publication: newsletter.

Dandansha
> Address: 4-5-4, Takamatsu, Nerima-ku, Tokyo 179. Phone: (03) 3999-6209. Activities: publication of works by women writers. Publication: *Gendai Ajia no josei sakka shirīzu* (Women Writers of Modern Asia).

DPI: Disabled Peoples' International Disabled Women's Network (DPI Josei Shōgaisha Nettowāku)
> Address: 178-3, Negishi-cho, Machida-shi, Tokyo 194. Phone: (0427) 91-0132. Activities: seminars for the disabled. Publication: newsletter.

Tokyo Rape Crisis Center (Tōkyō Gōkan Kyūen Sentā)
Address: P.O. Box 7, Joto Post Office, Koto-ku, Tokyo 136. Phone:
(03) 3207-3692. Activities: telephone counseling. Publication: newsletter; *Reepu kuraishisu* (Rape Crisis).

Tokyo Women's Christian University, Center for Women's Studies
(Tōkyō Joshi Daigaku, Joseigaku Kenkyūjo)
Address: 2-6-1, Zenfuku-ji, Suginami-ku, Tokyo 167. Phone: (03)
3395-1211, Ext. 283. Fax: (03) 5382-8670. Activities: lectures; seminars. Publications: annual report; *Women's Studies: Kenkyū*
hōkokusho (Report on Women's Studies).

Shinjuku Women's Information Center (Tōkyō-to Shinjuku Kuritsu Fujin
Jōhō Sentā)
Address: 16 Araki-cho, Shinjuku-ku, Tokyo 160. Phone: (03)
3341-0801. Fax: (03) 3341-0740. Activities: library service; lectures;
counseling service; function rooms. Publication: *Fujin jōhō*
(Women's Information; quarterly).

Tokyo Women's Information Center (Tōkyō-to Fujin Jōhō Sentā)
Address: Central Plaza 15F, 1-1, Kagurakashi, Shinjuku-ku, Tokyo
162. Phone: (03) 3235-1186. Fax: (03) 3268-1503. Activities: library service; counseling service; function rooms.

Domesu Press (Domesu Shuppan)
Address: 1-3-15, Komagome, Toshima-ku, Tokyo 170. Phone:
(03)-3944-5651. Activities: publications on women's history. Publications: *Sakuhin no naka no onna-tachi* (Women in Literature);
Kindai Nihon kangoshi zen yonkan (The History of Nursing in
Modern Japan, Vols. 1–4); *Nihon fujin mondai shiryō shūsei zen*
jukkan (Reports on Japanese Women's Issues, Vols. 1–10).

U.S.-Japan Women's Center (Nichibei Josei Sentā)
Address: 3-19-8, Kamikitazawa, Setagaya-ku, Tokyo 156. Phone:
(03) 3302-5020, 3469-5064. Activities: publication in U.S. and
Japan. Publication: *U.S.-Japan Women's Journal.*

Japan Nursing Association (Nihon Kango Kyōkai)
Address: 5-8-2, Jingumae, Shibuya-ku, Tokyo 150. Phone: (03)
3400-8331. Activities: working for a better working condition for
nurses; information service. Publications: *Kango e no michi* (The
Way to Nursing; pamphlet); other publications.

Christian Women's Temperance Union (Nihon Fujin Kyōfukai)
Address: 2-23-5, Hyakunin-chō, Shinjuku-ku, Tokyo 169. Phone: (03) 3361-0934. Fax: (03) 3361-1160. Activities: working for peace, gender and human rights based on Christianity. Publication: *Fujin shinpō* (Women's News; monthly).

Women's Studies Association of Japan (Nihon Josei Gakkai)
Address: c/o Gakkai Jimu Sentā, 2-4-16, Yayoi, Bunkyō-ku, Tokyo 113. Phone: (03) 3817-5801. Fax: (03) 3817-5800. Activities: information service for researchers; conferences. Publications: *Gakkai nyūsu* (Association News; quarterly); *Nihon Joseigaku Gakkaishi*) (Journal of the Women's Sudies Association of Japan).

Japanese Association of Sex Education: JASE (Nihon Seikyōiku Kyōkai)
Address: Miyata Bldg. 2E, 1-3, Jinbo-chō, Kanda, Chiyoda-ku, Tokyo 101. Phone: (03) 3291-7726. Fax: (03) 3291-6238. Activities: research resources on sex education; information service. Publication: *Gendai seikyōiku kenkyū geppō* (Modern Sex Education Report; monthly).

Japan Women's Forum (Nihon Fujin Mondai Konwakai)
Address: Kaneko Bldg. 3F, 1-47-4, Uehara, Shibuya-ku, Tokyo. Phone: (03) 3466-8252. Activities: symposiums; counseling service. Publication: newsletter; *Nihon no otoko-tachi wa ima katarō, otoko-tachi to* (Japanese Men, Now: Let's Talk With Men).

Japan Women Conference (Nihon Fujin Kaigi)
Address: 1-33-3, Hongō, Bunkyō-ku, Tokyo 113. Phone: (03) 3816-1862. Activities: center for various women's activities on peace, labor and human rights, and the body. Publications: *Fujin shinbun* (Women's Newspaper); *Josei kaihō e* (For Women's Liberation) by Yamamoto Kikue.

Association Against Prostitution (Baibaishun Mondai ni Torikumukai)
Address: Kyōfukaikan, 2-23-5, Hyakunin-chō, Shinjuku-ku, Tokyo 169. Phone: (03) 5386-4041. Activities: research on issues of prostitution and environment with an emphasis on child prostitution, sex tours, and comfort women. Publication: newsletter.

Pad Women's Office (Pado Women's Ofisu)
Address: Tōto Rejidensu 410, 4-28-5, Yoyogi, Shibuya-ku, Tokyo 151. Phone: (03) 3370-8440. Fax: (03) 3370-8440. Activities:

women's publishing company. Publications: *Josei jōhō* (Women's Information; monthly); *Josei jōhō nenkan* (Almanac of Women's Information).

Counseling Group for Filipino Brides (Firipin no Hanayome o Kangaerukai)
Address: c/o Fujin Minshu Kurabu, 3-31-18, Jingumae, Shibuya-ku, Tokyo 150. Phone: (03) 3402-3238. Activities: campaign against the importation of women.

Women's Cooperative Law Office (Fujin Kyōdo Hōritsu Jimusho)
Address: Mezon Kaneko 202, 1-45-11, Higashi Ikebukuro, Toshima-ku, Tokyo 170. Phone: (03) 3985-3308. Fax: (03) 3971-5565. Activities: support for independence of women and co-operation; counseling services; Publication: *Tou tou* (newsletter).

Women's Association for Buraku Liberation (Buraku Mondai o Kangaerukai)
Address: c/o Buraku Kaihō Dōmei Chūō Honbu, 3-5-11, Roppongi, Minato-ku, Tokyo. Activities: working against discrimination toward burakumen and women. Publication: newsletter.

Women's Democratic Club Femine (Fujin Minshu Kurabu Femin)
Address: 3-31-18, Jingumae, Shibuya-ku, Tokyo 150. Phone: (03) 3402-3244. Activities: women's networking; working on women's issues, environment, and education. Publication: *Femin* (weekly magazine).

National Liaison Association for Maternal Health (Boshi Hōken Zenkoku Renrakukai)
Address: c/o Mouri Iin, 3-30-10, Jingumae, Shibuya-ku, Tokyo. Phone: (03) 3408-6948. Activities: campaign against revision of Maternity Health Law. Publications: numerous.

Ms. Crayon House
Address: 3-8-15, Kita Aoyama, Minato-ku, Tokyo 107. Phone: (03) 3406-6492. Fax: (03) 3407-9568. Activities: bookstore specializing in children's and women's books. Publication: *Crayon House tsūshin* (Crayon House Newsletter).

Regumi Studio Tokyo (Regumi Sutajio Tōkyō)
Address: c/o JOKI, Nakazawa Bldg. 3F, 23 Araki-chō, Shinjuku-ku, Tokyo 160. Phone: (03) 3226-8314. Activities: campaign for lesbian

culture and liberation; parties. Publication: *Regumi tsūshin* (Regumi Monthly Newsletter).

From the Body: Liaison Against Revision of the Eugenics Protection Law 1982 (Watashi wa Karada kara 1982 Yūsei Hogohō Kaiaku Soshi Renrakukai)
> Address: c/o JOKI, Nakazawa Bldg. 3F, 23 Araki-chō, Shinjuku-ku, Tokyo 160. Activities: campaign against reform of the Eugenics Protection Law and abortion-related publications. Publications: *Watashi no karada nyūsu* (Women's Body News); *Bosei o kaidoku suru)* (Decode Motherhood).

Agora
> Address: 1-9-6, Shinjuku, Shinjuku-ku, Tokyo 160. Phone: (03) 3354-3941. Fax: (03) 3354-9014. Activities: collection of women's information; seminars. Publications: *Gekkan: Agora* (The Monthly: Agora); *Tokushū: Agora* (Special Issue: Agora).

Glossary

» » » »

AGORA   A feminist journal founded in 1972. See Interview with
Saitō Chiyo for more details.

AMAE   Formed from the verb *amaeru*, which means to avail oneself
of another's kindness or to wish to be pampered. As a psychological term, the word *amae* refers to the wish to be dependent
on and indulged by others. It was popularized as a psychological concept by Doi Takeo. See his *Anatomy of Dependence*,
Trans, John Bester (Tokyo: Kodansha International, 1973).
The term is frequently used to describe what some consider a
fundamental dynamic in Japanese sociofamilial relationships.

AMATERASU   The Sun Goddess. The Japanese imperial household
traced its heavenly lineage back to this goddess under state
Shinto.

AMPO   The U.S.-Japan Security Treaty (*Nichibei anzen hoshō
jōyaku*). Popular protests against the reratification of this
treaty led to widespread demonstrations in the late 1950s.

BAKUFU   Literally, "camp office." The name given to the military
government of the shogun during the Tokugawa Period
(1603–1867).

BOSEIAI   The love of a mother for her child.

CHIHEI   A leftist journal with a strong editorial focus on issues of contemporary political reform and minority group politics.

CHIKAN   Best translated as "pervert," the term gained wide usage as a popular description for men who take advantage of close bodily contact and anonymity in crowded Japanese peak-hour trains to touch women's bodies.

DOI TAKAKO   When elected chairperson of the Japan Socialist Party in 1986, she became the first women to lead a Japanese political party structure.

DOI TAKEO   Author of *Anatomy of Dependence* (*Amae no kōzō*), best known for his theory of *amae* (see above).

EDO PERIOD   Also known as the Tokugawa Period (1603–1867).

EMPEROR   In Japanese the emperor is usually referred to simply by the term *tennō* (emperor) or *tennō heika* (His Majesty, the Emperor). If it is necessary to distinguish between different emperors, the name given to the particular emperor's reign is used. The late Emperor Hirohito is referred to as the Shōwa (Enlightened Peace) emperor, and the present emperor, Akihito, as the Heisei (Peace and Prosperity) emperor.

EQUAL EMPLOYMENT OPPORTUNITY LAW   Implemented in 1986. For details of the debates surrounding this legislation, see my article "Altered States," in Andrew Gordon, *Postwar Japan as History* (Berkeley and Los Angeles: University of California Press, 1993).

EUGENICS PROTECTION LAW   Extensive sections of this law still carry influences of the wartime policies of eugenics and the privileging of women's reproductive labor over paid work-force participation. The Economic Reasons Clause, which allows women to seek an abortion on economic grounds, has been strongly contested by conservatives since its introduction into the postwar Constitution.

GŌKAN   One of the characters used to write this Japanese word for "rape" denotes three women in a cluster and carries the meaning of lewd or licentious. Feminists thus argue that the very word for rape in Japanese encodes the guilt of the female victim.

HANAKOZOKU   A name frequently used to designate a generation of middle-class Japanese women who read the magazine *Hanako*. This consumer magazine has a strong focus on luxury goods and an upwardly mobile lifestyle and is seen to lead trends among a highly status-conscious group of affluent women consumers.

LAFCADIO HEARN   The American journalist and novelist Lafcadio Hearn (1850–1904) arrived in Japan in 1890 and remained there for the rest of his life. During this time, he taught English and lectured on English literature at Tokyo University. He also wrote a total of twelve books about Japan. Some of his most well-known works are *Glimpses of Unfamiliar Japan* (1894); *Kwaidan: Stories and Studies of Strange Things* (1904); and *Japan: An Attempt at Interpretation* (1904).

HEIAN PERIOD   Late eighth to late twelfth century.

HIRATSUKA RAICHŌ   1878–1971. Founder of the journal *Seitō* (Bluestocking). She was a central figure in both the pre- and postwar "motherhood debates" (*bosei ronsō*).

HYŌRONKA   A term used to designate a professional social critic/writer. Today these public figures frequently play a central role in popularizing academic and theoretical debates through the popular media.

IE   Designates both the physical structure of the home/house and the sociofamilial structure of relationships between members of the household.

ISE SHRINE   The Shinto shrine at Ise in Mie Prefecture is the principal monument to the Sun Goddess (Amaterasu) and a traditional destination of pilgrimages. It is of central importance to the legitimacy of the imperial household under state Shinto.

KANA   The *hiragana* and *katakana* syllabic-based writing systems.

KANAI   Literally, "of the inside of the house," the term is used by a man to refer to his wife.

KANSAI   The Osaka-Kobe-Kyoto coastal plain region.

KARUCHĀ SENTĀ Neighborhood- or community-based culture centers funded variously by prefectural or municipal government or, in some instances, by private enterprise. These centers of adult education focus on a largely female audience for specialized culture courses.

KOJIKI The *Kojiki* (Record of Ancient Matters) was written in A.D. 712 and is Japan's earliest surviving written "history." It consists of a mythical account of Japan's creation as well as genealogical information about the imperial family. It is available in translation by Donald L Philippi, *Kojiki* (Princeton: Princeton University Press, 1969).

LDP Liberal Democratic Party, the conservative party alliance that has dominated postwar Japanese electoral politics.

MARUYAMA MASAO A well-known Japanese political scientist and the author of various influential studies of Japanese intellectual history and political thought.

MAZĀKON A term coined by Ueno Chizuko (see her interview) to designate the English "mother complex." Ueno uses the term to describe what she interprets as an excessive level of emotional investment and dependency on the part of Japanese mothers in relation to their children — in particular, their sons.

MEIJI PERIOD 1868–1912.

MINIKOMI Japanese contracted form of the English "mini-communication," used to describe the extensive communication network established by Japanese feminists from the 1970s to the present. The network is seen as an alternative to "mass communication."

MIZUKO JIZŌ Iconic statues made or bought by women who have undergone an abortion. The figures are placed at a designated site of spirit worship, and prayers are offered for the fetus. See the translation of Miya Yoshiko for more details.

MIZUSHŌBAI Term for sex and entertainment industry. Popularly translated as "water trade."

MOTOORI NORINAGA An eighteenth-century Japanese scholar

whose interpretations and commentary on the Japanese classical tradition positioned him as the head of one of the two Japanese "schools" (traditions) of Nativism.

NHK   The Japanese National Broadcasting Corporation.

NAKANE CHIE   A social anthropologist and the author of the well-known text *Japanese Society*, in which she develops her concept of *tate shakai* (vertical society).

NAKASONE YASUHIRO   The head of the ruling LDP and prime minister of Japan from 1979–87.

NISHIDA KITARŌ   1870–1945. A well-known philosopher whose work on subjectivity, knowledge, and action had a significant impact on the state of modern Japanese philosophy. His followers went on to found the Kyoto School.

OKUSAN   Literally, "person at the back of the house," the term translates as "wife."

ORE   A first-person designator usually used only by a male speaker in a situation of low formality or high intimacy.

O-TENTO-SAMA   A term for the sun that combines a sense of reverence and playful intimacy toward this popular deity.

PKO   Peace Keeping Operations. The debate surrounding the PKO Bill gained extensive public attention in relation to the Gulf War and the U.N. Cambodia initiative.

RITSURYŌ REFORMS   A series of reforms undertaken to create a centralized imperial state along the T'ang Chinese model. The foundation for these reforms was laid in 702 with the promulgation of the Taihō code, which included a penal (*ritsu*) and a civil (*ryō*) code.

SAIGYŌ   1118–1190. A poet whose works appear in the *Shin-kokinshu*, compiled in 1205.

SEI SHŌNAGON   *The Pillow Book* (*Makura no sōshi*) is traditionally attributed to this woman writer of the Heian court (ca.966–ca.1027).

SEPPUKU   Also called *harakiri*. Ritual suicide by disembowelment.

SHINJUKU RIBU SENTĀ   See listing of feminist organizations.

SHOGUN   Title of the political leader of the bakufu government of Tokugawa Japan.

SHŌWA PERIOD   1925–89.

TAISHŌ PERIOD   1912–26.

TALE OF GENJI   Early eleventh-century work in the *monogatari* (narrative tale) style, attributed to Murasaki Shikibu, a woman writer of the Heian court. This long tale is often referred to as the first "novel."

TANAKA MITSU   A leading Japanese feminist activist and writer. Author of the path-breaking feminist treatise *To the Women of Life* (*Inochi no onna-tachi e*), first published in 1972.

TENKŌ   Usually translated as "turncoating," the term is used to describe the act of changing allegiances, as exemplified by the number of Japanese politicians and intellectuals who *tenkō*-ed during the Second World War and the Occupation period.

TOKUGAWA PERIOD   The period of government of the Tokugawa shoguns (1600–1867). Since their capital was in Edo (modern Tokyo), the era is also known as the Edo period.

YOSANO AKIKO   1878–1942. A feminist activist and poet. She was Hiratsuka Raichō's main adversary in the Taishō Period "motherhood debate."

YOSHIWARA   Name of the "entertainment" or licensed district of brothels, bars and teahouses located in Tokyo (old Edo) and dating from the Edo period to 1958 when prostitution was criminalized.

INDEX

» » » »

References to chronology entries are followed by the letter "c."

Designer: Barbara Jellow
Compositor: Keystone Typesetting, Inc.
Text: 10/14 Sabon
Display: Sabon
Printer: BookCrafters, Inc.
Binder: BookCrafters, Inc.